Jethro T
Aqualun

Music transcriptions by Addi Booth and Ryan Maziarz

ISBN 0-634-07850-X

7777 W. BLUEMOUND RD. P.O. BOX 13819 MILWAUKEE, WI 53213

Aqualung

Music by Ian Anderson
Lyrics by Jennie Anderson

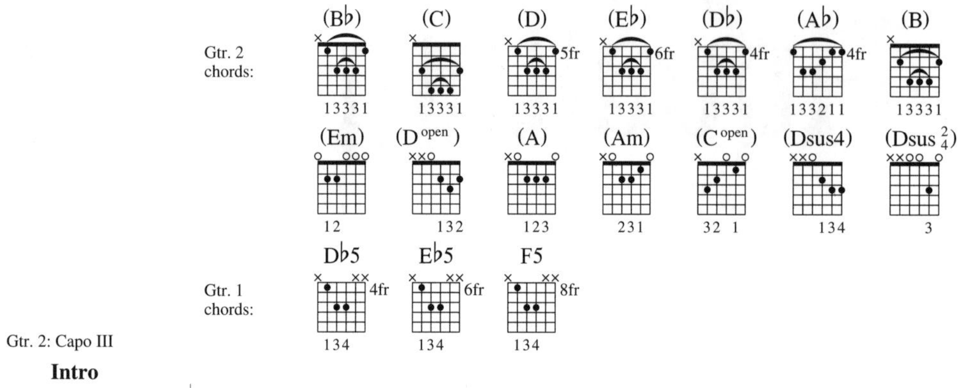

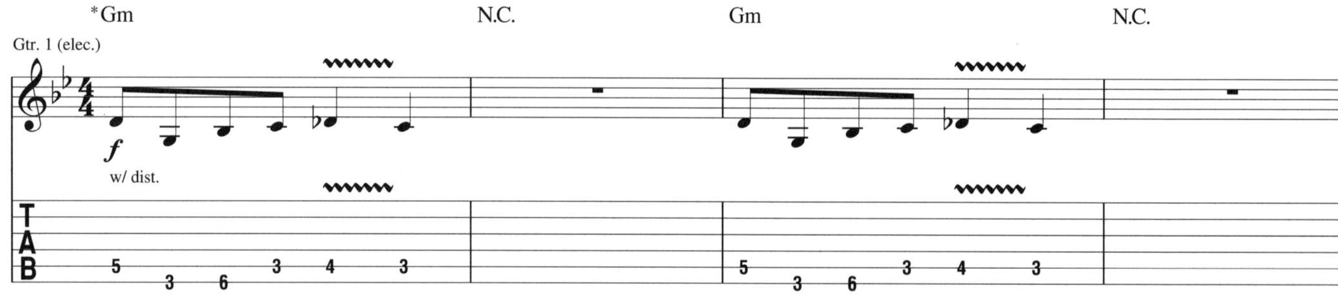

*Chord symbols reflect implied harmony.

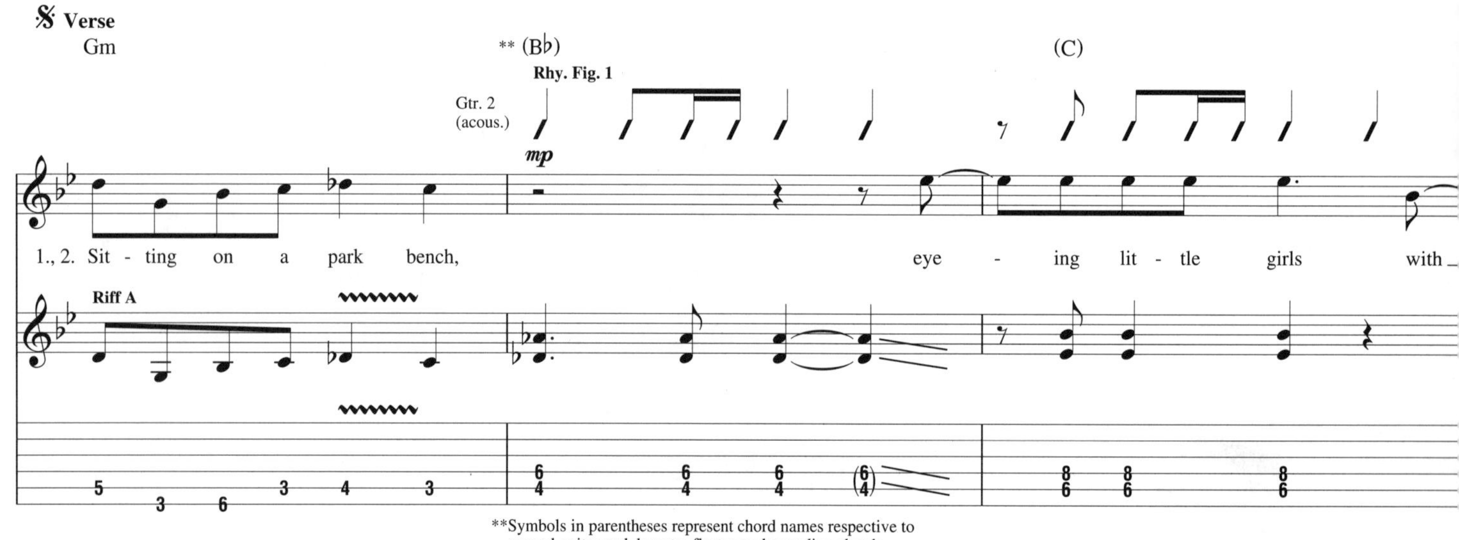

**Symbols in parentheses represent chord names respective to capoed guitar and do not reflect actual sounding chords.

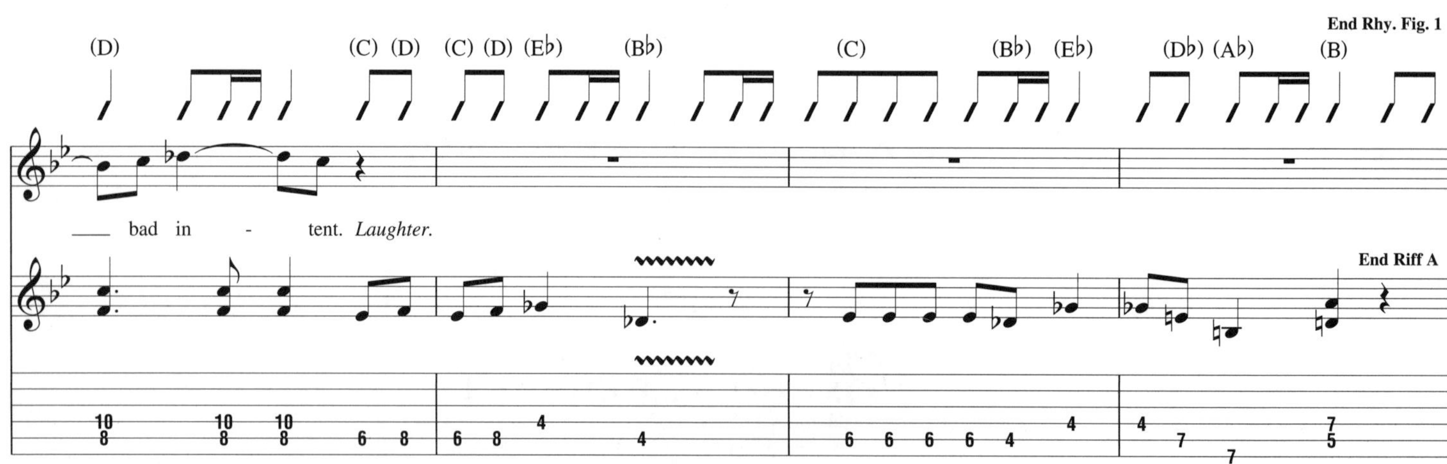

Gtr. 1: w/ Riff A (3 times)
Gtr. 2: w/ Rhy. Fig. 1
(Em)
* D♭ (B♭)
E♭ (C)
F (D)
E♭ F (C) (D)
Rhy. Fill 1
End Rhy. Fill 1
Gtr. 2
Snot's run - ning down his nose, greas - y fin - gers smear - ing shab - by clothes
*Symbols in parentheses represent chord names respective to capoed guitar. Symbols above reflect actual sounding chords.
E♭ F G♭ D♭ (C) (D) (E♭) (B♭)
E♭ (C)
D♭ G♭ (B♭) (E♭)
E B D (D♭) (A♭) (B)
Gtr. 2: w/ Rhy. Fill 1
Gm (Em)
Hey, Aq - ua - lung. Dry - ing in the cold sun,
Gtr. 2: w/ Rhy. Fig. 1
D♭ (B♭)
E♭ (C)
F (D)
E♭ F (C) (D)
watch - ing as the fril - ly pant - ies run.
Riff A1
Gtr. 3 (elec.)
f
w/ dist.
3 3 3
5 5 5
7 7 7 5 7
E♭ F G♭ D♭ (C) (D) (E♭) (B♭)
E♭ (C)
D♭ G♭ (B♭) (E♭)
E B D (D♭) (A♭) (B)
Hey, Aq - ua - lung.
End Riff A1
5 7 3 3
5 5 5 5 3 3
3 6 6 4
Gtr. 2: w/ Rhy. Fill 1
Gtr. 3 tacet
Gm (Em)
Gtr. 2: w/ Rhy. Fig. 1 (1st 5 meas.)
Gtr. 3: w/ Riff A1
D♭ (B♭)
E♭ (C)
Feel - ing like a dead duck, spit - ting out pie - ces of his

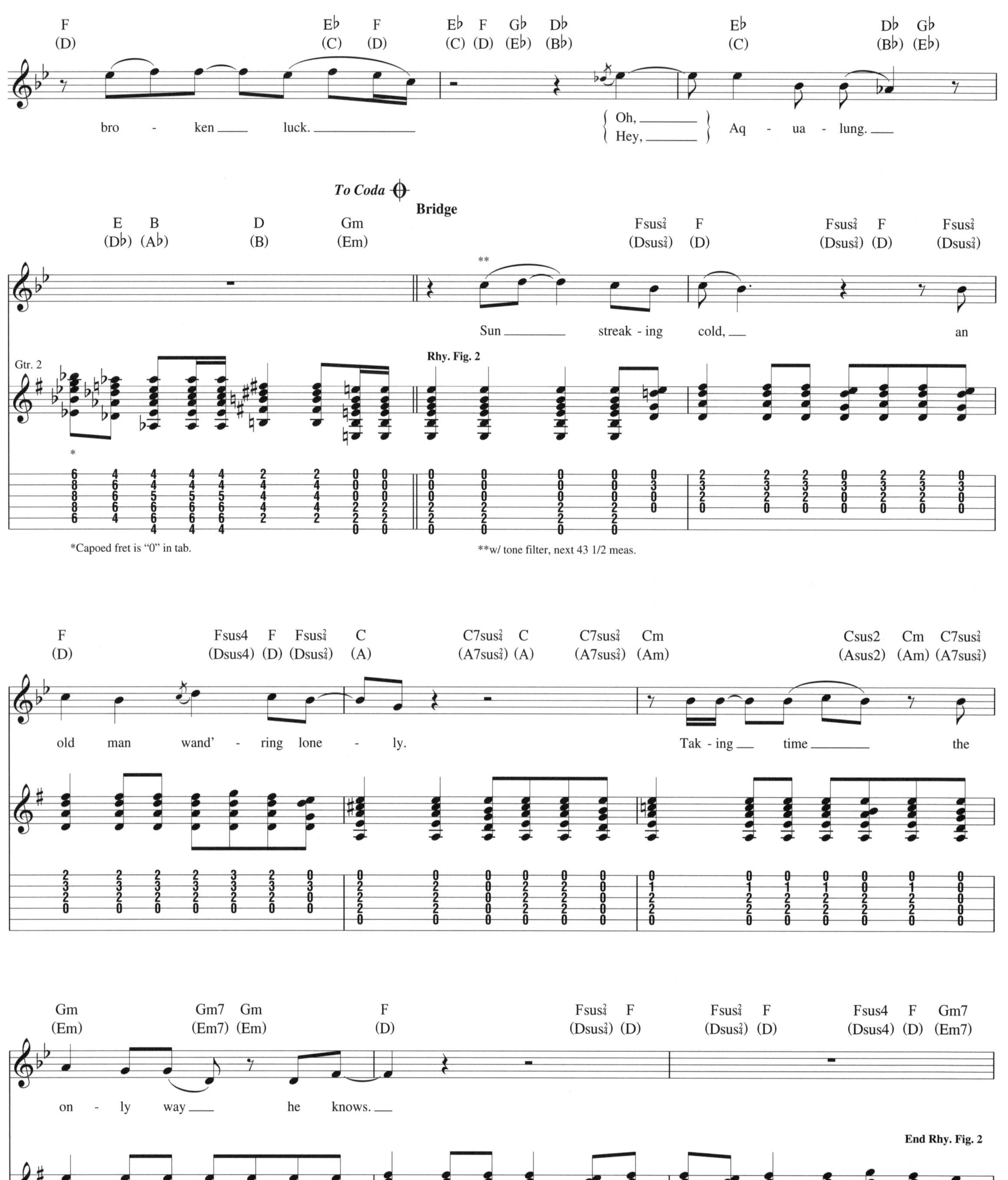
F (D)
E♭ (C)
F (D)
E♭ (C) F (D) G♭ (E♭) D♭ (B♭)
E♭ (C)
D♭ (B♭) G♭ (E♭)
bro - ken luck.
Oh, / Hey,
Aq - ua - lung.
To Coda
Bridge
E (D♭) B (A♭) D (B) Gm (Em)
Fsus2/4 (Dsus2/4) F (D)
Sun streak - ing cold, an
Gtr. 2
Rhy. Fig. 2
*Capoed fret is "0" in tab.
**w/ tone filter, next 43 1/2 meas.
F (D) Fsus4 (Dsus4) F (D) Fsus2/4 (Dsus2/4) C (A)
C7sus2/4 (A7sus2/4) C (A) C7sus2/4 (A7sus2/4) Cm (Am)
Csus2 (Asus2) Cm (Am) C7sus2/4 (A7sus2/4)
old man wand' - ring lone - ly.
Tak - ing time the
Gm (Em) Gm7 (Em7) Gm (Em) F (D)
Fsus2/4 (Dsus2/4) F (D) Fsus4 (Dsus4) F (D) Gm7 (Em7)
on - ly way he knows.
End Rhy. Fig. 2

Gtr. 2: w/ Rhy. Fig. 2
Gm (Em) Fsus2/4 (Dsus2/4) F (D) Fsus2/4 (Dsus2/4) F (D) Fsus2/4 (Dsus2/4) F (D) Fsus4 (Dsus4) F (D) Fsus2/4 (Dsus2/4) C (A) C7sus2/4 (A7sus2/4) C (A) C7sus2/4 (A7sus2/4)
Leg hurt - ing bad, as he bends to pick a dog - end. He
*Sung behind the beat.
Cm (Am) Csus2 (Asus2) Cm (Am) C7sus2/4 (A7sus2/4) Gm (Em) Gm7 (Em7) Gm (Em) F (D) Fsus2/4 (Dsus2/4) F (D) Fsus2/4 (Dsus2/4) F (D) Fsus4 (Dsus4) F (D) Gm7 (Em7)
goes down to the bog and warms his feet.
Fsus2/4 (Dsus2/4) F (D) Fsus2/4 (Dsus2/4) F (D) Fsus2/4 (Dsus2/4) F (D) Gm7 (Em7)
Gtr. 2
Gtr. 2: w/ Rhy. Fig. 2 (2 times)
Gm (Em) Fsus2/4 (Dsus2/4) F (D) Fsus2/4 (Dsus2/4) F (D) Fsus2/4 (Dsus2/4) F (D) Fsus4 (Dsus4) F (D) Fsus2/4 (Dsus2/4)
Feel - ing a - lone, the ar - my's up the road.
C (A) C7sus2/4 (A7sus2/4) C (A) C7sus2/4 (A7sus2/4) Cm (Am) Csus2 (Asus2) Cm (Am) C7sus2/4 (A7sus2/4) Gm (Em) Gm7 (Em7) Gm (Em)
Sal - va - tion a la mode and a cup of
F (D) Fsus2/4 (Dsus2/4) F (D) Fsus2/4 (Dsus2/4) F (D) Fsus4 (Dsus4) F (D) Gm7 (Em7) Gm (Em) Fsus2/4 (Dsus2/4)
tea. Aq - ua - lung, my
F (D) Fsus2/4 (Dsus2/4) F (D) Fsus2/4 (Dsus2/4) F (D) Fsus4 (Dsus4) F (D) Fsus2/4 (Dsus2/4) C (A) C7sus2/4 (A7sus2/4) C (A) C7sus2/4 (A7sus2/4)
friend, don't you start a - way un - eas - y. You

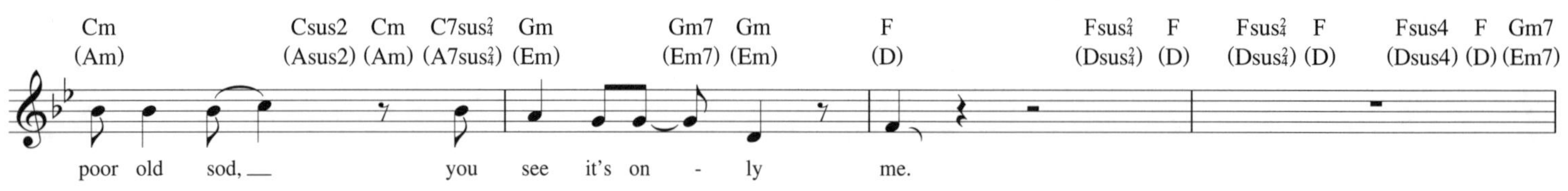
Cm
(Am)
Csus2
(Asus2)
Cm
(Am)
C7sus4
(A7sus4)
Gm
(Em)
Gm7
(Em7)
Gm
(Em)
F
(D)
Fsus4
(Dsus4)
F
(D)
Fsus4
(Dsus4)
F
(D)
Fsus4
(Dsus4)
F
(D)
Gm7
(Em7)
poor old sod, you see it's on - ly me.

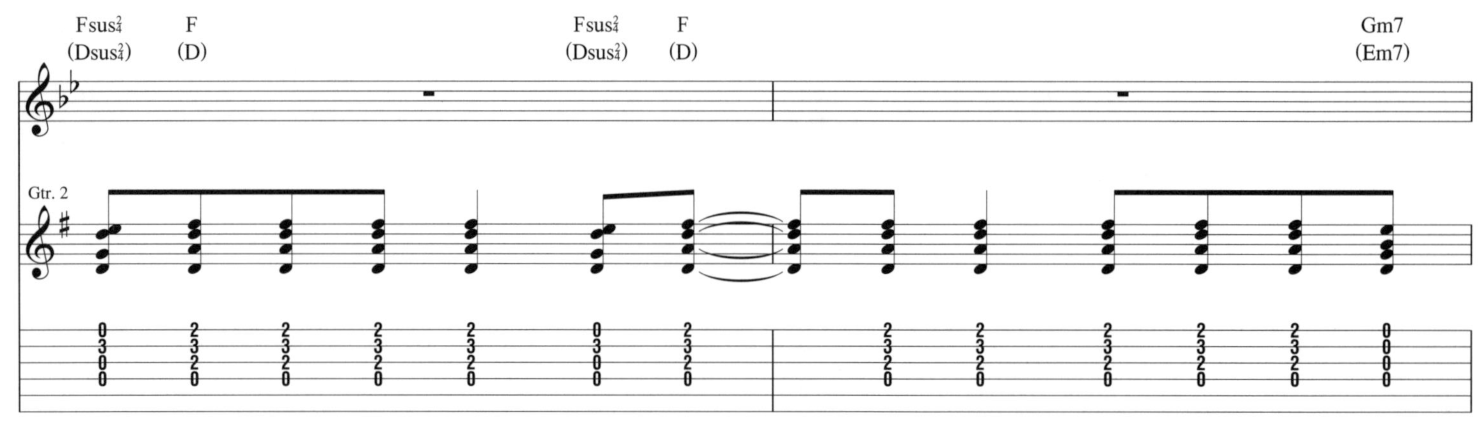
Fsus4
(Dsus4)
F
(D)
Fsus4
(Dsus4)
F
(D)
Gm7
(Em7)
Gtr. 2

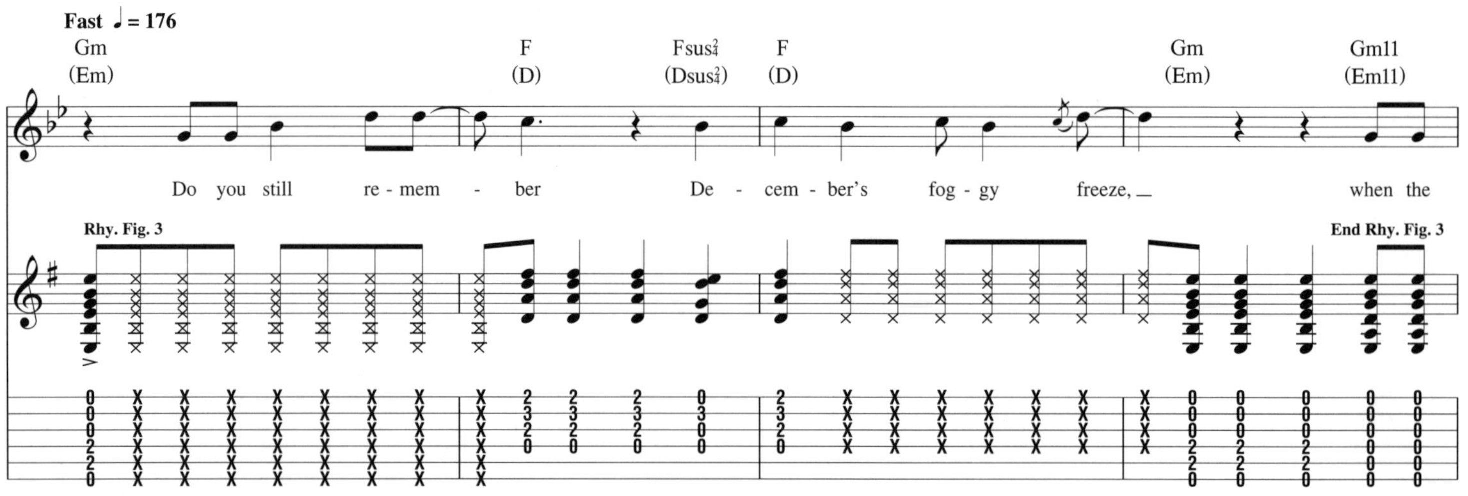
Fast ♩ = 176
Gm
(Em)
F
(D)
Fsus4
(Dsus4)
F
(D)
Gm
(Em)
Gm11
(Em11)
Do you still re - mem - ber De - cem - ber's fog - gy freeze, when the
Rhy. Fig. 3
End Rhy. Fig. 3

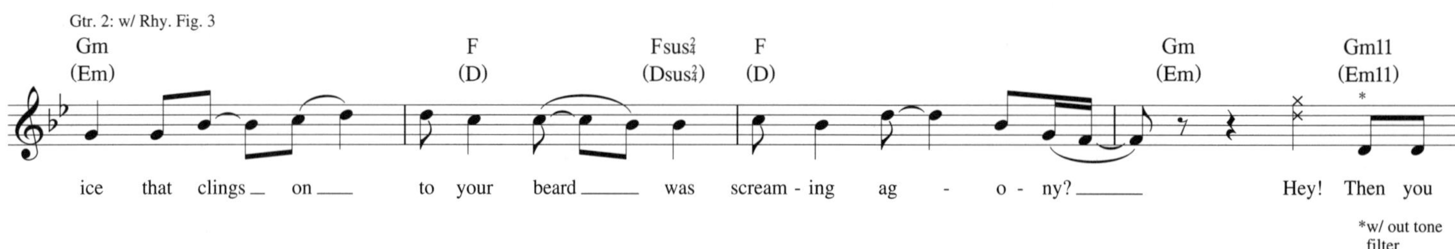
Gtr. 2: w/ Rhy. Fig. 3
Gm
(Em)
F
(D)
Fsus4
(Dsus4)
F
(D)
Gm
(Em)
Gm11
(Em11)
ice that clings on to your beard was scream - ing ag - o - ny? Hey! Then you
*w/ out tone filter

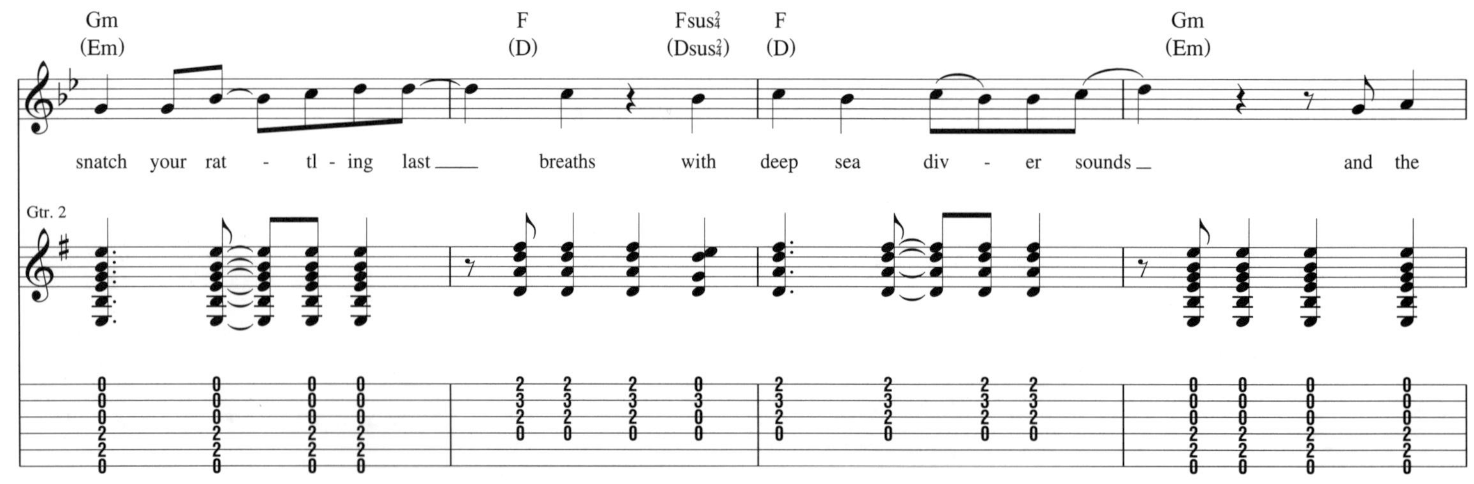
Gm
(Em)
F
(D)
Fsus4
(Dsus4)
F
(D)
Gm
(Em)
snatch your rat - tl - ing last breaths with deep sea div - er sounds and the
Gtr. 2

Cm (Am)
F (D)
Fsus2/4 (Dsus2/4)
flow - ers bloom like mad - ness in the spring.
F (D)
Fsus4 (Dsus4)
F (D)
Fsus2/4 (Dsus2/4)
F (D)
Fsus2/4 (Dsus2/4)
F (D)
Gm7 (Em7)
Gm (Em)
Sun streak - ing
Rhy. Fig. 4
F (D)
Fsus2/4 (Dsus2/4)
F (D)
C (A)
C7sus2/4 (A7sus2/4)
Cm (Am)
cold, an old man wand' - ring lone - ly, tak - ing time the
Gm (Em)
F (D)
Fsus2/4 (Dsus2/4)
F (D)
Fsus4 (Dsus4)
F (D)
Fsus2/4 (Dsus2/4)
on - ly way he knows.
End Rhy. Fig. 4

Gtr. 2: w/ Rhy. Fig. 4
Gm (Em) F (D) Fsus2/4 (Dsus2/4) F (D) C (A) C7sus2/4 (A7sus2/4)
Leg hurt - ing bad, as he bends to pick a dog - end. He
Cm (Am) Gm (Em) F (D) Fsus2/4 (Dsus2/4) F (D) Fsus4 (Dsus4) F (D) Fsus2/4 (Dsus2/4)
goes down to the bog and warms his feet.
F (D) Fsus4 (Dsus4) F (D) Fsus2/4 (Dsus2/4) Gm (Em)
Whoa, ho, ho, no. Feel - ing a - lone,
Gtr. 2
Rhy. Fig. 5
F (D) Fsus2/4 (Dsus2/4) F (D) C (A) C7sus2 (A7sus2)
the ar - my's up the road. Sal -
End Rhy. Fig. 5
Gtr. 2: w/ Rhy. Fig. 4 (last 4 meas.)
Cm (Am) Gm (Em) F (D) Fsus2/4 (Dsus2/4)
va - tion a la mode and a cup of tea.
Gtr. 2: w/ Rhy. Fig. 5
F (D) Fsus4 (Dsus4) F (D) Fsus2/4 (Dsus2/4) Gm (Em) F (D) Fsus2/4 (Dsus2/4)
Aq - ua - lung, my friend, don't you
Gtr. 2: w/ Rhy. Fig. 4 (last 4 meas.)
F (D) C (A) C7sus2 (A7sus2) Cm (Am)
start a - way un - eas - y. You poor old sod, you

Gm
(Em)
F
(D)
Fsus2/4
(Dsus2/4)
F
(D)
Fsus4
(Dsus4)
F
(D)
Fsus2/4
(Dsus2/4)
see it's on - ly me,
me.
(D open)
Gtr. 2
Oh, ho, ho, ho, oh,
Gtr. 1
Interlude
(Em)
(D open)
no.
(A)
*Gtrs. 1 & 3
*Composite arrangement
(Am)
(Em)
fdbk.
let ring
fdbk.

Gtr. 3 tacet
(D open)
Gtr. 1
let ring
Guitar Solo
(Em)
(C open)
(D open)
(Em)
Rhy. Fig. 6
End Rhy. Fig. 6
Gtr. 2: w/ Rhy. Fig. 6 (2 times)
Gm
(Em)
E♭
(C)
F
(D)
Gm
(Em)
fdbk.
Pitch: G
E♭
(C)
F
(D)
Gm
(Em)
let ring
(Em)
(C open)
(D open)
(Dsus4)
(D open)
(Dsus4)
(D open)
Gtr. 2
Gtr. 1
let ring
let ring
let ring

Gtr. 2: w/ Rhy. Fig. 6 (3 1/2 times)
(D open)
(Dsus4)
(D open)
Gm
(Em)
E♭
(C)
let ring
F
(D)
let ring
Gm
(Em)
E♭
(C)
F
(D)
Gm
(Em)
E♭
(C)
F
(D)
let ring
Gm
(Em)
E♭
(C)
(D open)
(Dsus4)
(D open)
(Dsus4)
(D open)
Gtr. 2
Gtr. 1
let ring
let ring

Bridge
A tempo
Gtr. 1 tacet
Gtr. 2: w/ Rhy. Fig. 2 (1 1/2 times)
Dee, dee, dee, dee, dee, dee, dee, dee, dee, dee.
Dee, dee, dee, dee, dee, dee, dee, dee, dee, dee.
Aq - ua - lung, my
friend, don't you start a - way un - eas - y.
You poor old sod, you see it's on - ly me, yeah.
Hmm.
Gtr. 2

D.S. al Coda

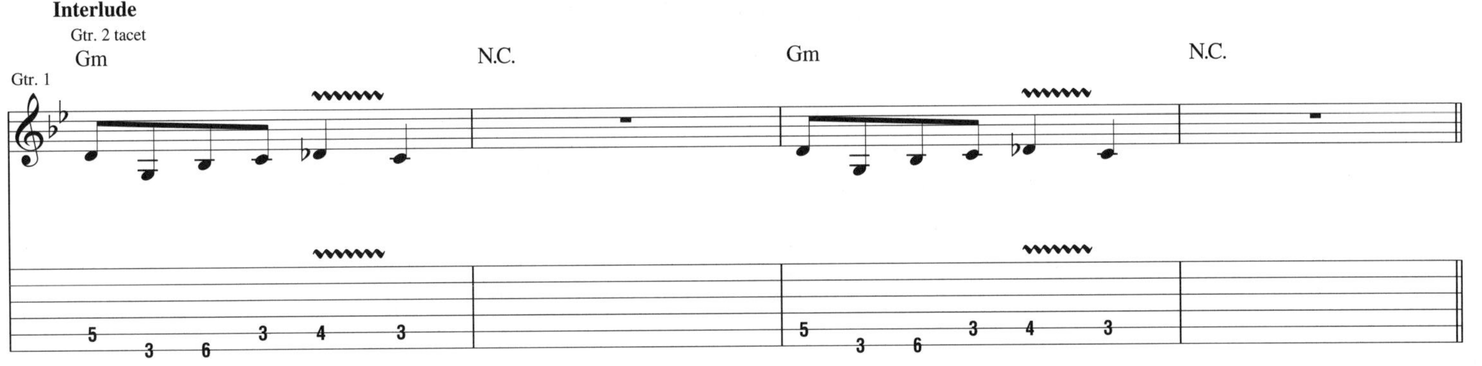
Interlude
Gtr. 2 tacet
Gm
N.C.
Gm
N.C.
Gtr. 1

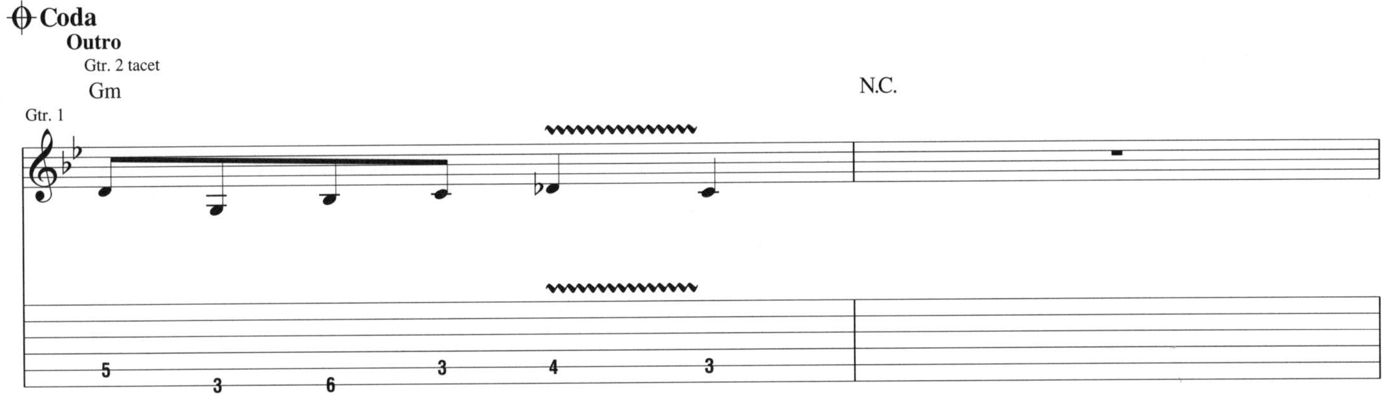
Coda
Outro
Gtr. 2 tacet
Gm
N.C.
Gtr. 1

Gm
N.C.
Gm
(cont. in slashes)

Free time
D♭5
E♭5
F5
Gtr. 1
Whoa, oh, oh, Aq - ua - lung.
Gtr. 3

Cross-Eyed Mary

Words and Music by Ian Anderson

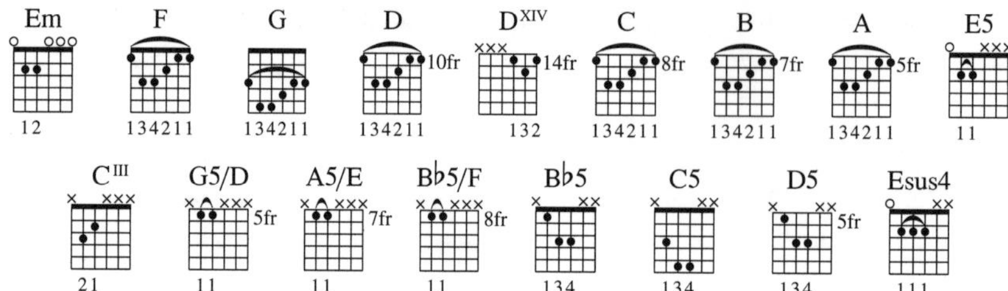

Intro
Moderately slow Rock ♩ = 84

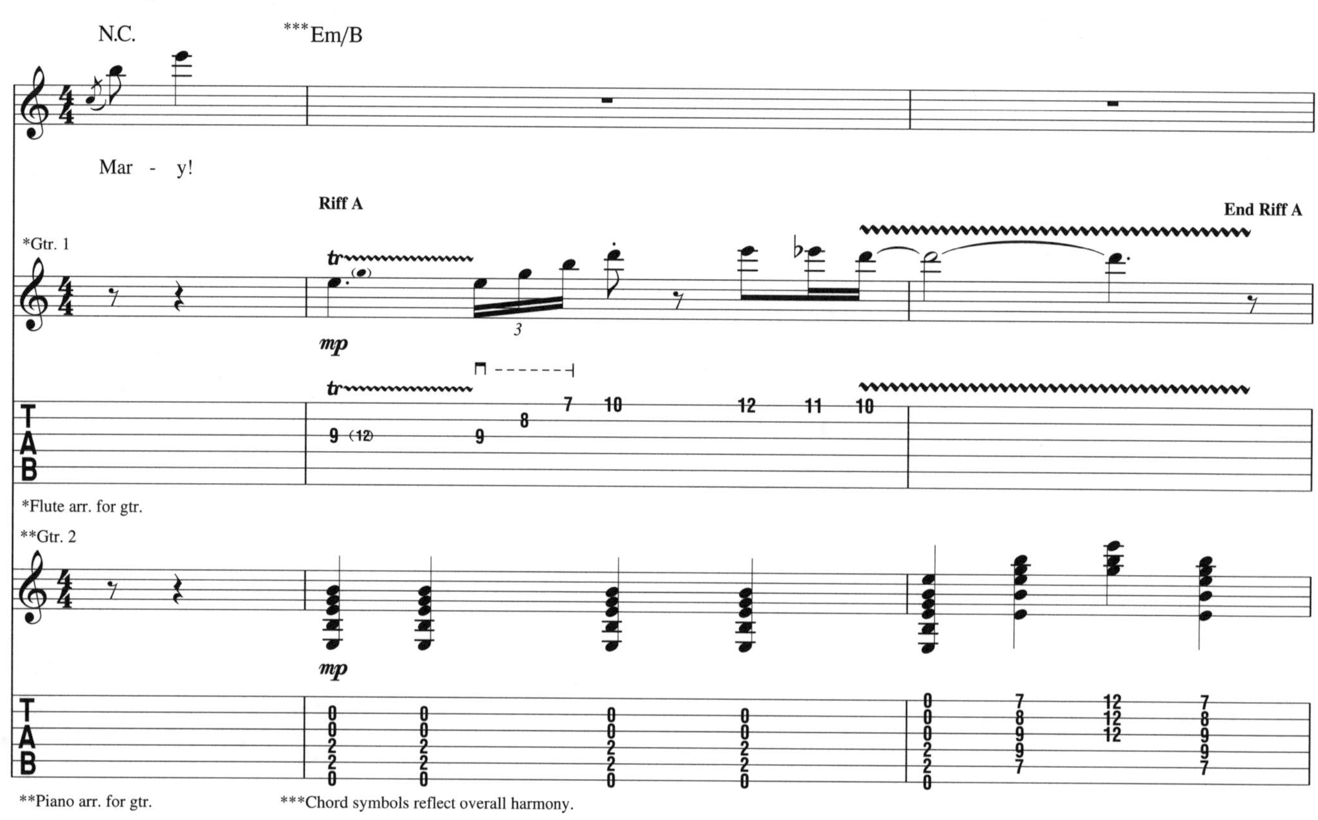

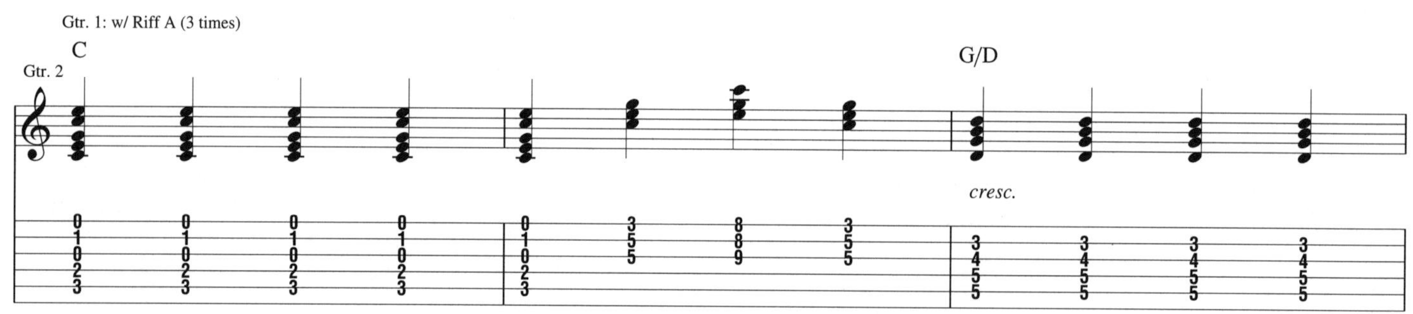

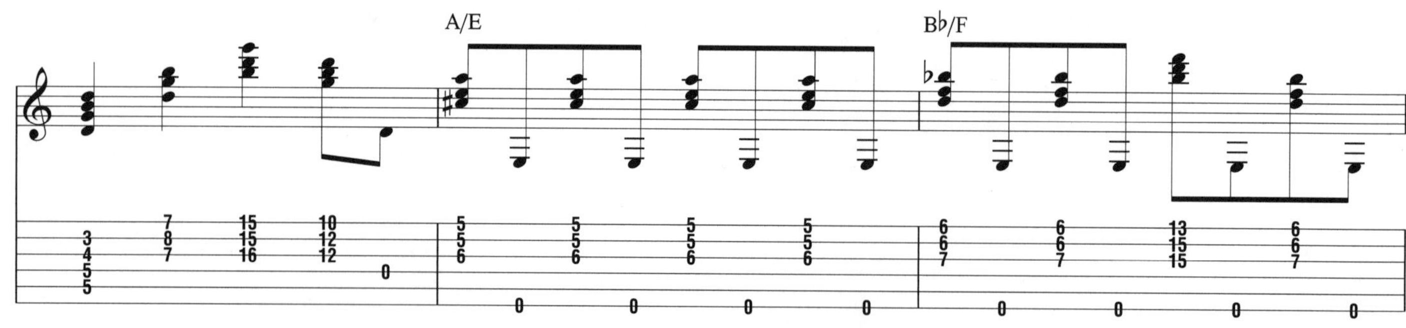

Gtr. 2 tacet
Em
Bb
Em
Gtr. 1
mf
Gtr. 3 (dist.)
mp
Bb
C
Ab
D
C
Cm

B♭
A7
Esus4
Verse
Gtrs. 1 & 3 tacet
Em
Rhy. Fig. 1
F
Gtr. 2
1. Who would be a poor man, a beg - gar - man, a thief,
Rhy. Fig. 1A
*Gtr. 4 (fuzz)
w/ wah-wah as filter
*Two gtrs. arr. for one.
G
D
D^XIV
D
End Rhy. Fig. 1
if he had a rich man in his hand?
End Rhy. Fig. 1A

Gtrs. 2 & 4: w/ Rhy. Figs. 1 & 1A
Em
F
And who would steal the can - dy from a laugh - ing ba - by's mouth if

G
D
he could take it from the mon - ey man?

Chorus
*Am
G5
Am
G5
Cross - eyed Mar - y, a goes jump - ing in a - gain. She
Rhy. Fig. 2
End Rhy. Fig. 2
Gtr. 4
*Chord symbols reflect implied harmony.

Gtr. 4: w/ Rhy. Fig. 2
Am
G5
Am
G5
signs no con - tract, but she al - ways plays the game. She

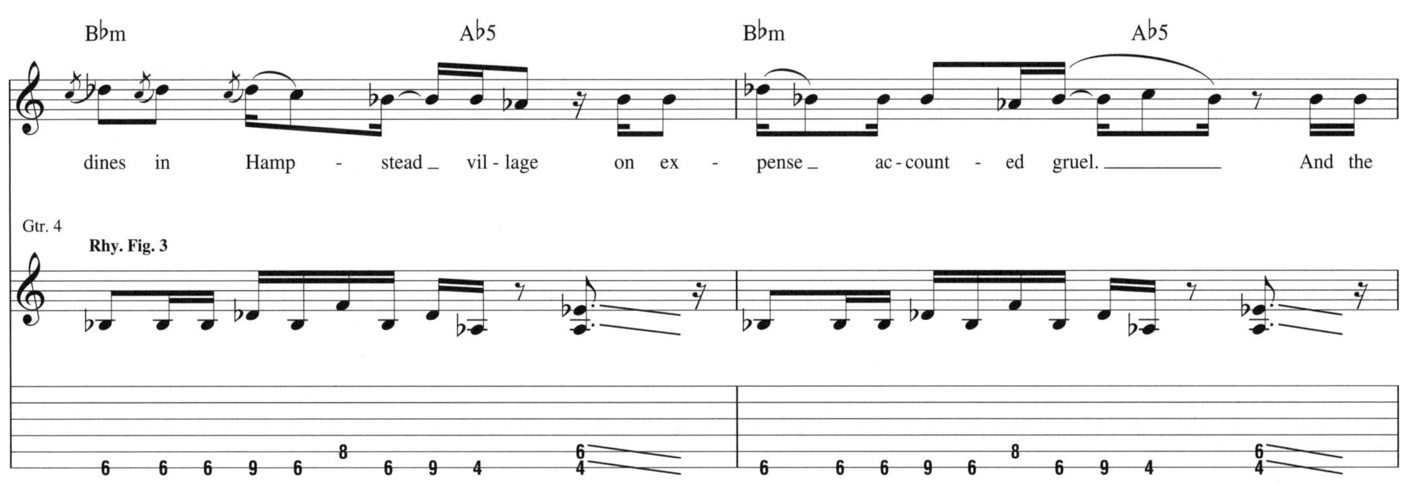
B♭m
A♭5
B♭m
A♭5
dines in Hamp - stead vil - lage on ex - pense ac - count - ed gruel. And the
Gtr. 4
Rhy. Fig. 3

To Coda
B♭m
A♭5
C
D
C D
B
A B
Rhy. Fig. 4
End Rhy. Fig. 4
Gtr. 2
(1st time, cont. in notation)
jack - knife bar - ber drops her off at school. Hey!
End Rhy. Fig. 3
Rhy. Fig. 4A
End Rhy. Fig. 4A
Verse
Gtr. 4: w/ Rhy. Fig. 1A (2 times)
Em
F
2. Laugh-ing in the play - ground, gets no kicks from lit - tle boys. Would
Rhy. Fig. 5
Gtr. 2
G
D
rath - er make it with a letch - ing grey.
End Rhy. Fig. 5
Gtr. 2: w/ Rhy. Fig. 5
Em
F
G
Or may-be her at - ten - tion is drawn by Aq-ua - lung, who watch-es through the rail - ings as they

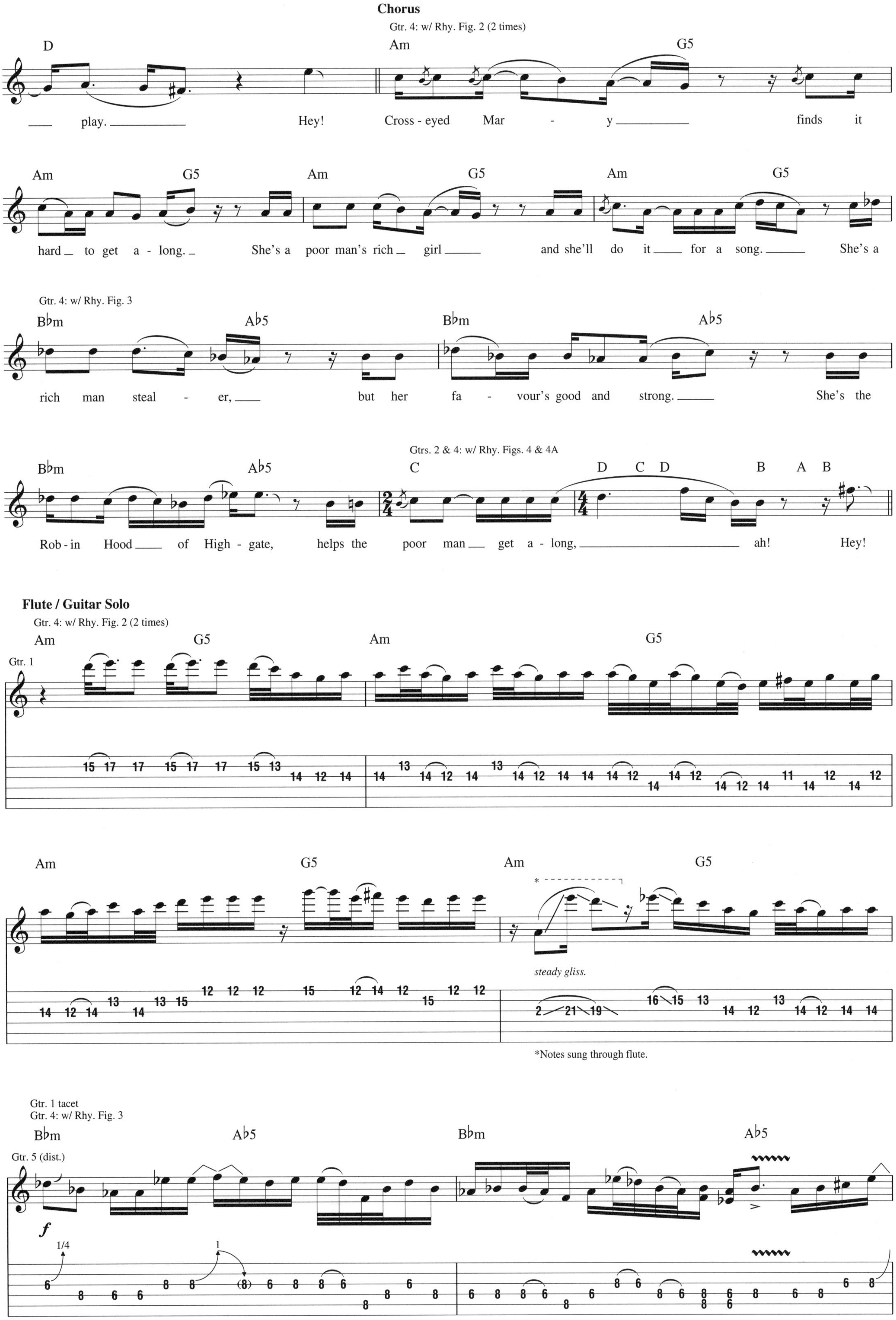

Chorus

Gtr. 4: w/ Rhy. Fig. 2 (2 times)

D | Am | G5

play. Hey! Cross-eyed Mar - y finds it

Am | G5 | Am | G5 | Am | G5

hard to get a - long. She's a poor man's rich girl and she'll do it for a song. She's a

Gtr. 4: w/ Rhy. Fig. 3

B♭m | A♭5 | B♭m | A♭5

rich man steal - er, but her fa - vour's good and strong. She's the

Gtrs. 2 & 4: w/ Rhy. Figs. 4 & 4A

B♭m | A♭5 | C | D C D | B A B

Rob - in Hood of High - gate, helps the poor man get a - long, ah! Hey!

Flute / Guitar Solo

Gtr. 4: w/ Rhy. Fig. 2 (2 times)

Am | G5 | Am | G5

Gtr. 1

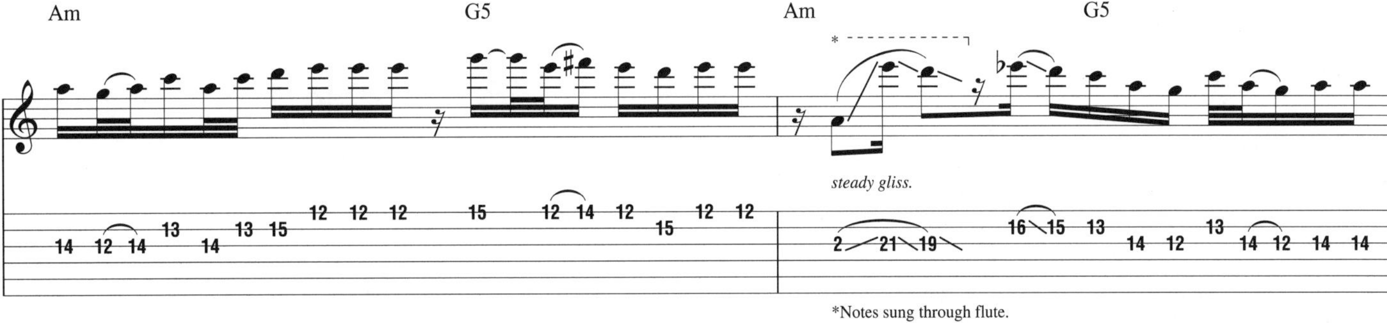

*Notes sung through flute.

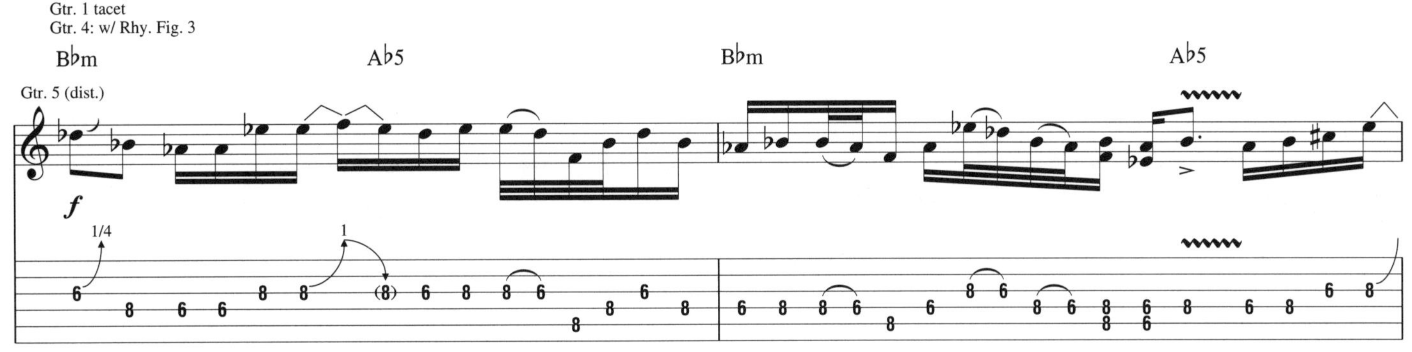

Gtrs. 2 & 4: w/ Rhy. Figs. 4 & 4A
B♭m
A♭5
C
D
C D
B A B
1
1/2
1

Verse

Gtr. 2: w/ Rhy. Fig. 1 (2 times)
Gtr. 5 tacet
Em
F
3. Laugh-ing in the play - ground, gets no kicks from lit - tle boys, would
Gtr. 4
Rhy. Fig. 6
P.M.

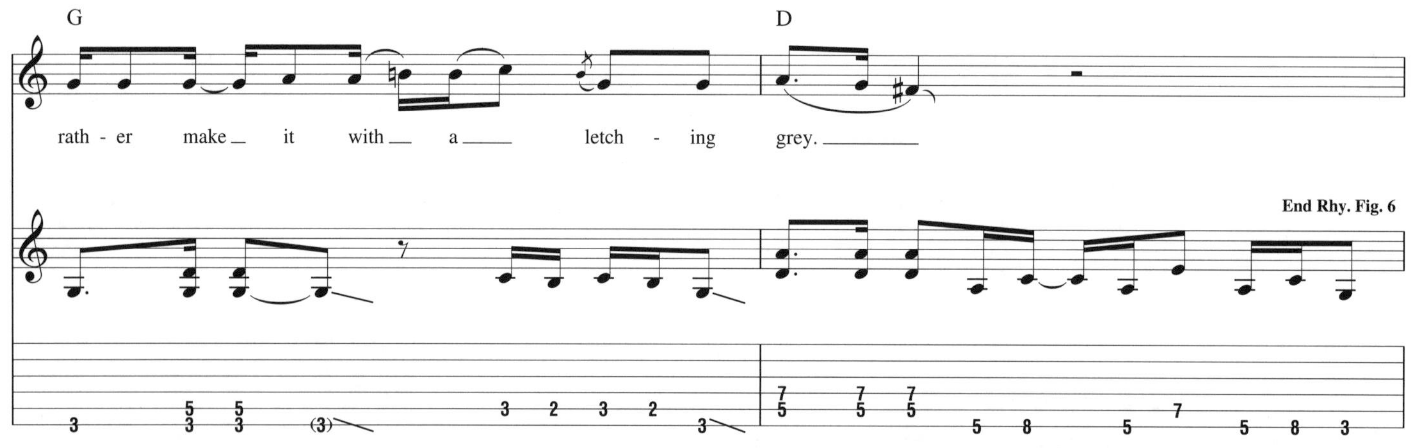
G
D
rath - er make it with a letch - ing grey.
End Rhy. Fig. 6

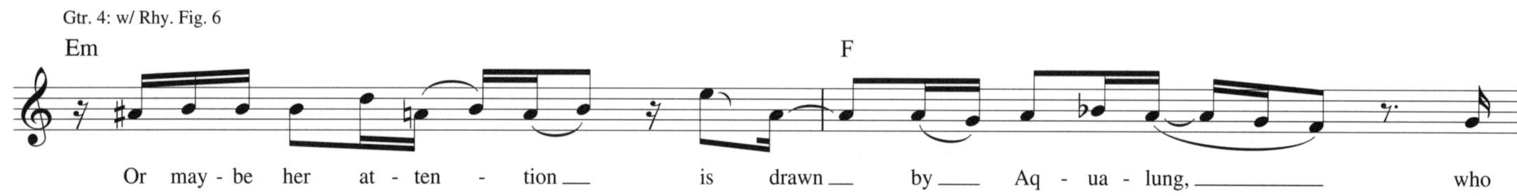
Gtr. 4: w/ Rhy. Fig. 6
Em
F
Or may - be her at - ten - tion is drawn by Aq - ua - lung, who

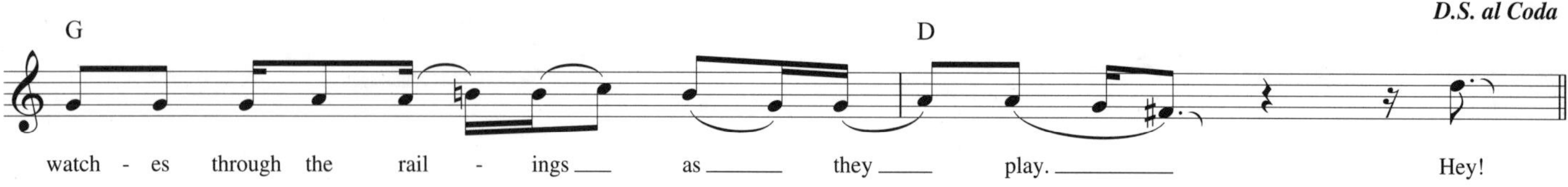
D.S. al Coda
G
D
watch - es through the rail - ings as they play. Hey!

Coda
Outro
Gtrs. 2 & 4 tacet
E5
C^III
Gtr. 3
Cross - eyed Mar - y.
Gtr. 1
Gtr. 1 tacet
G5/D
Gtr. 5 tacet
A5/E
B♭/F
Gtr. 5
Gtr. 2
Gtr. 2 tacet
E5
B♭5
C5
D5
rit.
Oh, Mar - y!
Oh,
Gtr. 1
rit.
Free time
Esus4
E5
oh, Cross-eyed Mar - y.
Yeow!

Cheap Day Return

Words and Music by Ian Anderson

Gtrs. 1 & 2: Capo VII

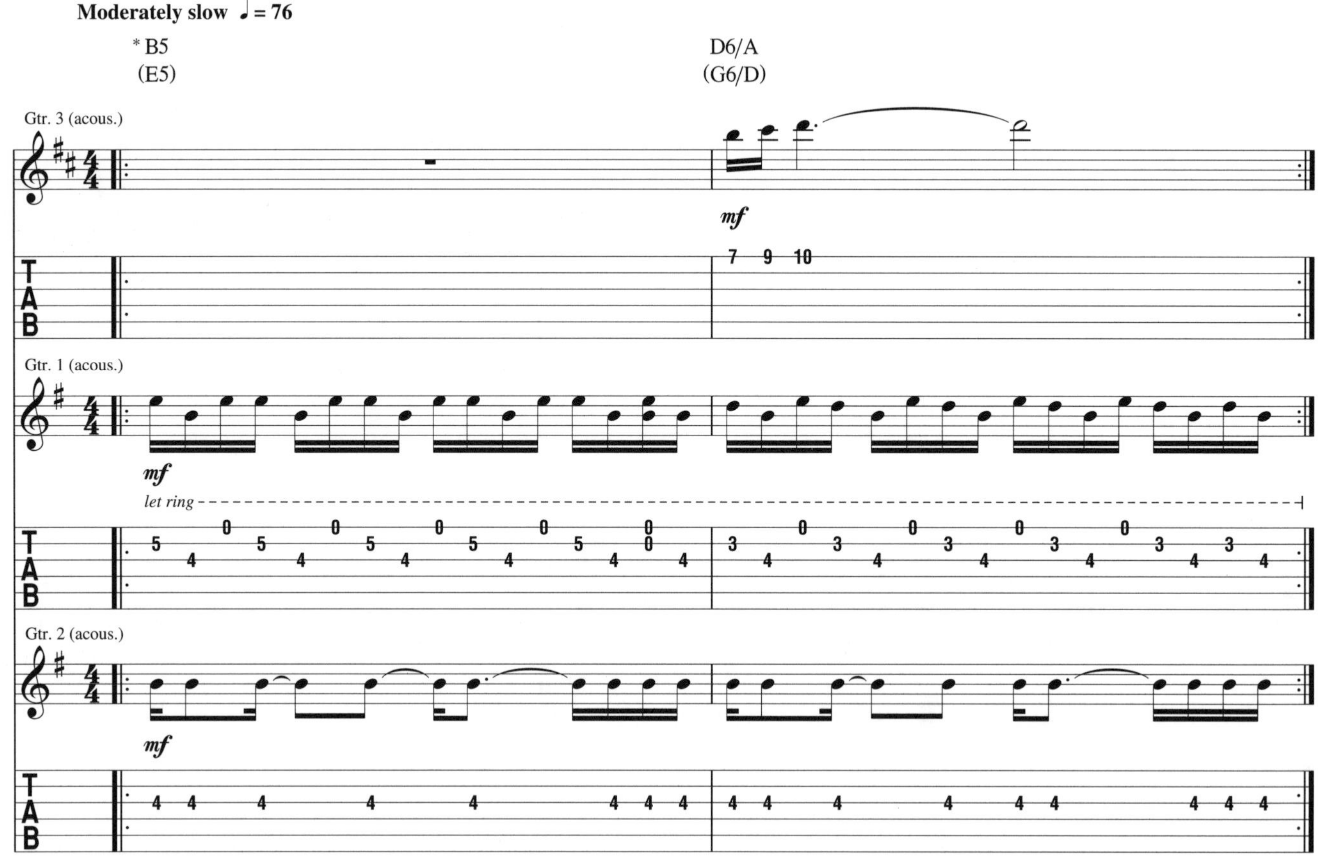

*Symbols in parentheses represent chord names respective to capoed guitar. Symbols above reflect actual sounding chords. Capoed fret is "0" in tab. Chord symbols reflect implied harmony.

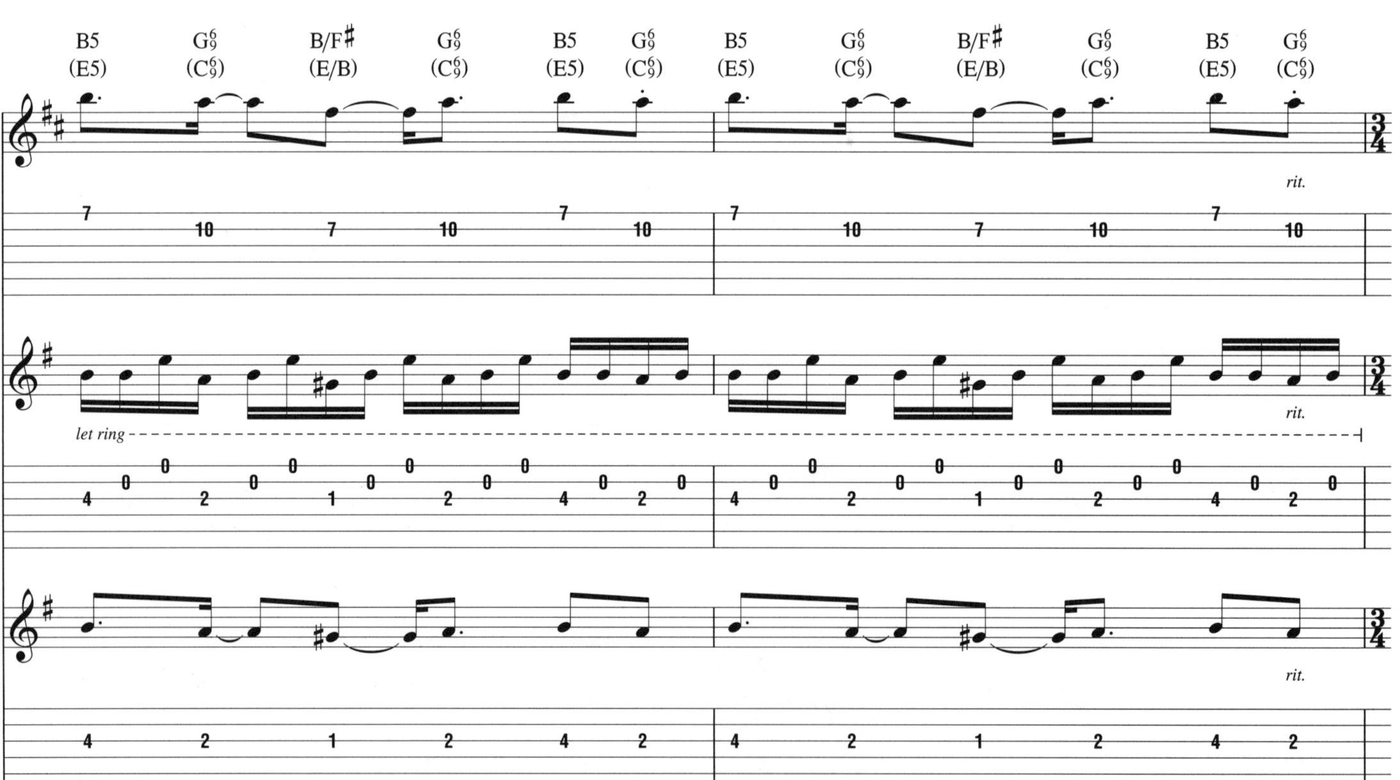

A tempo
Gtr. 2 tacet
Bm
(Em)
N.C.
Bm9
(Em9)
N.C.
Gtr. 3
Gtr. 2
divisi
Gtr. 1
let ring
A
(D)
N.C.
A tempo
Bm
(Em)
rit.
Verse
G
(C)
A
(D)
D
(G)
A/C♯
(D/F♯)
Bm
(Em)
On Pres - ton plat - form do your soft shoe shuf - fle dance.
1/2

G (C) A (D) D (G) A/C♯ (D/F♯) E (A)

Brush a-way the cig-'rette ash that's fall-ing down your pants.

1

let ring

G (C) A (D) D (G) A/C♯ (D/F♯) Bm (Em)

And then you sad-ly won-der, does the nurse treat your old man the way she, sh, should?

let ring

A
(D)

G
(C)

Gsus2
(Csus2)

She made you tea, asked for your au - to-graph.

1/2

mp let ring

mf let ring

let ring

Outro

D
(G)

A/C♯
(D/F♯)

Bm
(Em)

A
(D)

Spoken: What a laugh.

let ring

let ring

mp let ring

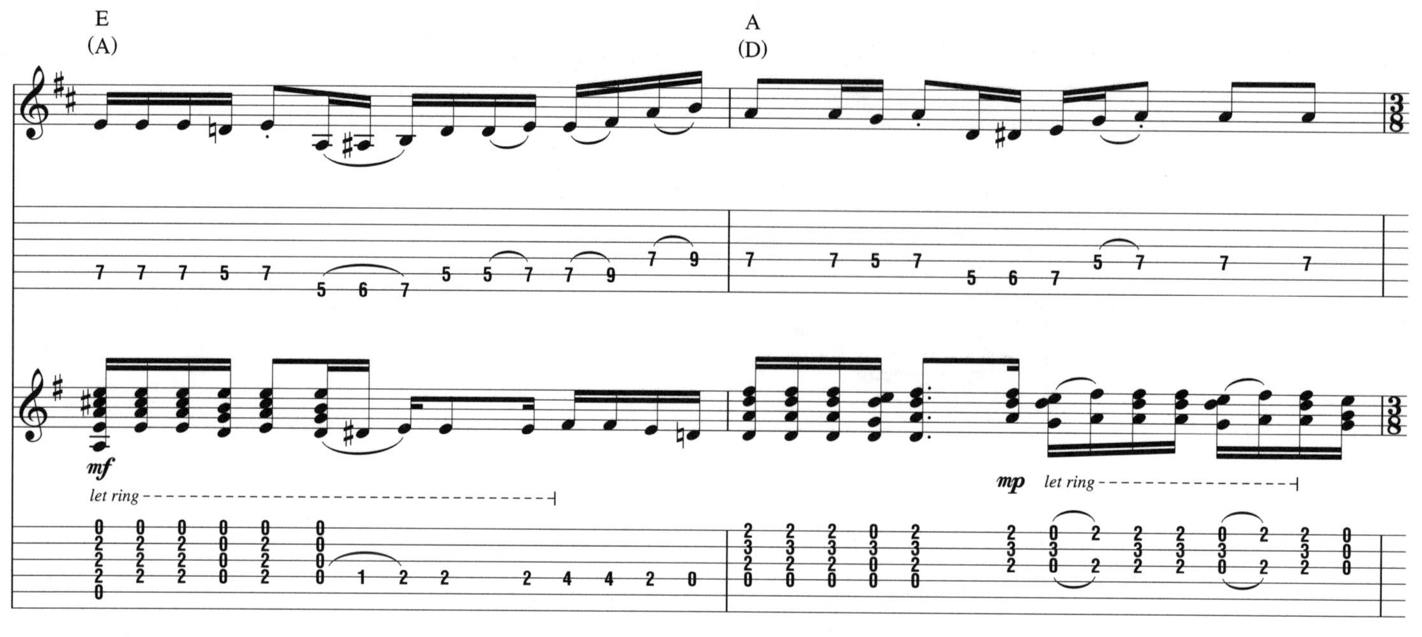
E
(A)
A
(D)
mf
let ring
mp
let ring

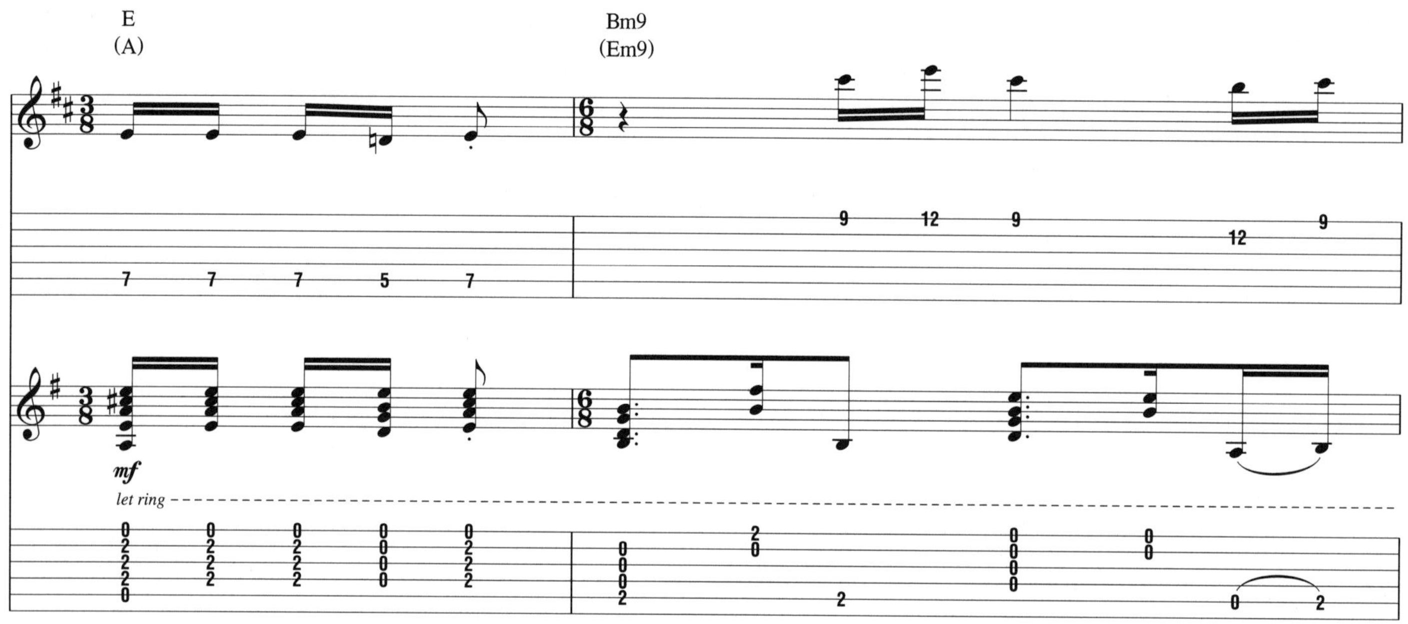
E
(A)
Bm9
(Em9)
mf
let ring

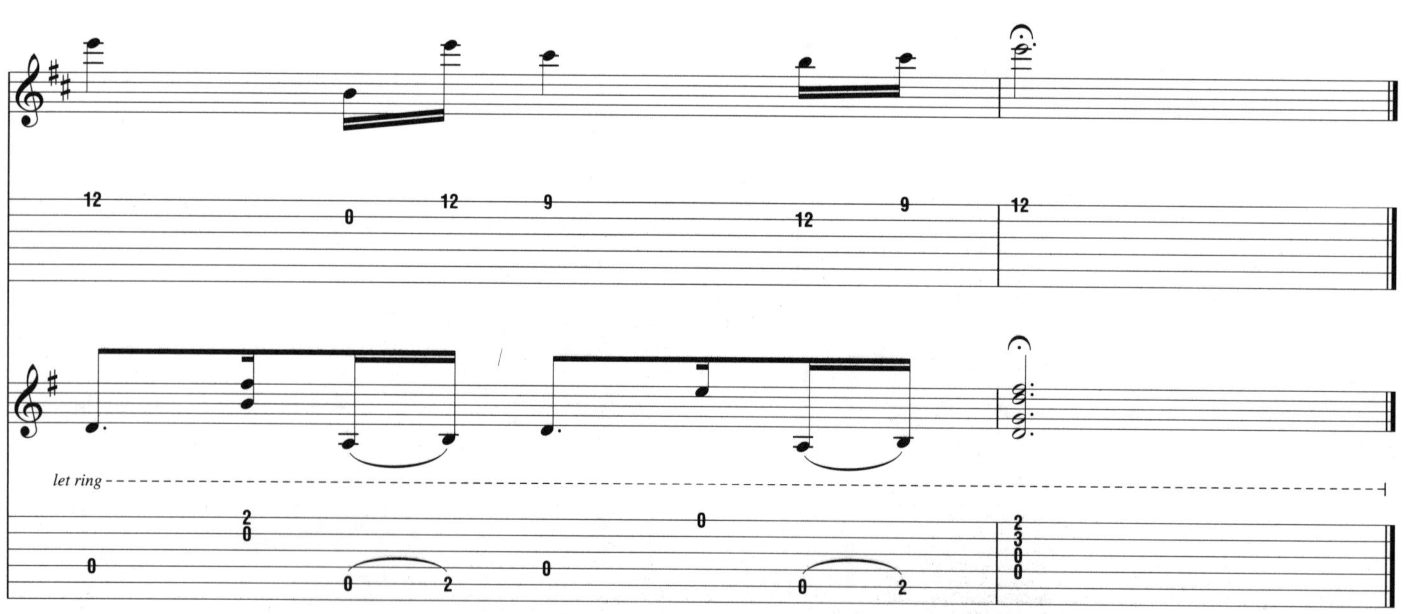
let ring

Mother Goose

Words and Music by Ian Anderson

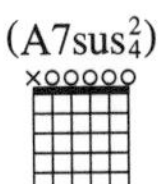

Gtrs. 1 & 2: Capo V

Intro

Moderately slow ♩ = 96

**Dsus2 (Asus2) — C5 (G5) — Dsus2 (Asus2) — C5 (G5)

Rhy. Fig. 1

*Gtrs. 1 & 2 (acous.)

mf

let ring throughout

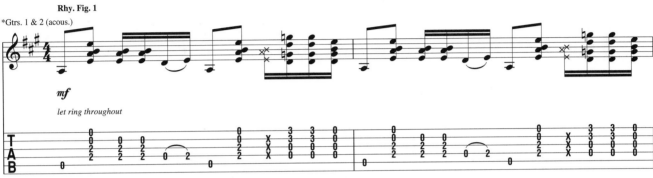

*Composite arrangement

**Symbols in parentheses represent chord names respective to capoed guitar. Symbols above reflect actual sounding chords. Capoed fret is "0" in tab. Chord symbols reflect basic harmony.

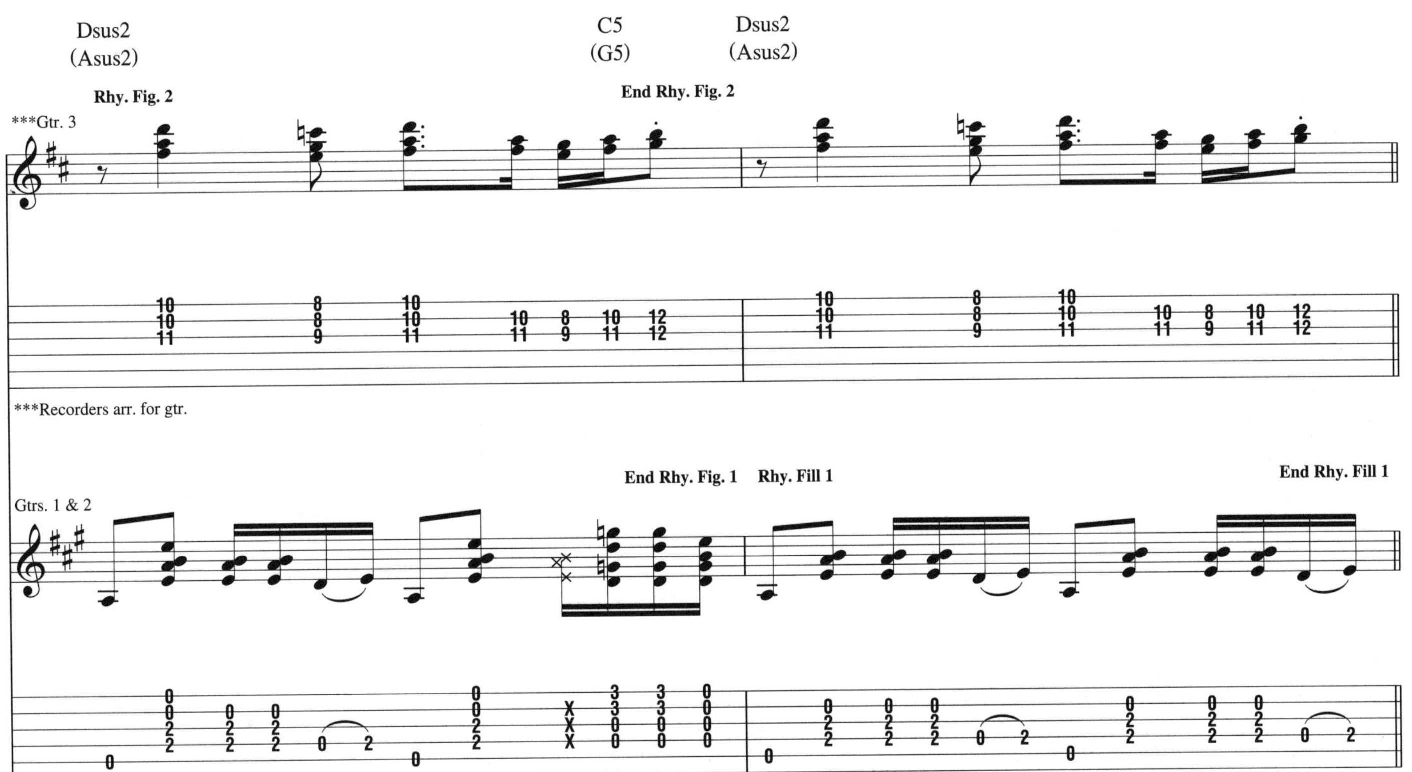

Verse
Gtr. 3 tacet
D7sus2
(A7sus2)
Dsus2
(Asus2)
F
(C)
1. As I did walk by Hamp - stead Fair I came up - on
2. And a beard - ed la - dy said to me, "If you
Gtrs. 1 & 2

G
(D)
F
(C)
G
(D)
G/F
(D/C)
Moth - er Goose, so I turned her loose and she was scream-
start your rav - ing and your mis - be - hav - ing you'll be

Gtr. 3: w/ Rhy. Fig. 2 (2 times)
Dsus2
(Asus2)
C5
(G5)
Dsus2
(Asus2)
C5
(G5)
- ing.
sor - ry."
Yeah.

D7sus2
(A7sus2)
Dsus2
(Asus2)
F
(C)
And a for - eign stu - dent said to me, "Was it
Then the chick - en - fan - ci - er came to play with his
Rhy. Fig. 3

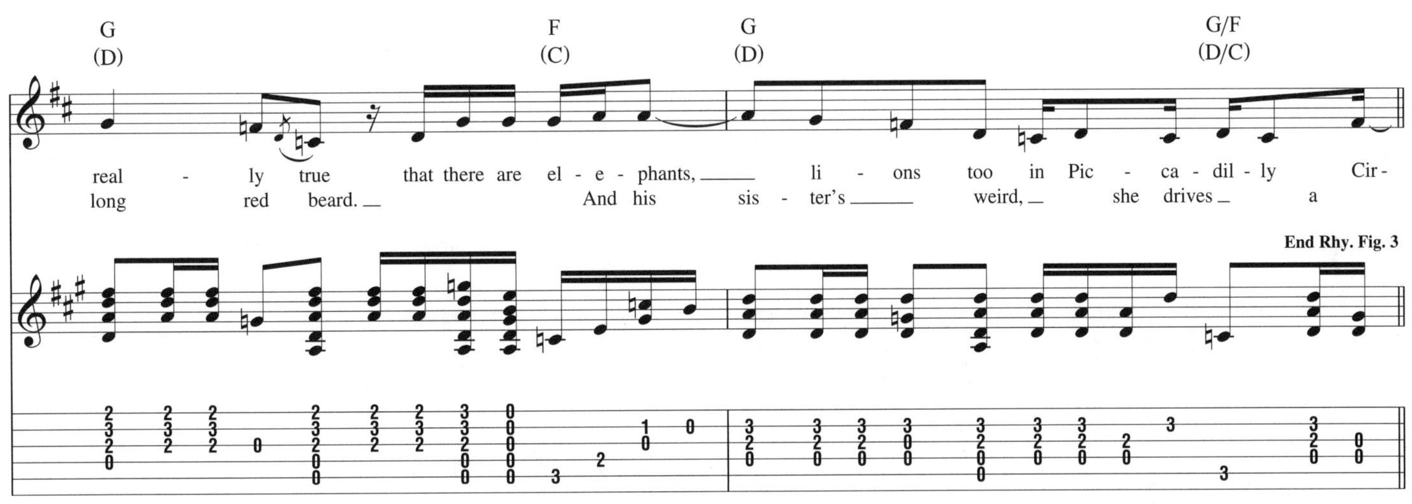
G
(D)
F
(C)
G
(D)
G/F
(D/C)
real - ly true that there are el - e - phants, li - ons too in Pic - ca - dil - ly Cir -
long red beard. And his sis - ter's weird, she drives a
End Rhy. Fig. 3

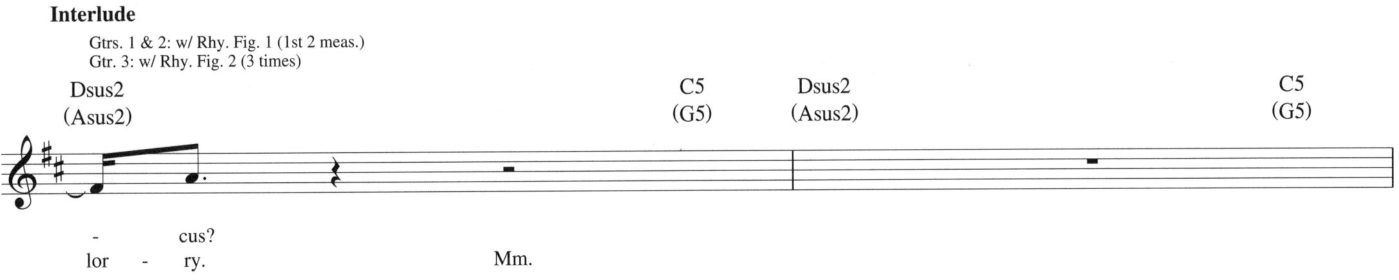
Interlude
Gtrs. 1 & 2: w/ Rhy. Fig. 1 (1st 2 meas.)
Gtr. 3: w/ Rhy. Fig. 2 (3 times)
Dsus2
(Asus2)
C5
(G5)
Dsus2
(Asus2)
C5
(G5)
- cus?
lor - ry. Mm.

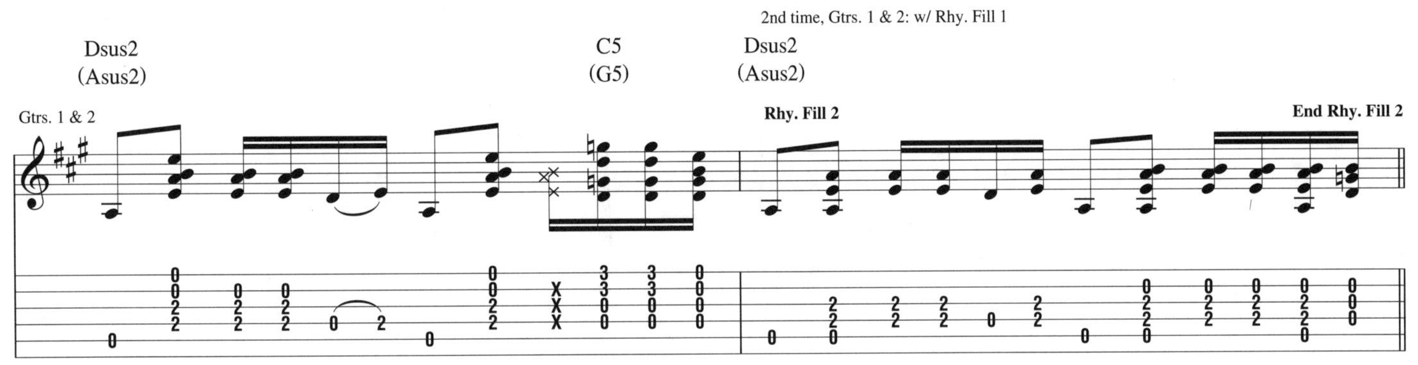
2nd time, Gtrs. 1 & 2: w/ Rhy. Fill 1
Dsus2
(Asus2)
C5
(G5)
Dsus2
(Asus2)
Gtrs. 1 & 2
Rhy. Fill 2
End Rhy. Fill 2

𝄋 Chorus

3rd time, Gtr. 4 tacet

G (D) D/F♯ (A/C♯) G (D) C/E (G/B) C (G) G (D)

1., 3. Walked down by the bath - ing pond to try and catch some su - un.
2. Laughed down by the put-ting green, I popped 'em in their ho - oles.

Gtrs. 1 & 2

Rhy. Fig. 4

D (A) D7sus4/2 (A7sus4/2) D (A) D7sus4/2 (A7sus4/2) G (D) D/F♯ (A/C♯) G (D)

Saw / Must a been at least a hun - dred school girls sob-bing in - to hand -
Four and twen-ty la - bor - ers were la - bor-ing and

End Rhy. Fig. 4

Gtrs. 1 & 2: w/ Rhy. Fig. 4

C/E (G/B) C (G) G (D) D (A) D7sus4/2 (A7sus4/2) D (A) D7sus4/2 (A7sus4/2)

- ker - chiefs as o - one. I
dig-ging up their go - old. I

To Coda 𝄌

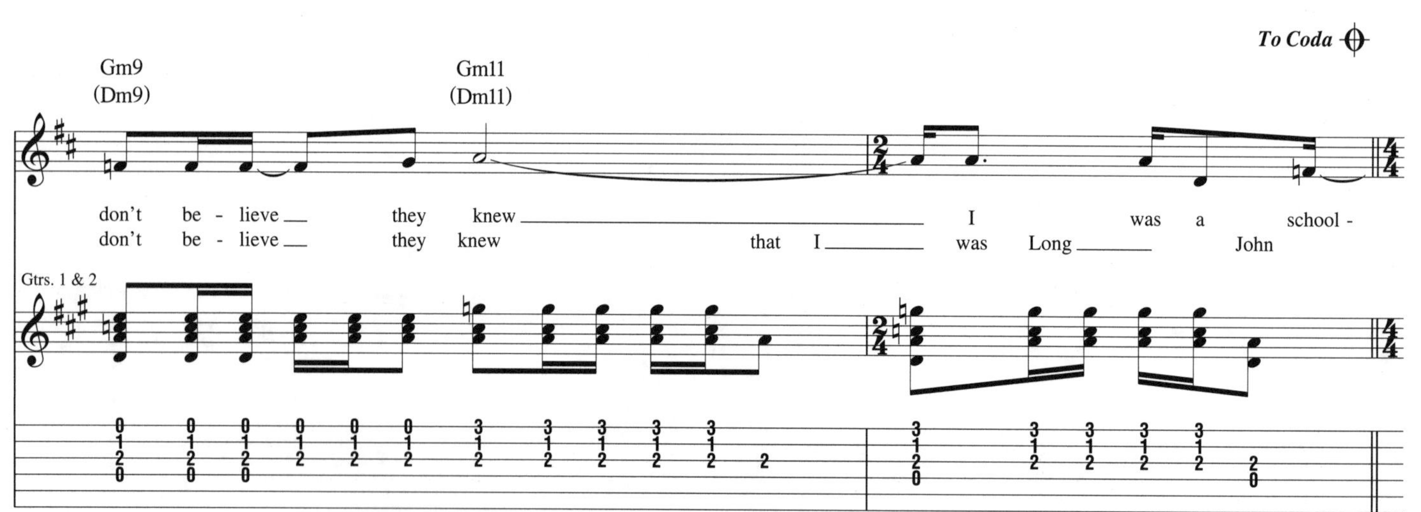

Interlude

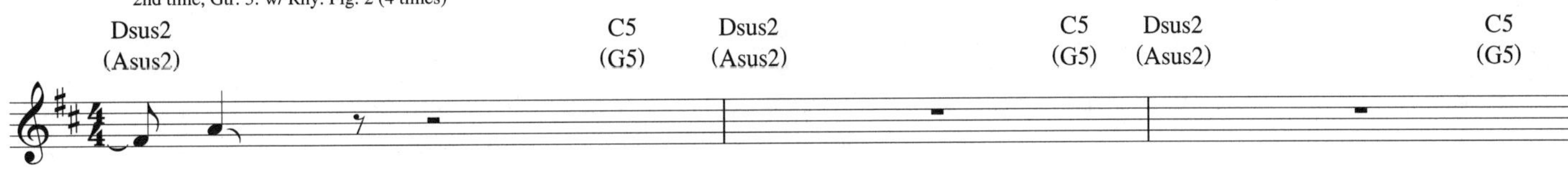
Gtrs. 1 & 2: w/ Rhy. Fig. 1
1st time, Gtr. 3: w/ Rhy. Fig. 2 (3 times)
2nd time, Gtr. 3: w/ Rhy. Fig. 2 (4 times)
Dsus2
(Asus2)
C5
(G5)
Dsus2
(Asus2)
C5
(G5)
Dsus2
(Asus2)
C5
(G5)
- boy
Sil - ver.

1.
2.
Dsus2
(Asus2)
Dsus2
(Asus2)
C5
(G5)
Rhy. Fill 3
Gtrs. 1 & 2

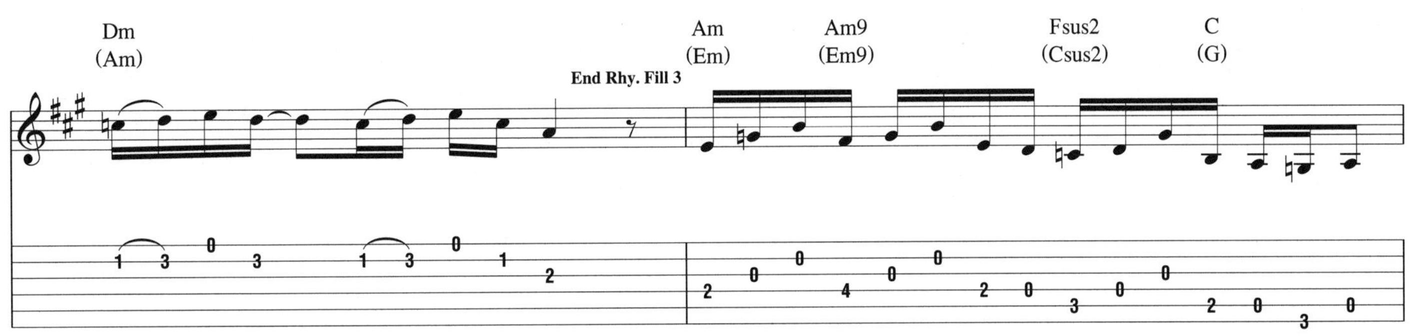
Dm
(Am)
End Rhy. Fill 3
Am
(Em)
Am9
(Em9)
Fsus2
(Csus2)
C
(G)

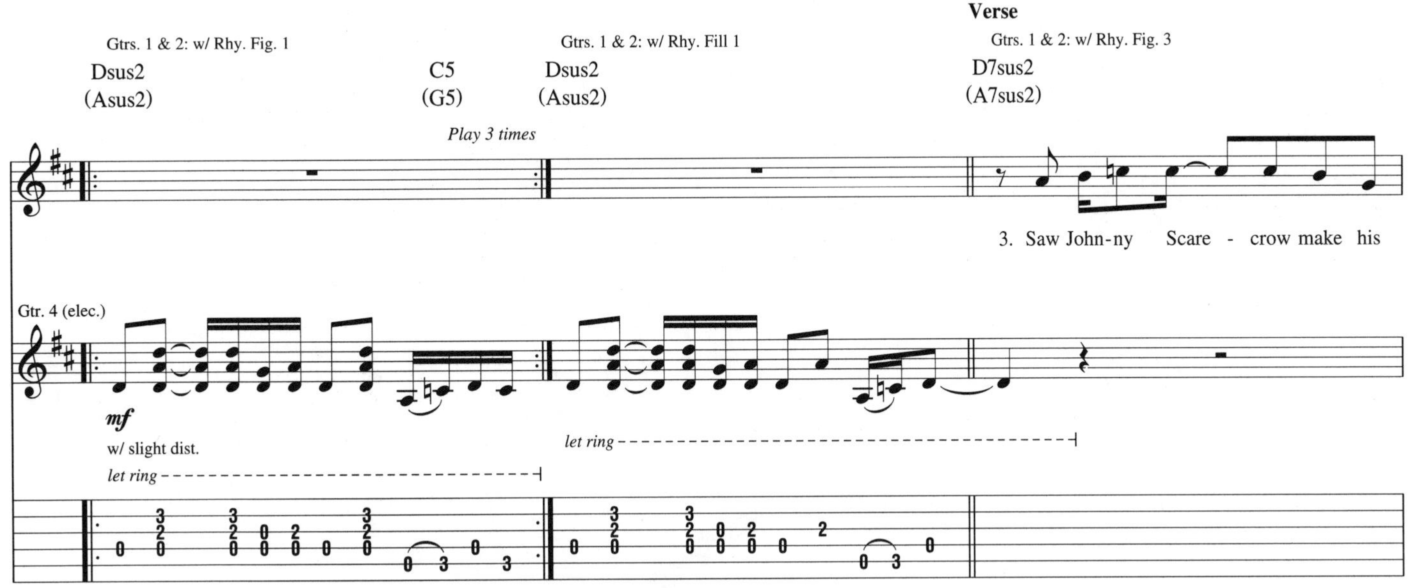
Gtrs. 1 & 2: w/ Rhy. Fig. 1
Dsus2
(Asus2)
C5
(G5)
Play 3 times
Gtrs. 1 & 2: w/ Rhy. Fill 1
Dsus2
(Asus2)
Verse
Gtrs. 1 & 2: w/ Rhy. Fig. 3
D7sus2
(A7sus2)
3. Saw John-ny Scare - crow make his
Gtr. 4 (elec.)
mf
w/ slight dist.
let ring
let ring

Gtr. 4 tacet
Dsus2
(Asus2)
F
(C)
G
(D)
F
(C)
G
(D)
G/F
(D/C)
rounds in his jet - black 'mac, which he won't give back, stole it from a

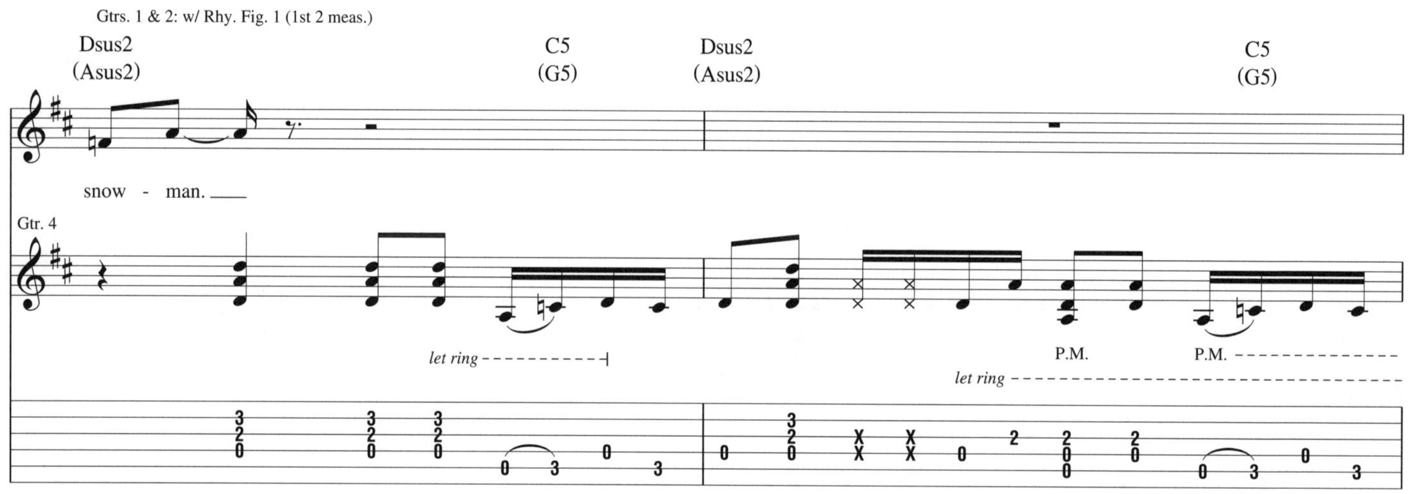
Gtrs. 1 & 2: w/ Rhy. Fig. 1 (1st 2 meas.)
Dsus2
(Asus2)
C5
(G5)
Dsus2
(Asus2)
C5
(G5)
snow - man.
Gtr. 4
let ring
P.M.
P.M.
let ring

Gtrs. 1 & 2: w/ Rhy. Fig. 3
D7sus2
(A7sus2)
Dsus2
(Asus2)
F
(C)
G
(D)
F
(C)
As I did walk by Hamp-stead Fair I came up - on Moth - er Goose, so I
P.M.
let ring

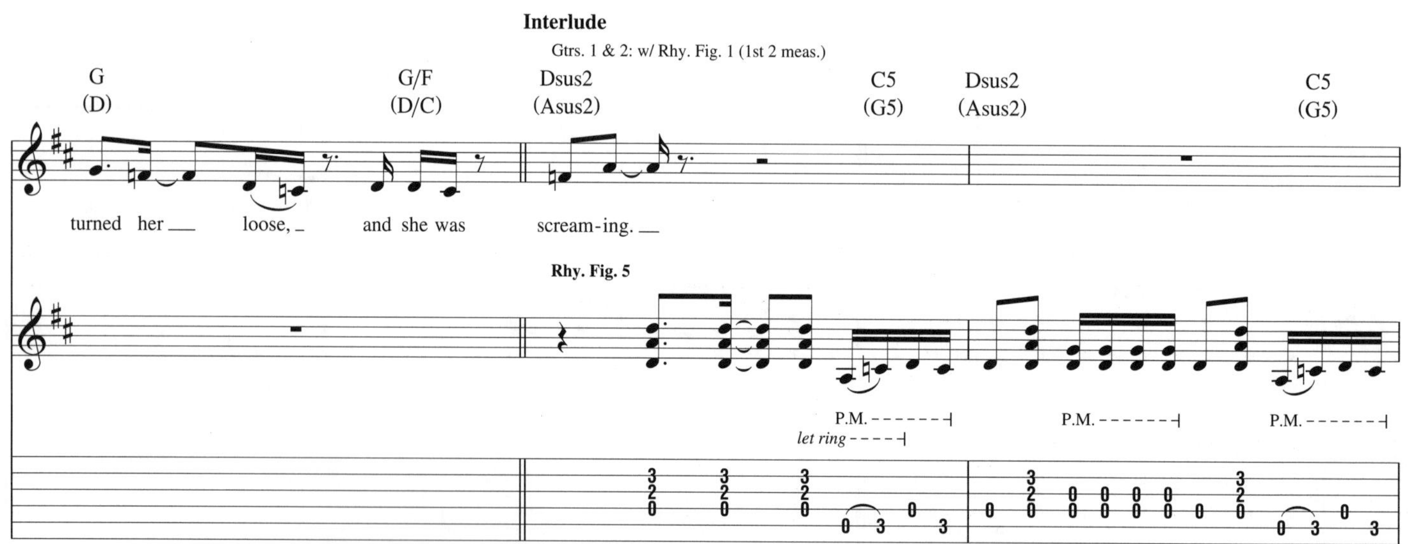
Interlude
Gtrs. 1 & 2: w/ Rhy. Fig. 1 (1st 2 meas.)
G
(D)
G/F
(D/C)
Dsus2
(Asus2)
C5
(G5)
Dsus2
(Asus2)
C5
(G5)
turned her loose, and she was scream-ing.
Rhy. Fig. 5
P.M.
let ring
P.M.
P.M.

D.S. al Coda

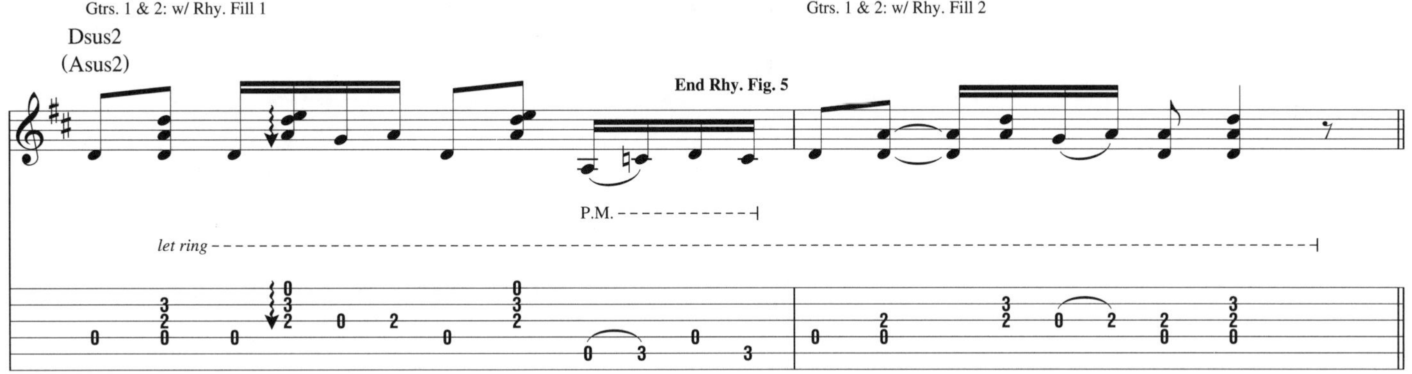
Gtrs. 1 & 2: w/ Rhy. Fill 1
Gtrs. 1 & 2: w/ Rhy. Fill 2
Dsus2
(Asus2)
End Rhy. Fig. 5
P.M.
let ring

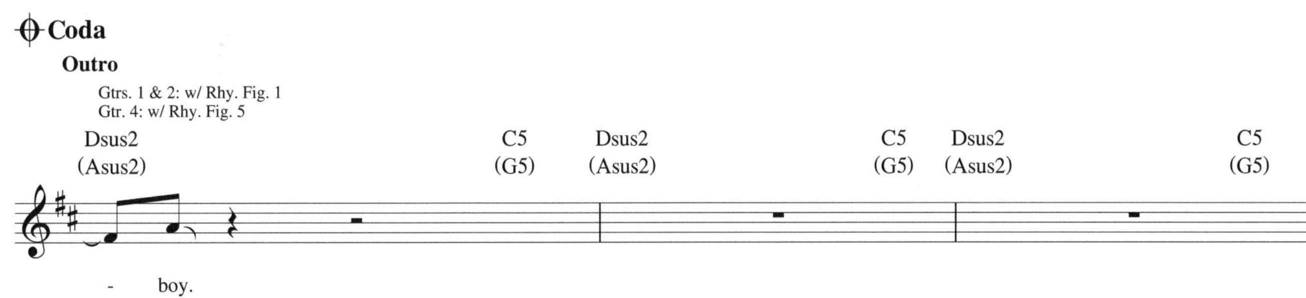
Coda
Outro
Gtrs. 1 & 2: w/ Rhy. Fig. 1
Gtr. 4: w/ Rhy. Fig. 5
Dsus2
(Asus2)
C5
(G5)
Dsus2
(Asus2)
C5
(G5)
Dsus2
(Asus2)
C5
(G5)
- boy.

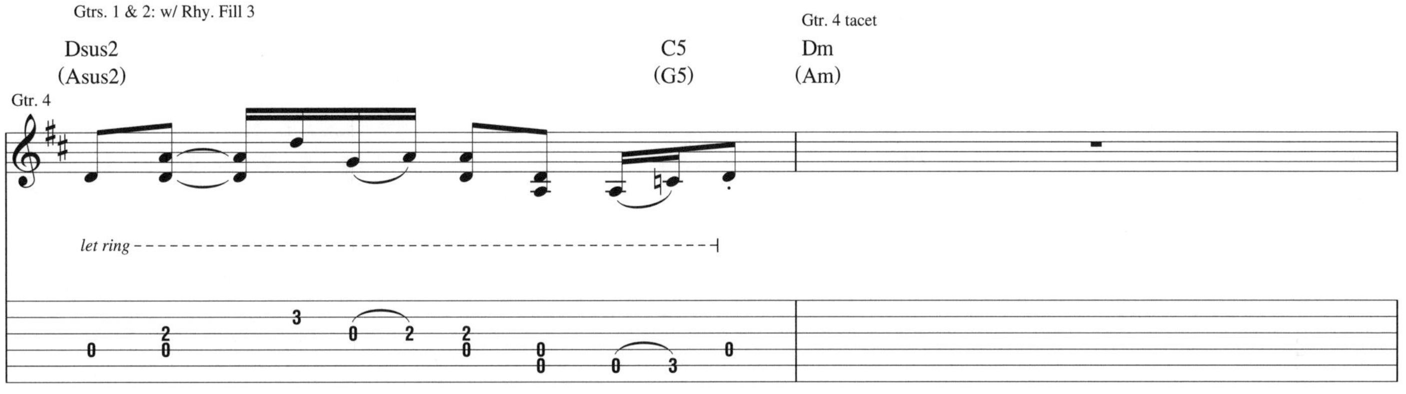
Gtrs. 1 & 2: w/ Rhy. Fill 3
Gtr. 4 tacet
Dsus2
(Asus2)
C5
(G5)
Dm
(Am)
Gtr. 4
let ring

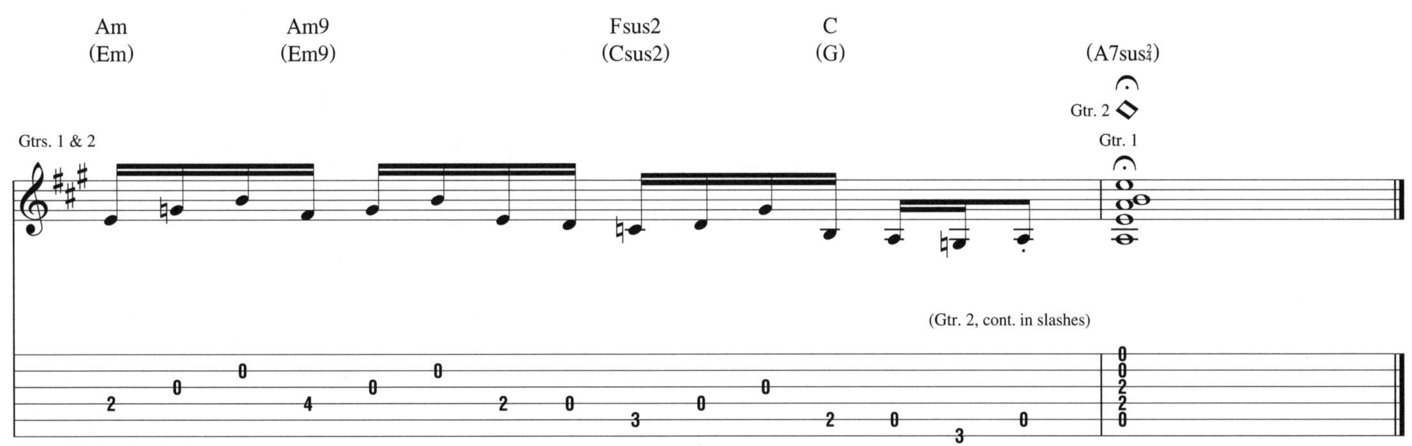
Am
(Em)
Am9
(Em9)
Fsus2
(Csus2)
C
(G)
(A7sus4)
Gtr. 2
Gtrs. 1 & 2
Gtr. 1
(Gtr. 2, cont. in slashes)

Wond'ring Aloud

Words and Music by Ian Anderson

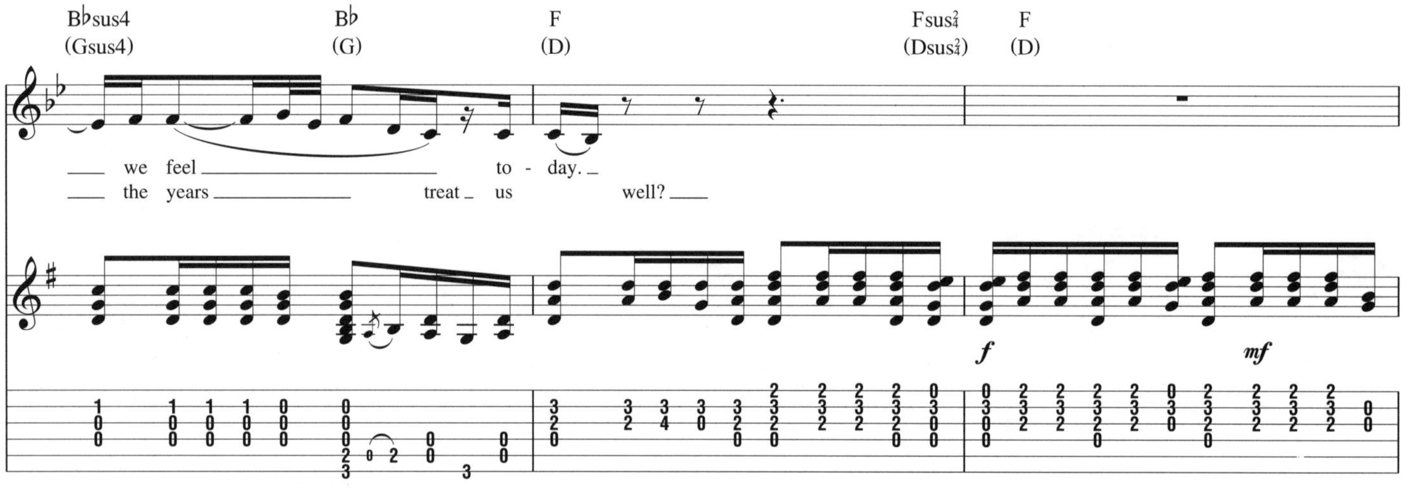

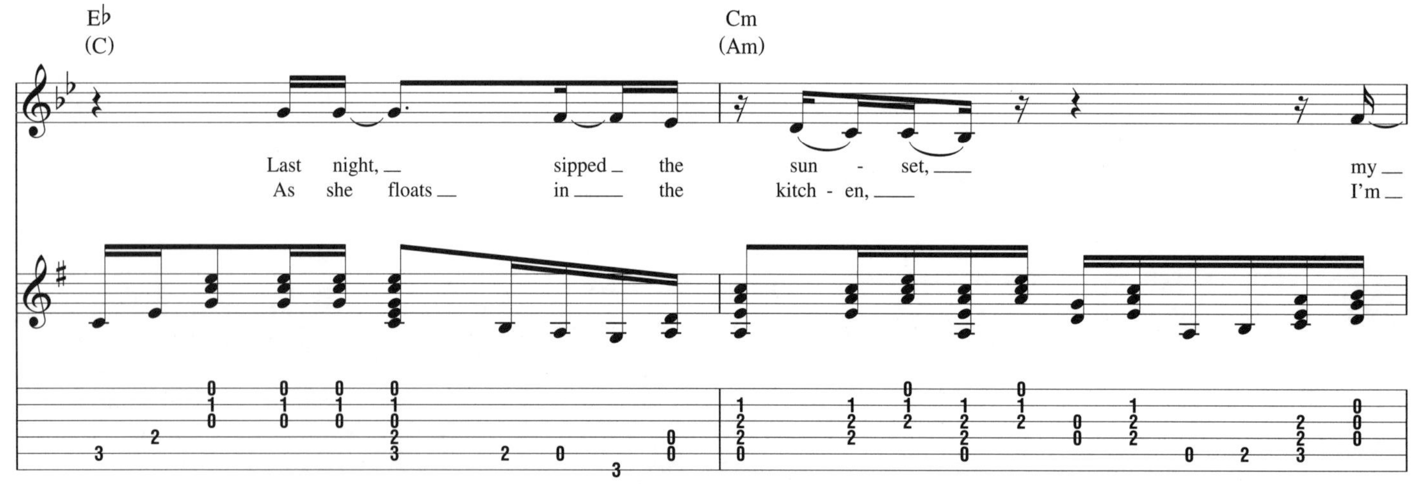

B♭add11
(Gadd11)
B♭
(G)
F
(D)
Fsus2/4
(Dsus2/4)
hand in her hair.
tast - ing the smell, (Laughed:) yeah,
F
(D)
B♭6
(G6)
E♭
(C)
f
mf
We are our own sav - iors as we start both our
of toast as the but - ter runs. Then she comes spill - ing
Gm
(Em)
hearts beat - ing li - i - ife
crumbs on the bed

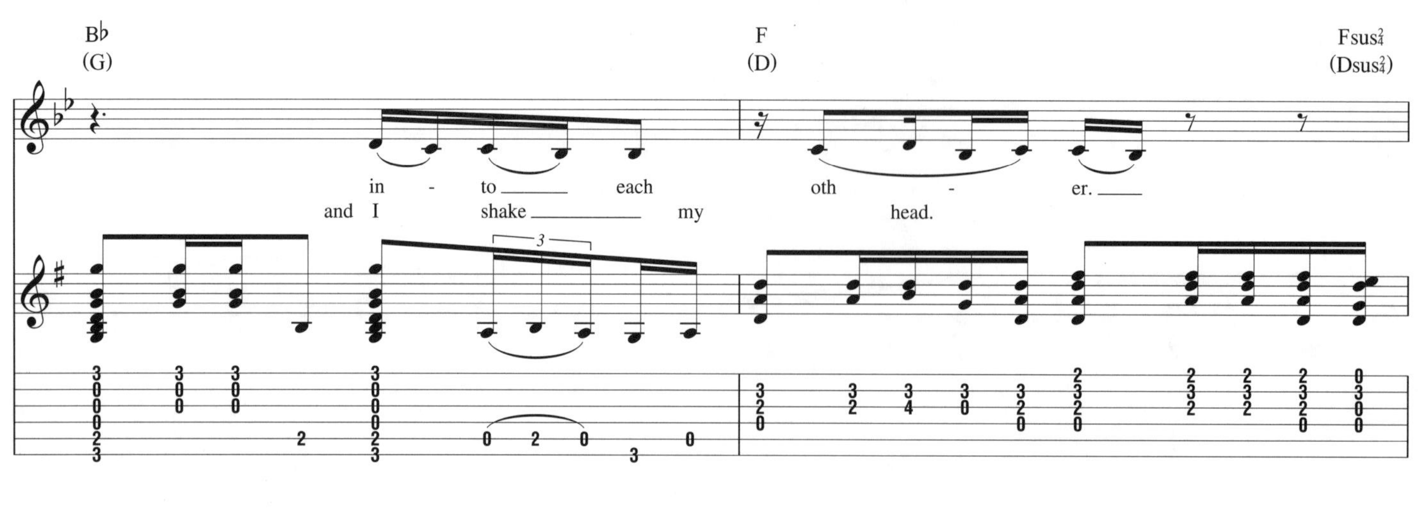
B♭
(G)
F
(D)
Fsus2/4
(Dsus2/4)
in - to each oth - er.
and I shake my head.

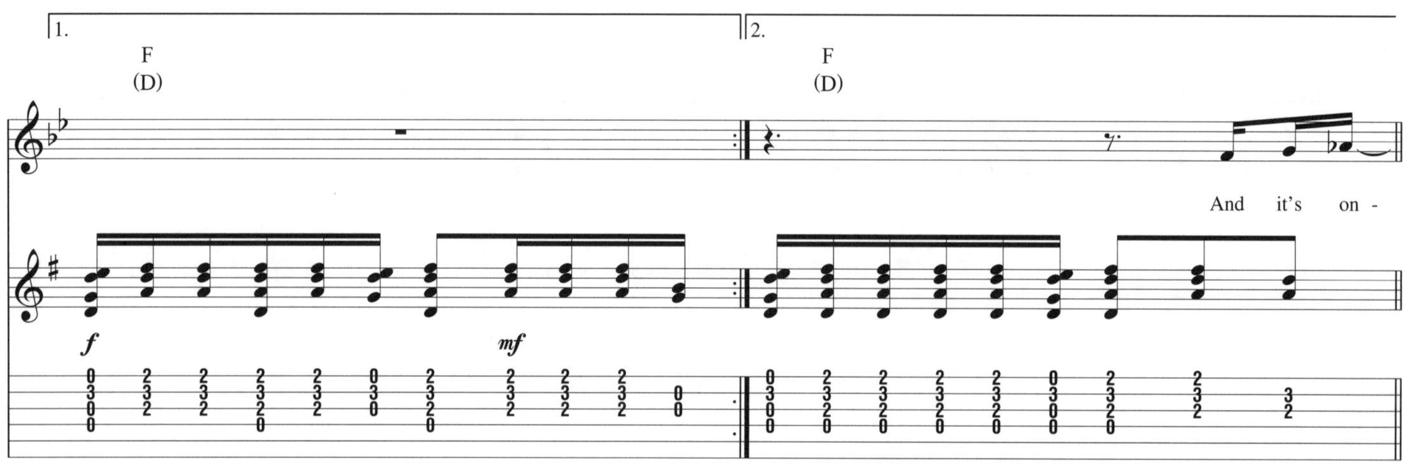
1.
F
(D)
2.
F
(D)
And it's on -
f
mf

Outro

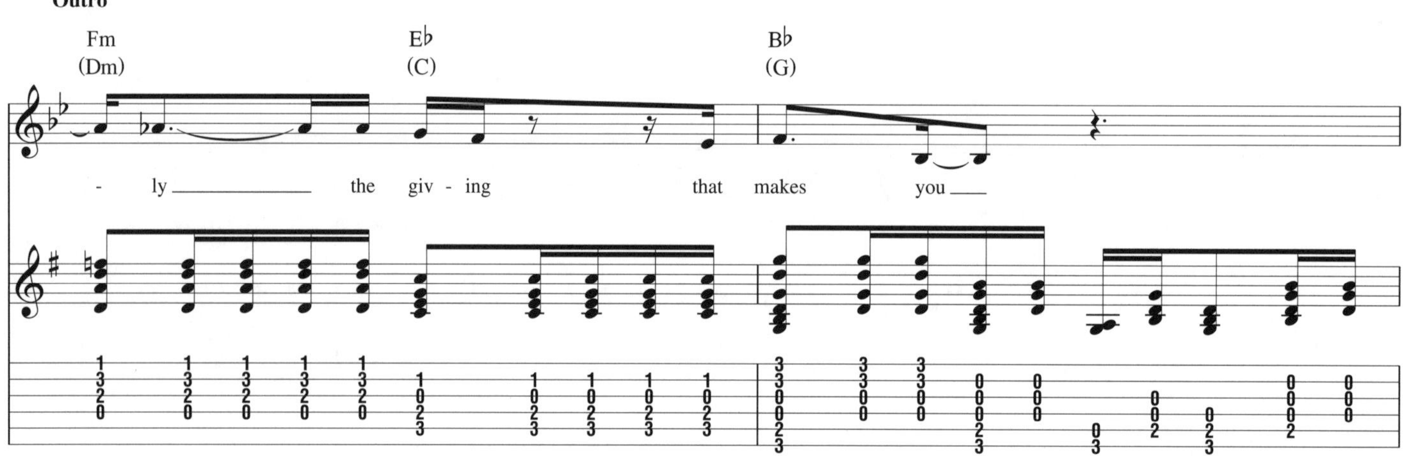
Fm
(Dm)
E♭
(C)
B♭
(G)
- ly the giv - ing that makes you

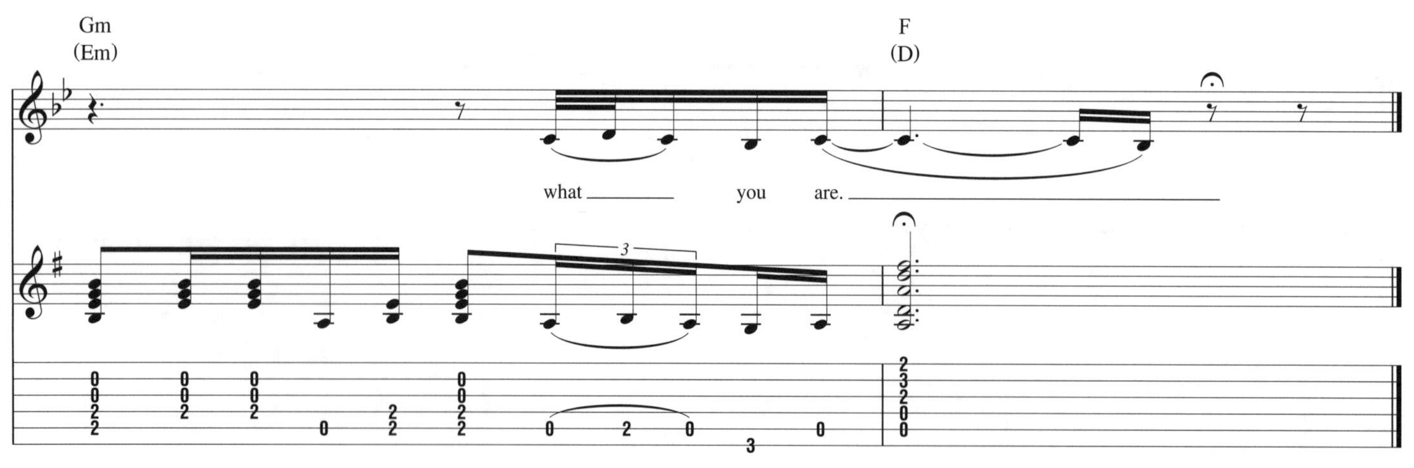
Gm
(Em)
F
(D)
what you are.

Up to Me

Words and Music by Ian Anderson

Intro
Moderately ♩ = 100

N.C. *E7♯9

Gtr. 1 (acous.)
(Laughing) 2 sec.
mf

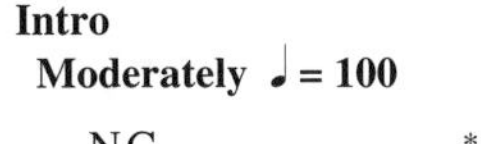

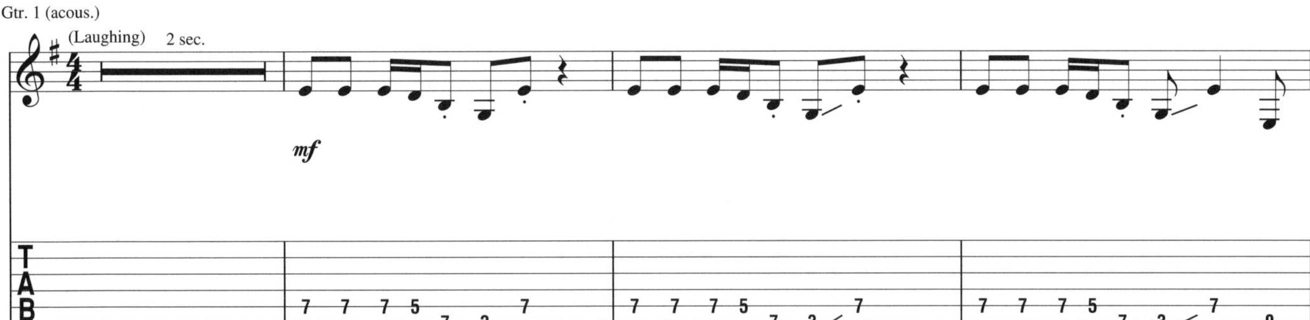

*Chord symbols reflect overall harmony.

Oh,
yeah,
hey.
Gtr. 2 (elec.)
f
w/ dist.
1 1/2
Gtr. 1

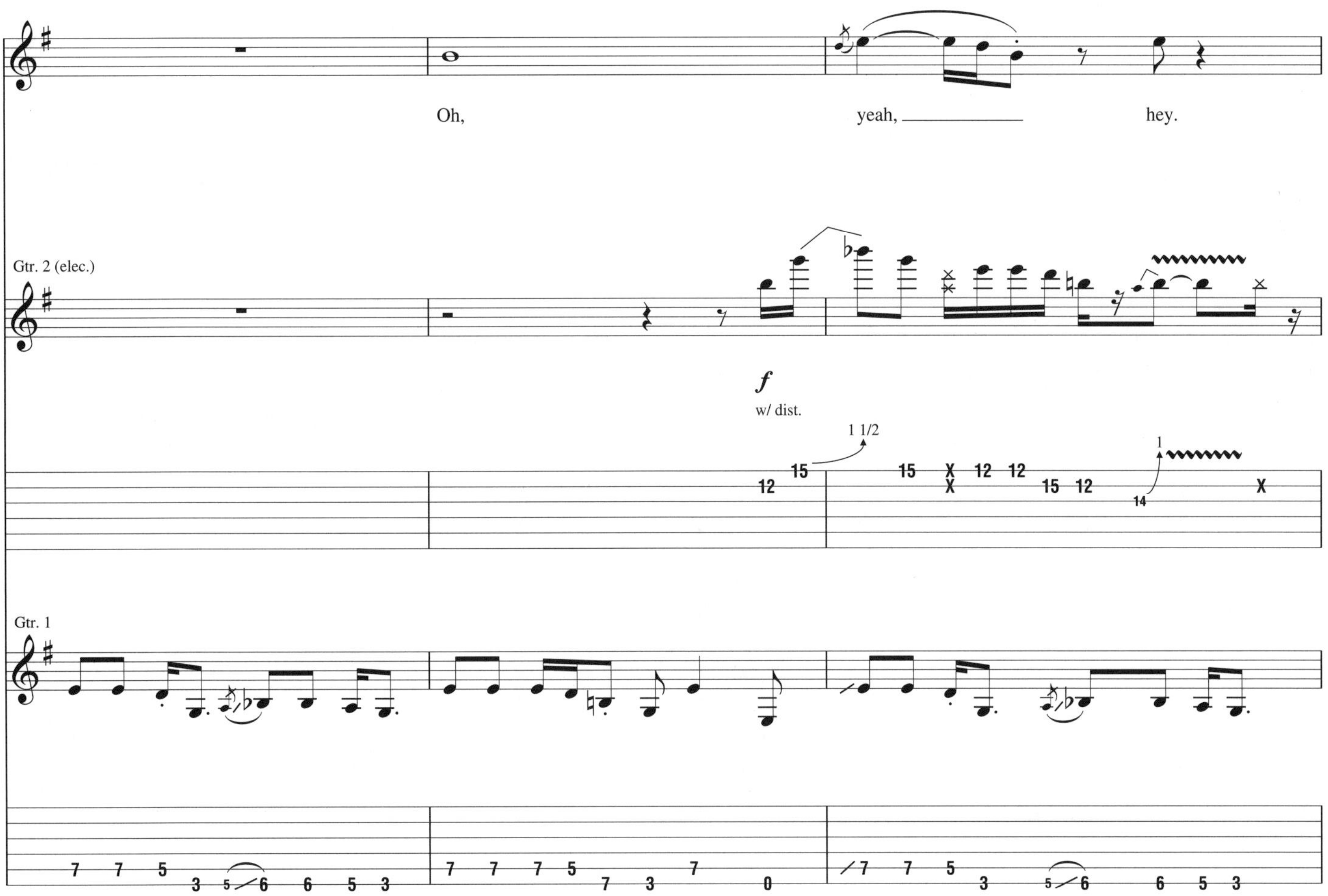

𝄋 Verse

Gtr. 2 tacet

Em

1. Uh, take you to the cin - e - ma ___ and
buy a sil - ver cloud to ride, ___
3. The rain - y sea - son comes to pass, ___ the

Gtr. 3 (acous.)

mf

Gtr. 1

End Riff A

let ring throughout

D C

leave you in a Wim - py Bar, you tell me that we've gone _ too far, come
pack the ten - nis club in - side, trou - ser cuffs ___ hung far too wide, well, it
day - glo pi - rate sinks _ at last, and if I laughed _ a bit ___ too fast, well,

let ring

let ring

Am D/F♯ Em

run - ning _ up ___ to _____ me. _____ Make the scene _ at Cous - in Jack's, leave
was up to me. _____ Tyres down _ on your bi - cy - cle, your nose
it was up to me. _____ Take you ______ to the cin - e - ma __ and

let ring

*T

*T = Thumb on 6th string

D
C
him to put the bot - tles back, mends his glass - es that I cracked, _ well,
_ feels _ like an ic - i - cle, _ the yel - low fin - gered smok - y girl _ is
leave you _ in a Wim - py Bar, you _ tell me _ that you've gone too far come
let ring
let ring

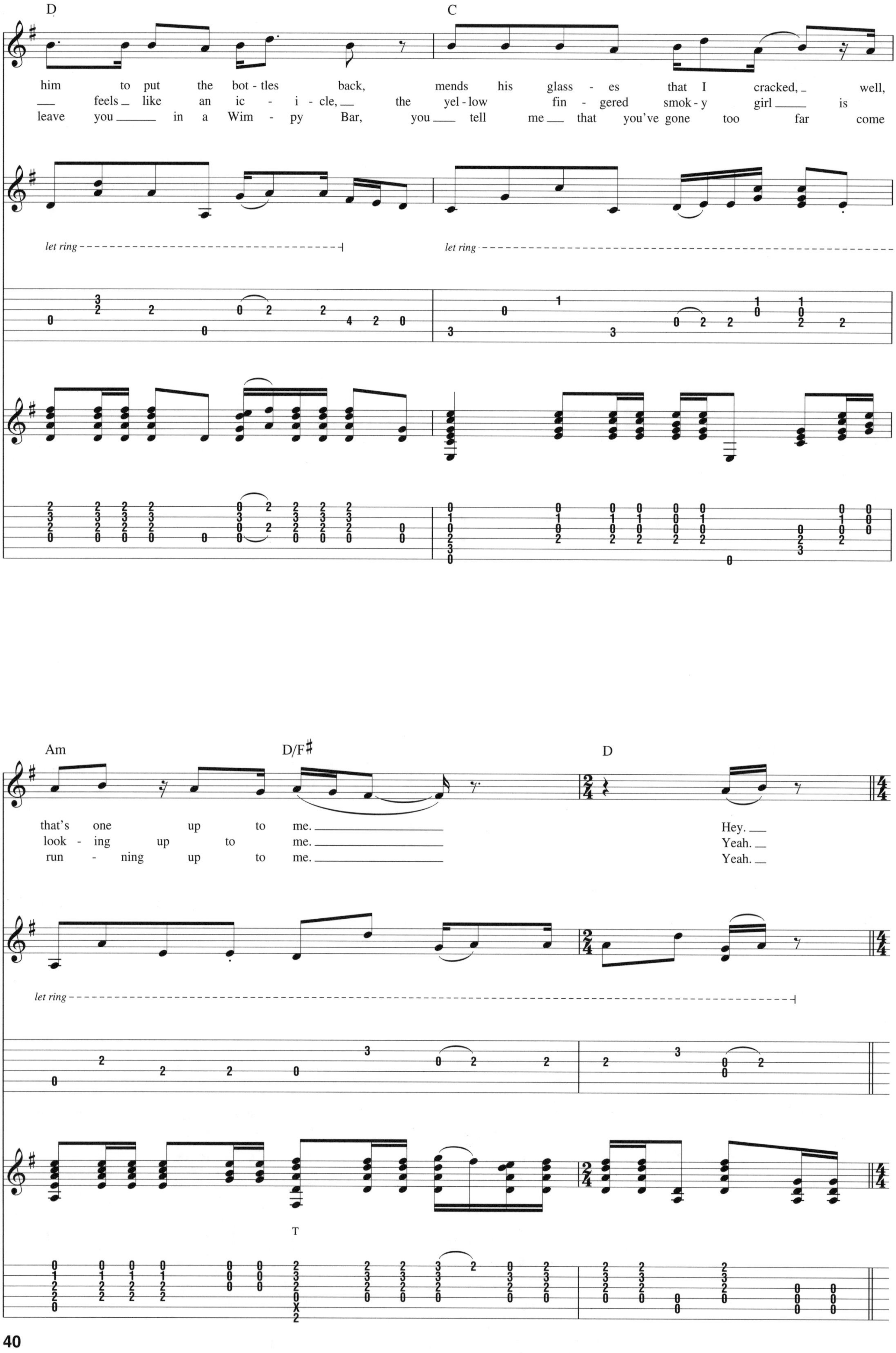

Am D/F♯ D

that's one up to me. _ Hey. _
look - ing up to me. _ Yeah. _
run - ning up to me. _ Yeah. _

let ring

T

Chorus

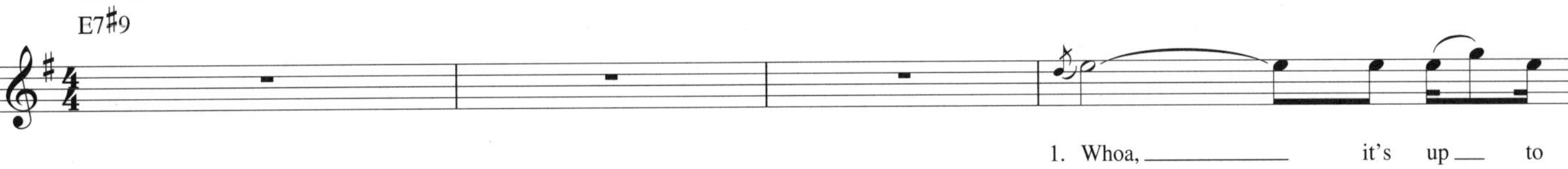
To Coda 1
Gtr. 1: w/ Riff A (4 times)
Gtr. 3 tacet
E7♯9
1. Whoa, it's up to
2. Hah.
3. Whoa, you know it's up

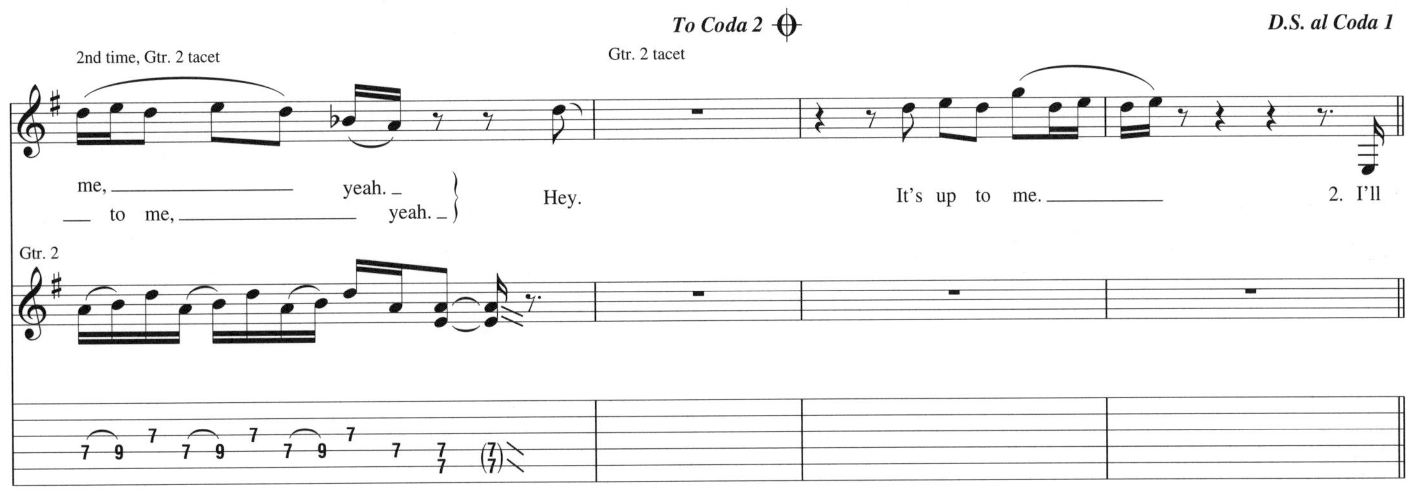
To Coda 2
D.S. al Coda 1
2nd time, Gtr. 2 tacet
Gtr. 2 tacet
me, yeah.
to me, yeah.
Hey.
It's up to me.
2. I'll
Gtr. 2

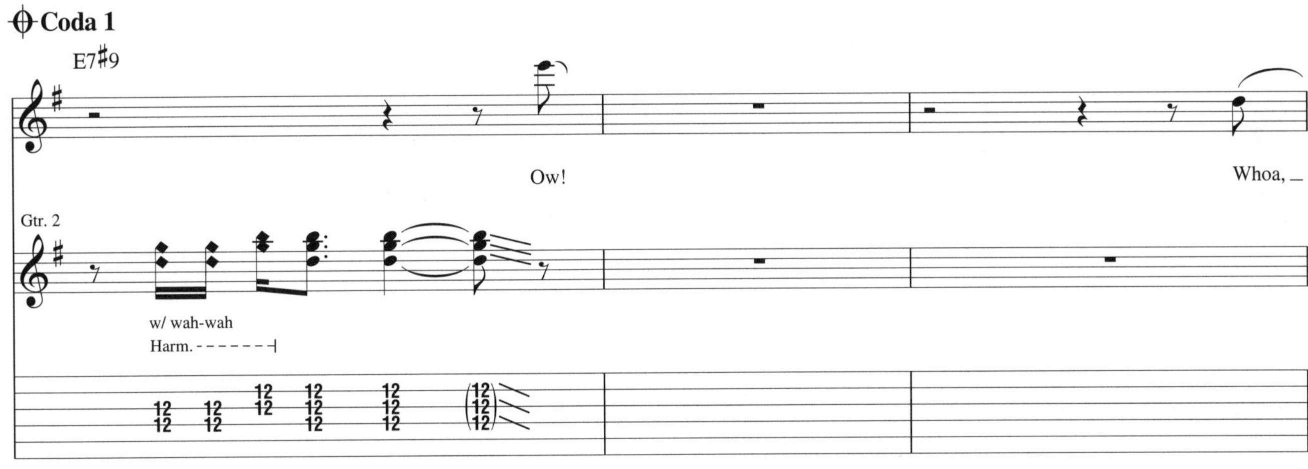
Coda 1
E7♯9
Ow!
Whoa,
Gtr. 2
w/ wah-wah
Harm.

you know it's up to me, yeah.
Hey.
let ring
1
1/2

Bridge

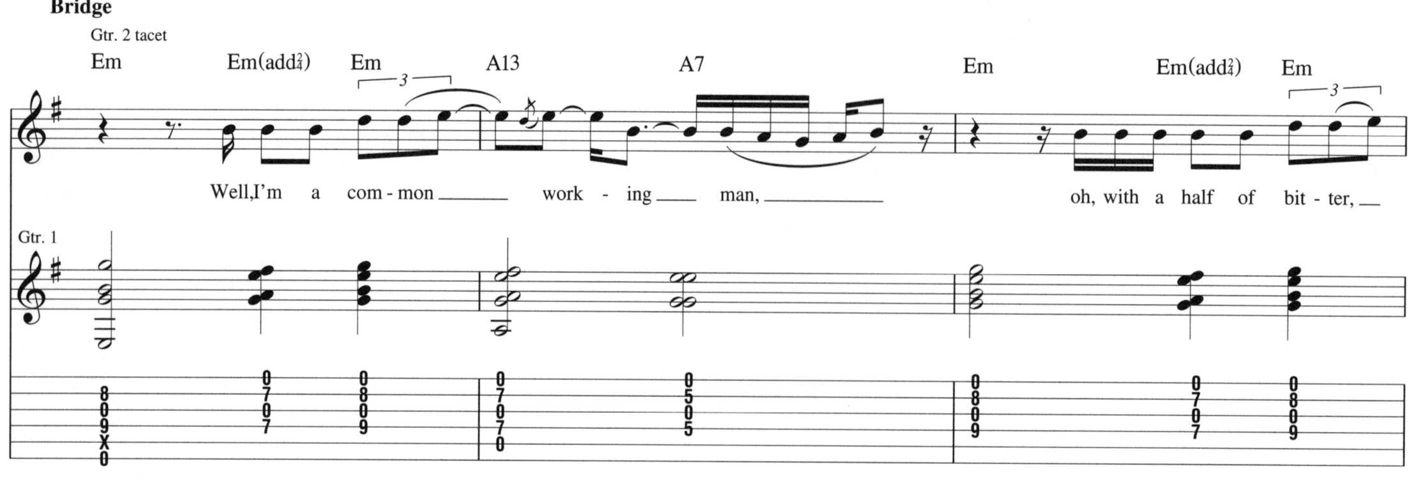
Gtr. 2 tacet
Em
Em(add9/4)
Em
A13
A7
Em
Em(add9/4)
Em
Well, I'm a com - mon work - ing man,
oh, with a half of bit - ter,
Gtr. 1

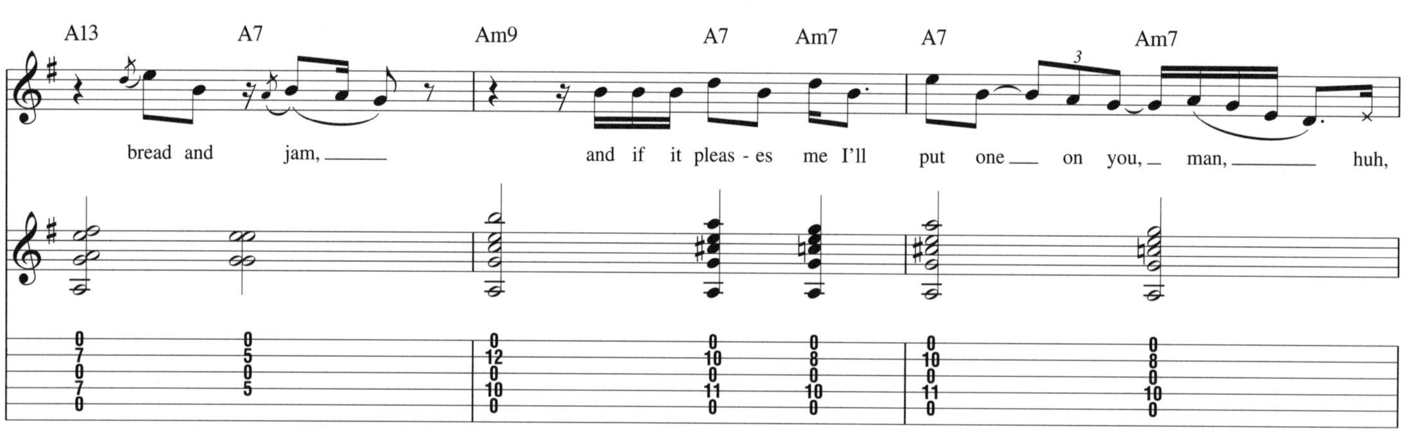
A13
A7
Am9
A7
Am7
A7
Am7
bread and jam,
and if it pleas - es me I'll put one on you, man, huh,

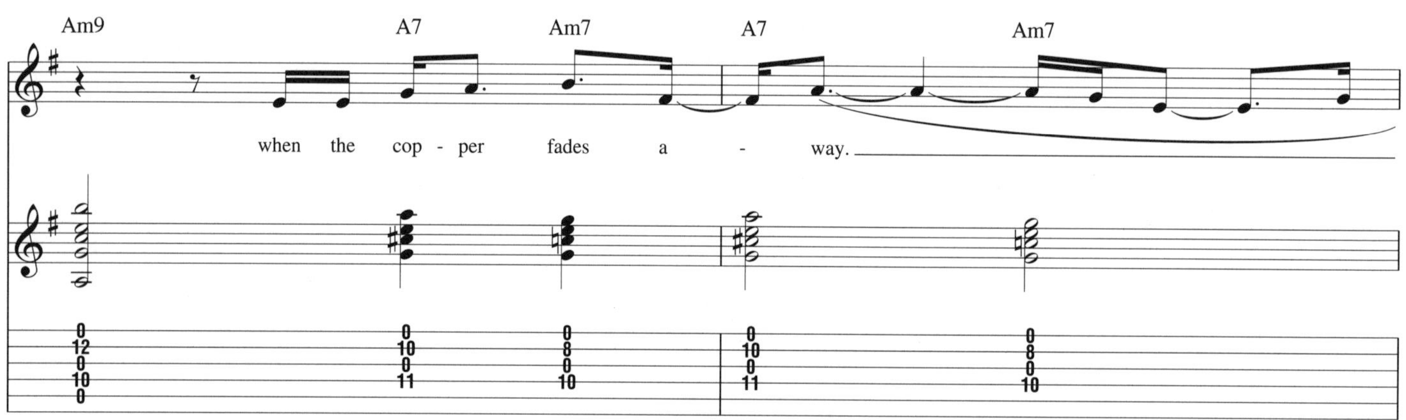
Am9
A7
Am7
A7
Am7
when the cop - per fades a - way.

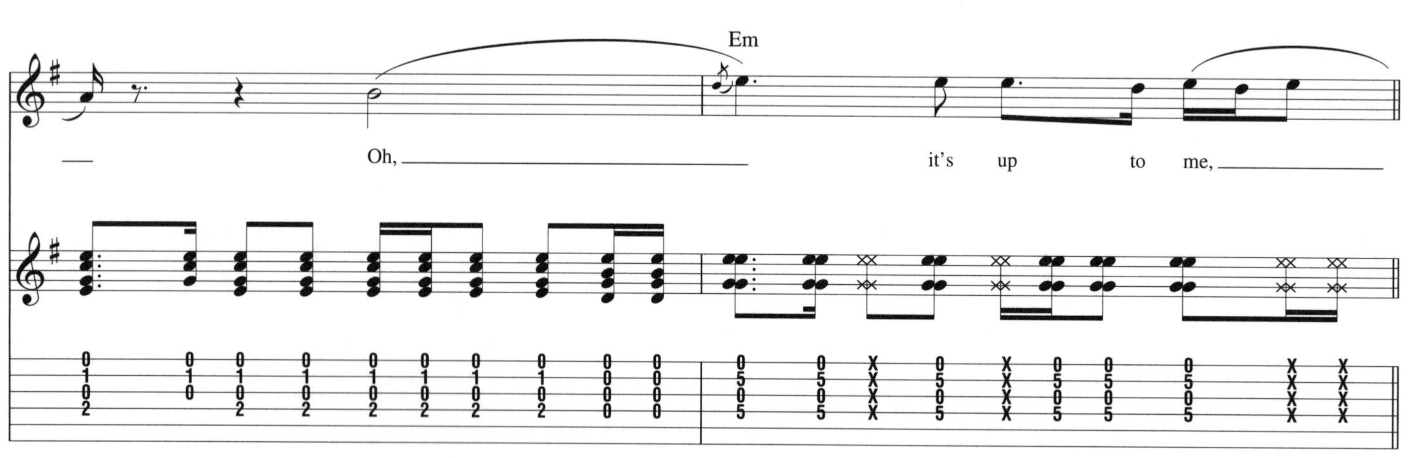
Em
Oh,
it's up to me,

Chorus

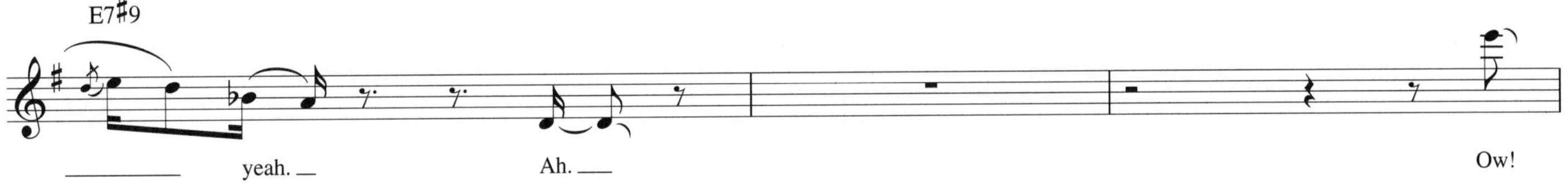
Gtr. 1: w/ Riff A (4 times)
E7#9
yeah.
Ah.
Ow!

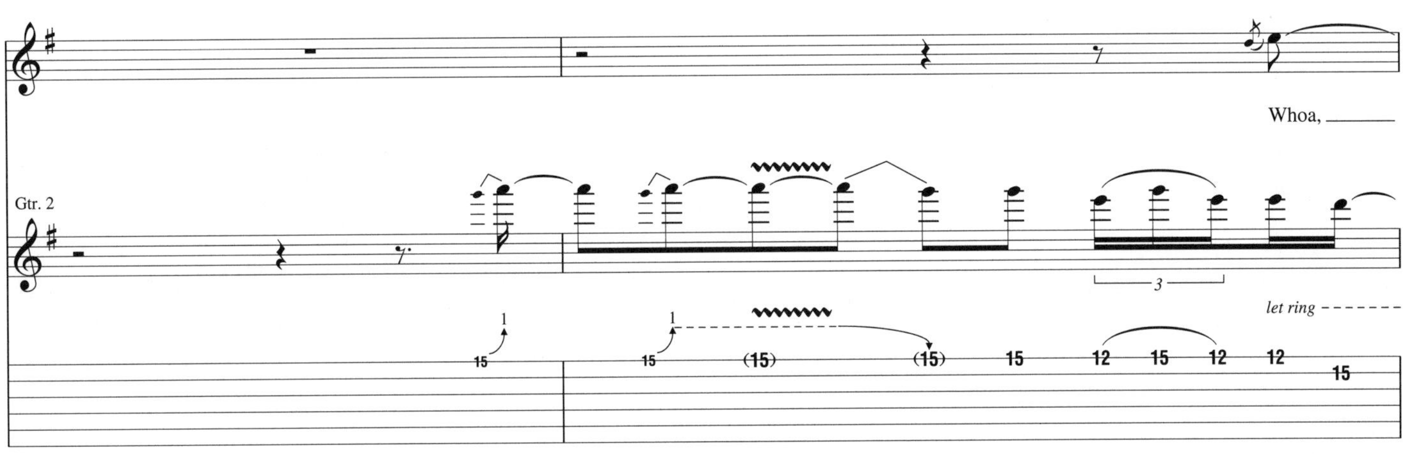
Whoa,
Gtr. 2
let ring
15 15 (15) (15) 15 12 15 12 12 15

D.S. al Coda 2
Gtr. 2 tacet
I said it's up to me, yeah.
let ring
(15)

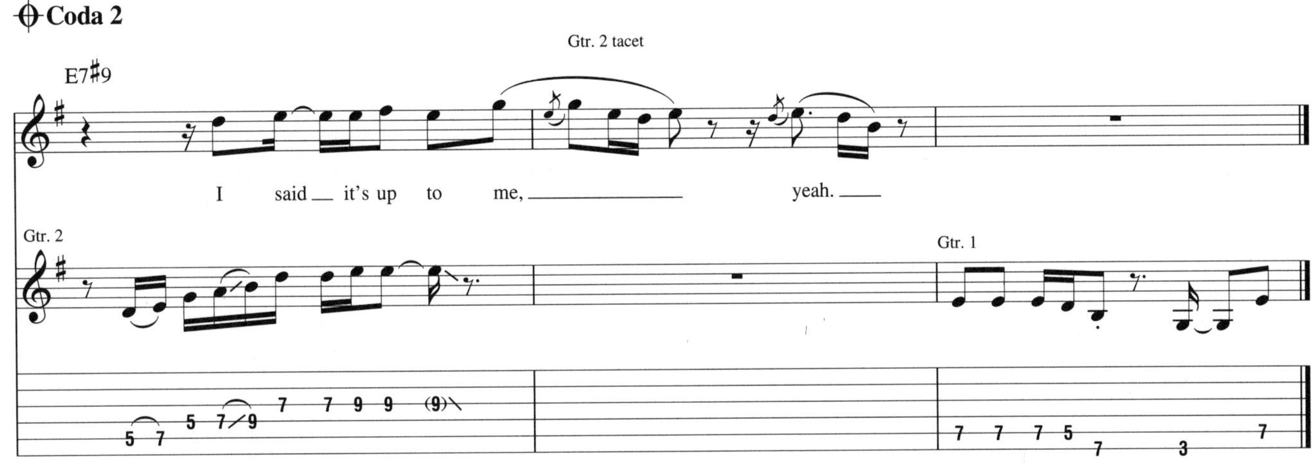
Coda 2
E7#9
Gtr. 2 tacet
I said it's up to me, yeah.
Gtr. 2
Gtr. 1
5 7 5 7 9 7 7 9 9 (9)
7 7 7 5 7 3 7

My God

Words and Music by Ian Anderson

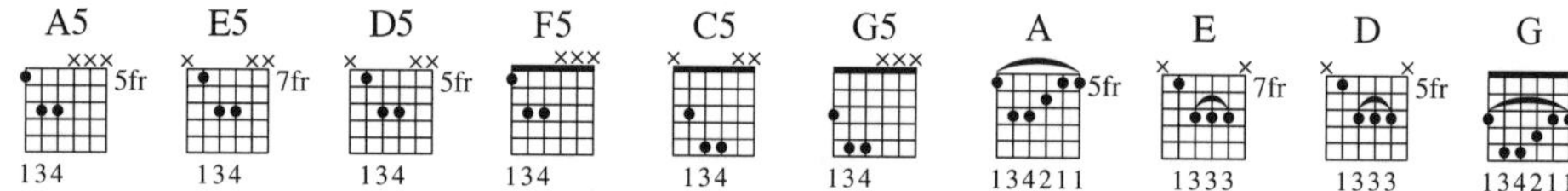

*Chord symbols reflect implied harmony.

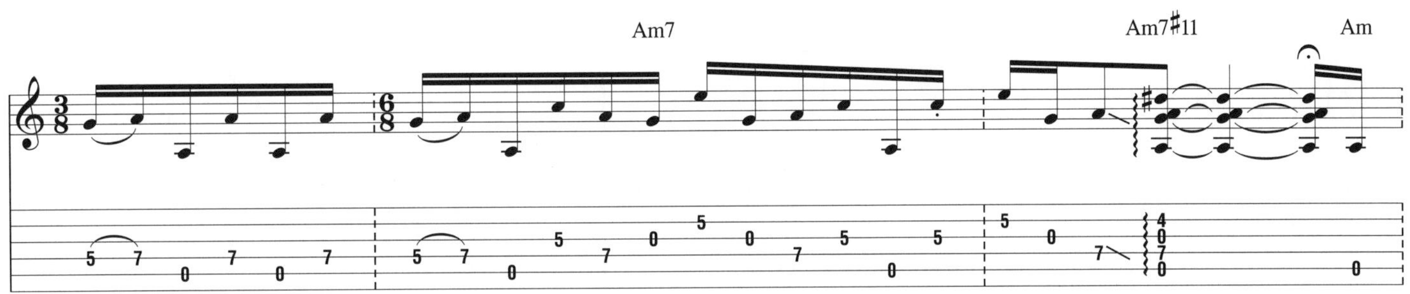

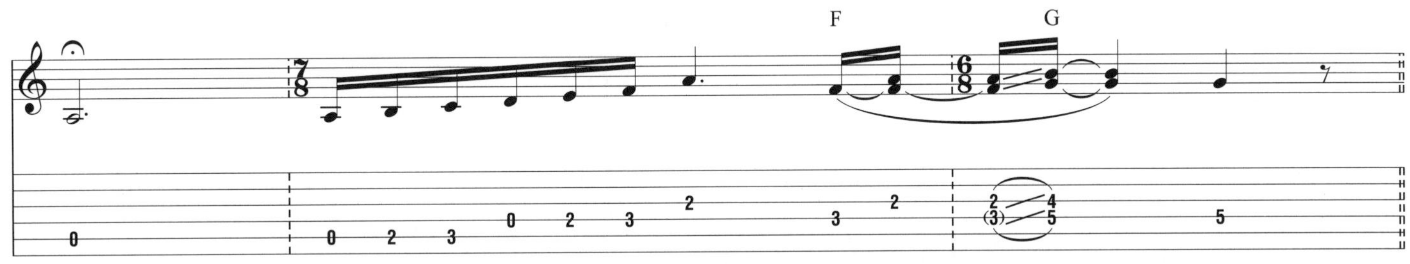

Slowly ♩. = 45

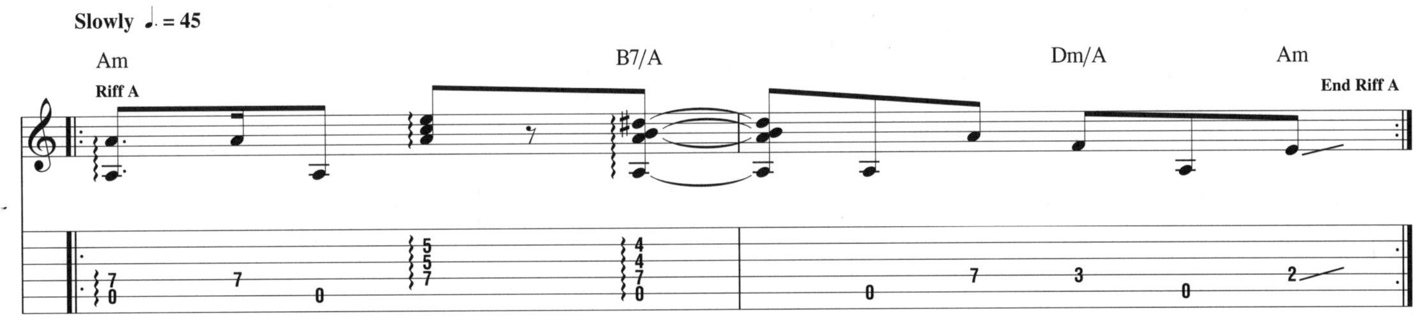

Verse

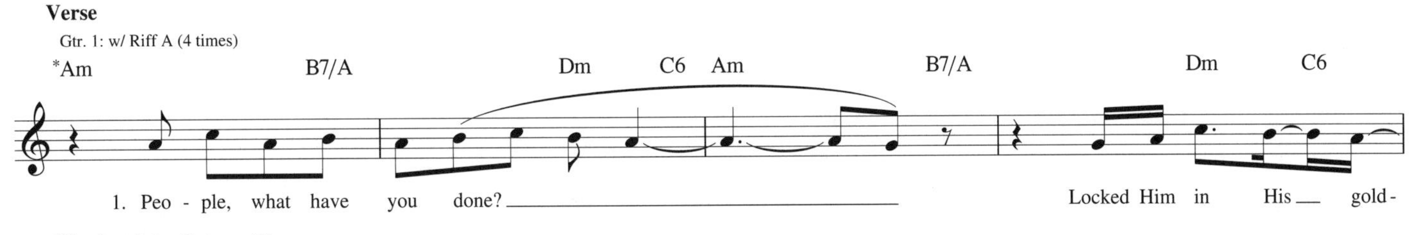

*Chord symbols reflect overall harmony.

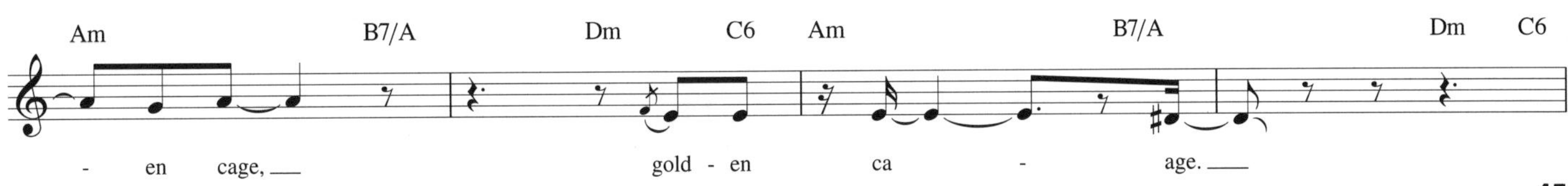

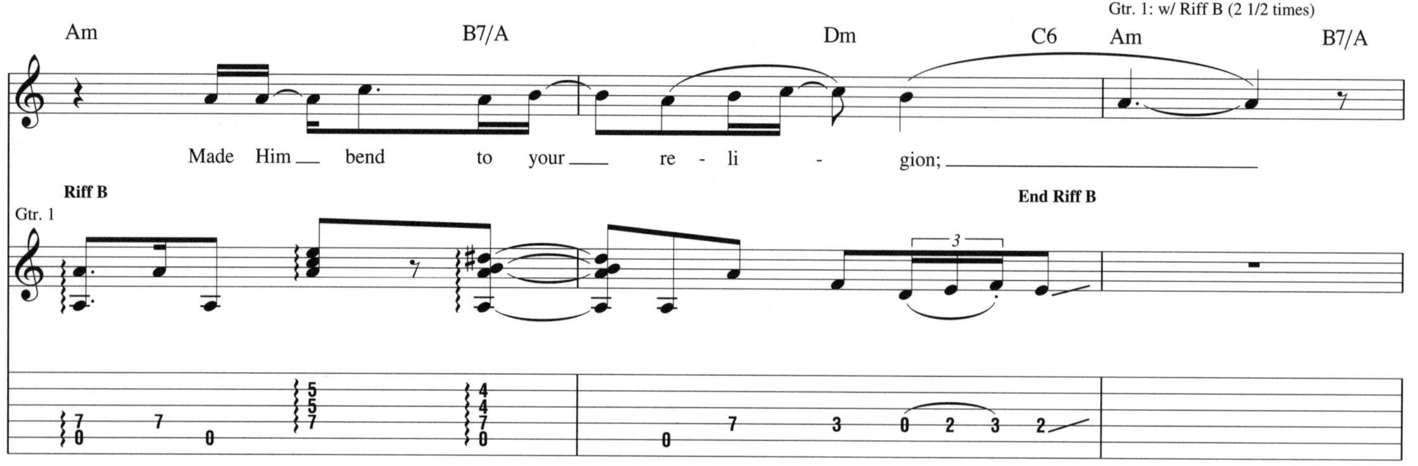
Gtr. 1: w/ Riff B (2 1/2 times)
Am
B7/A
Dm
C6
Am
B7/A
Made Him bend to your re - li - gion;
Riff B
Gtr. 1
End Riff B

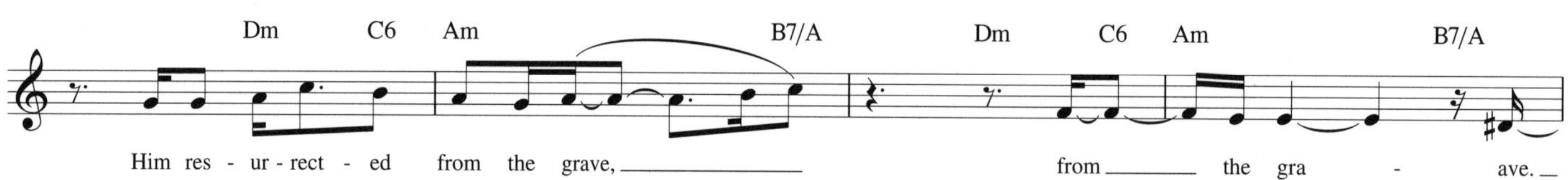
Dm
C6
Am
B7/A
Dm
C6
Am
B7/A
Him res - ur - rect - ed from the grave, from the gra - ave.

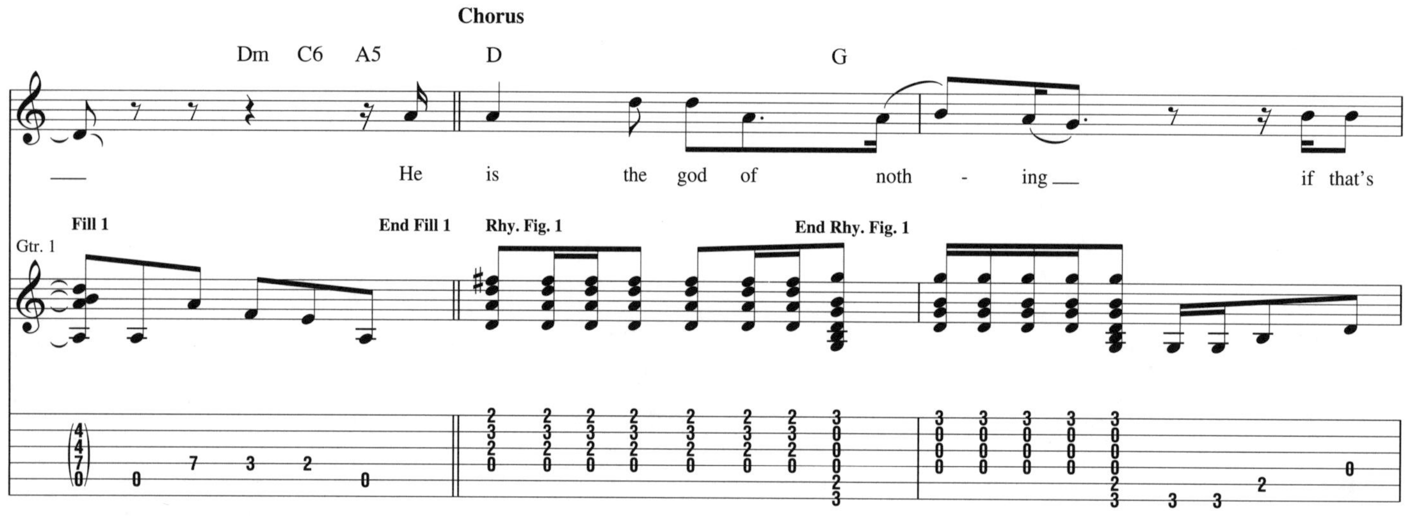
Chorus
Dm
C6
A5
D
G
He is the god of noth - ing if that's
Fill 1
End Fill 1
Rhy. Fig. 1
End Rhy. Fig. 1
Gtr. 1

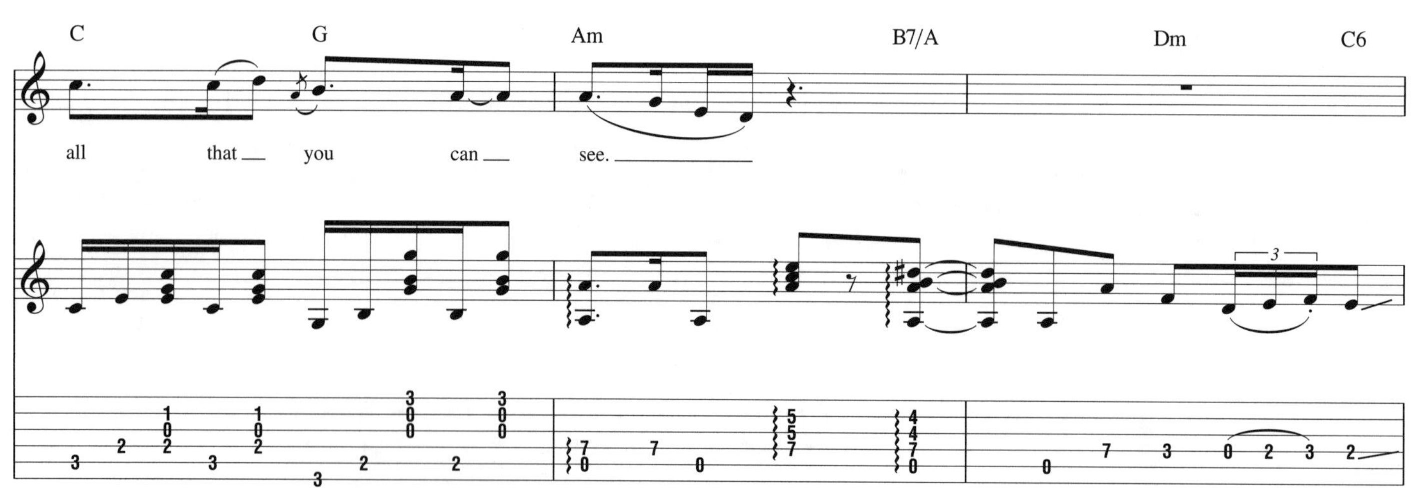
C
G
Am
B7/A
Dm
C6
all that you can see.

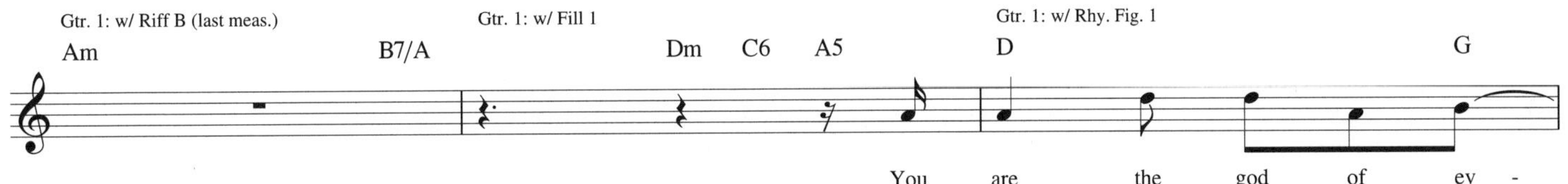

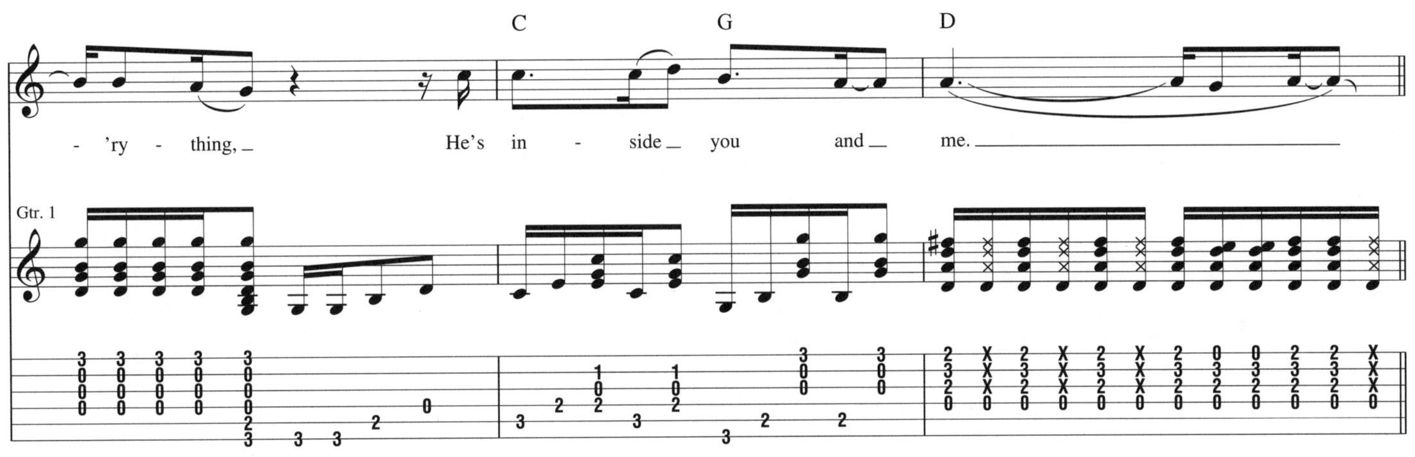

Interlude

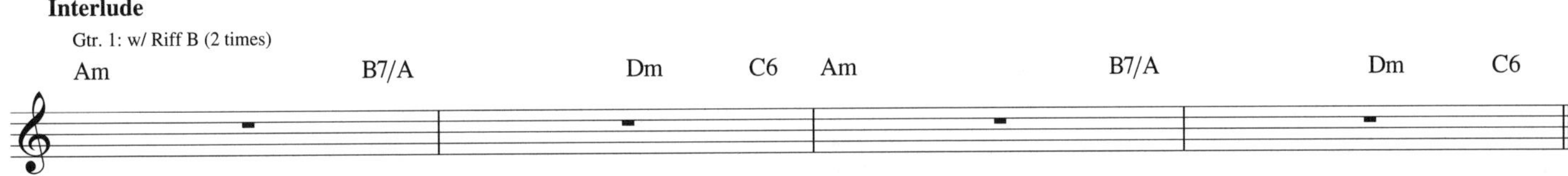

Verse

Gtr. 2: w/ Riff C (2 times)
Am B7/A Dm C6 Am B7/A Dm C6
you from your so - cial grac - es, whoa, and the sins
con - fus - es me as to who and where and why, as to how

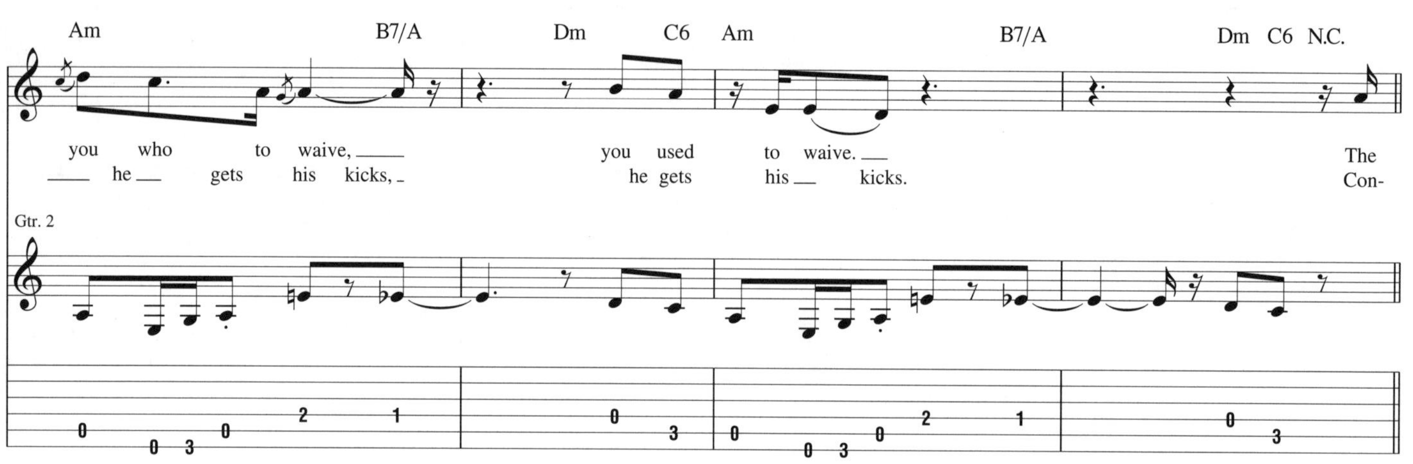
Am B7/A Dm C6 Am B7/A Dm C6 N.C.
you who to waive, you used to waive. The
he gets his kicks, he gets his kicks. Con-
Gtr. 2

Chorus

D G C5 G5
blood - y church of Eng - land, in chains of his - to -
fess - ing to the end - less sin, the end - less whin - ing
let ring
let ring

Am B7/A Dm C6 Am B7/A Dm C6 N.C.
ry, re -
sound, ha, ha. You'll be
P.M.

Guitar Solo

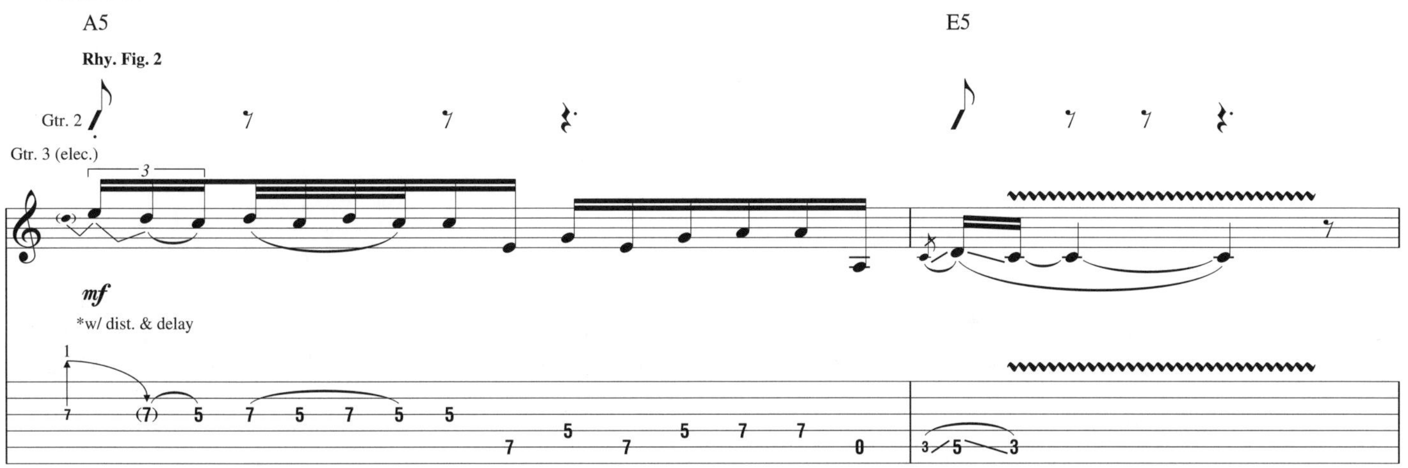

*Delay set for sixteenth-note regeneration w/ 1 repeat.

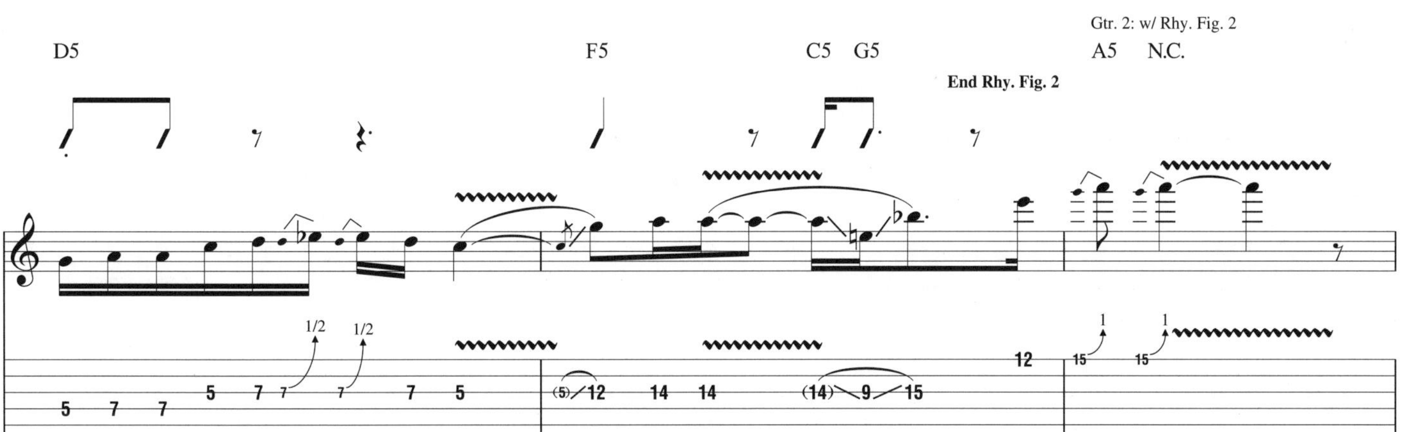

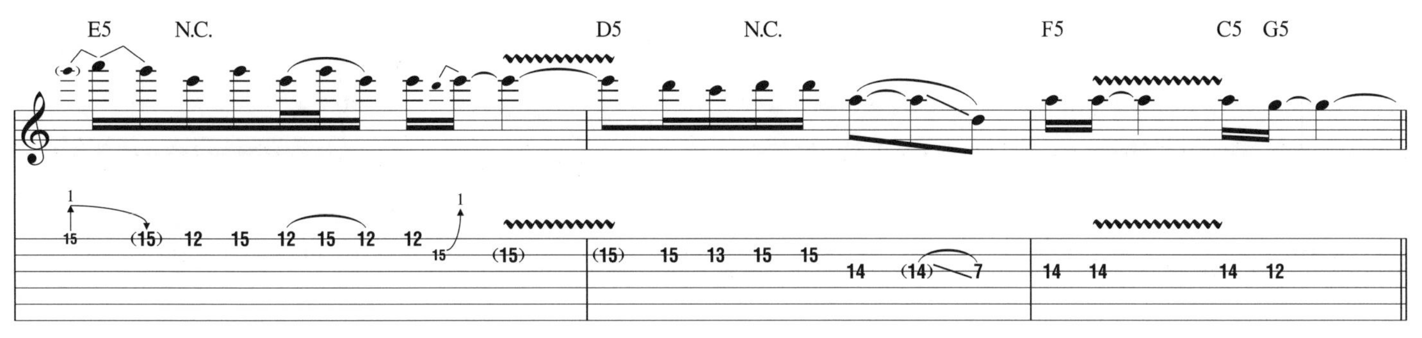

Interlude

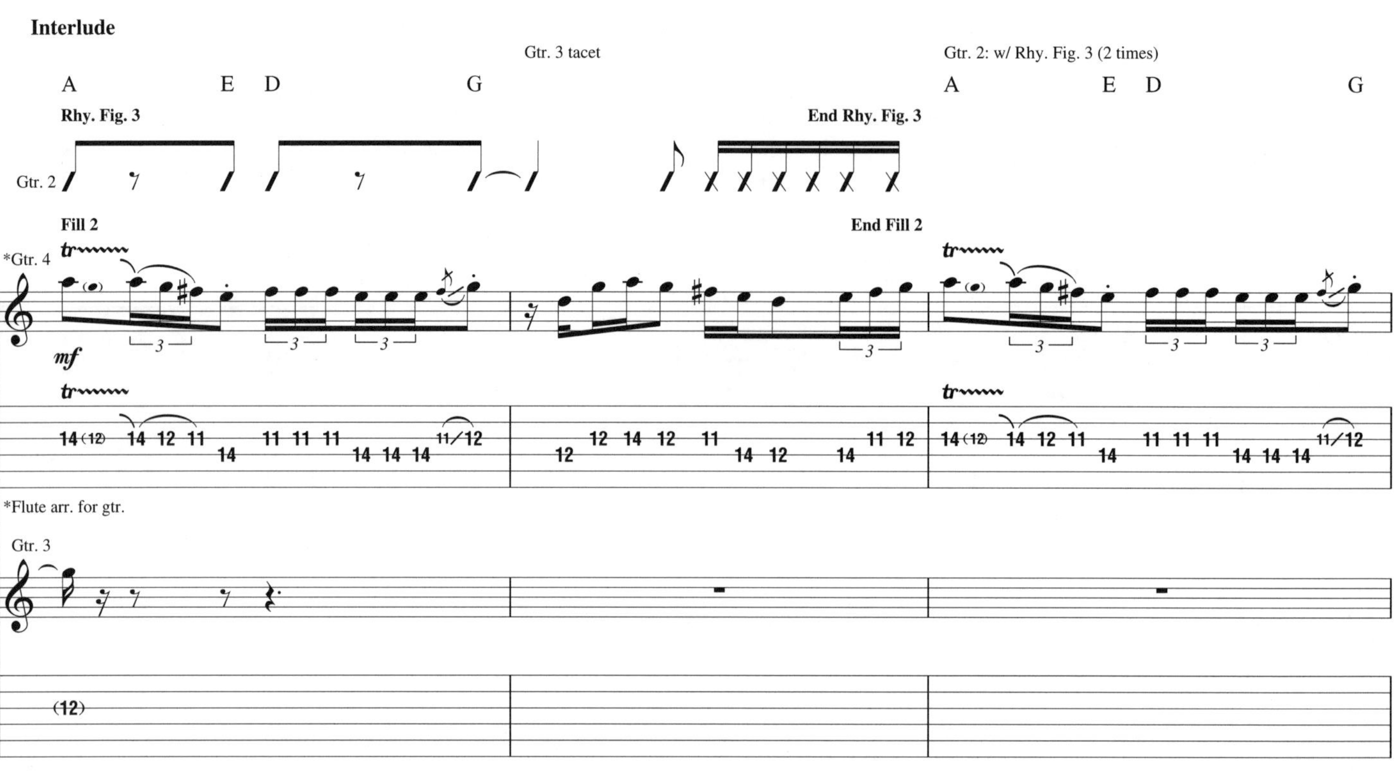
Gtr. 3 tacet
Gtr. 2: w/ Rhy. Fig. 3 (2 times)
A E D G A E D G
Rhy. Fig. 3
End Rhy. Fig. 3
Gtr. 2
Fill 2
End Fill 2
*Gtr. 4
tr
mf
14 (12) 14 12 11 14 11 11 11 14 14 14 11 12
12 12 14 12 11 14 12 14 11 12
14 (12) 14 12 11 14 11 11 11 14 14 14 11 12
*Flute arr. for gtr.
Gtr. 3
(12)

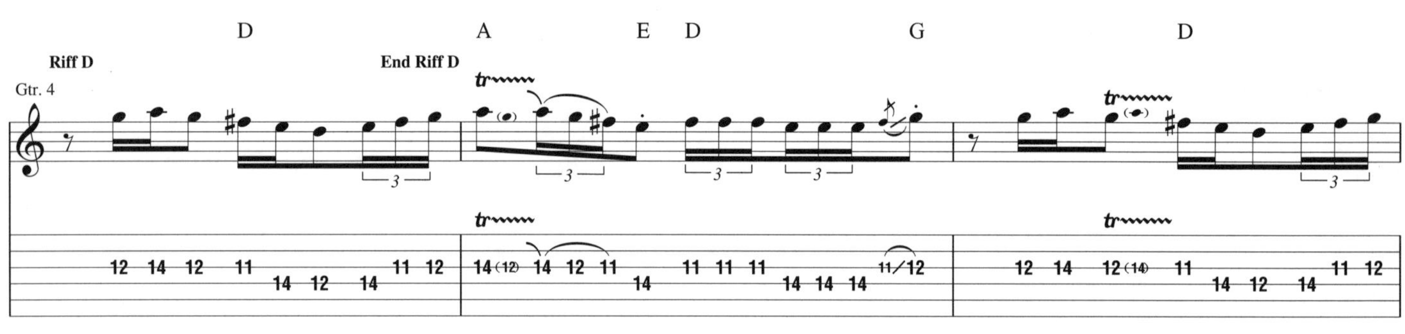
D A E D G D
Riff D
End Riff D
Gtr. 4
tr
12 14 12 11 14 12 14 11 12
14 (12) 14 12 11 14 11 11 11 14 14 14 11 12
12 14 12 (14) 11 14 12 14 11 12

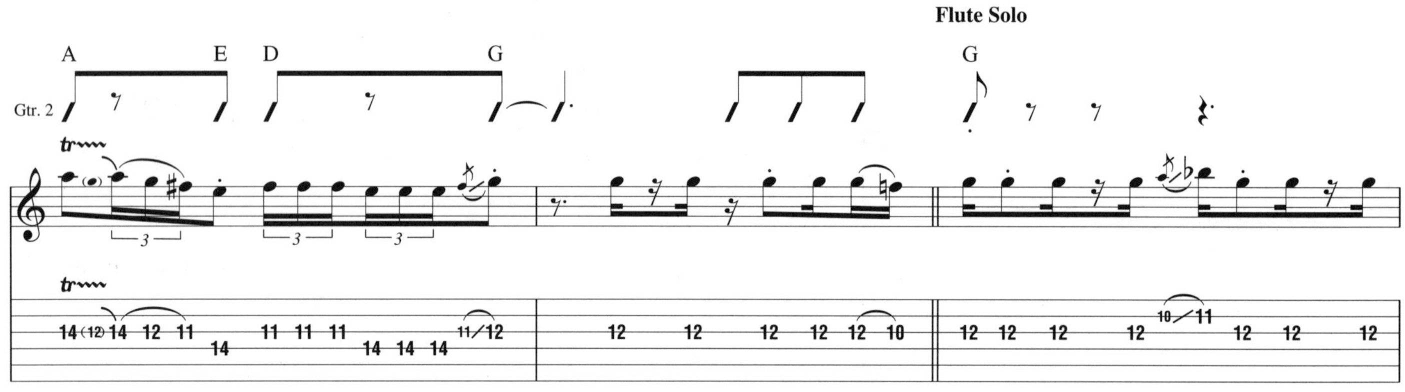
Flute Solo
A E D G G
Gtr. 2
tr
14 (12) 14 12 11 14 11 11 11 14 14 14 11 12
12 12 12 12 12 10
12 12 12 12 10 11 12 12 12

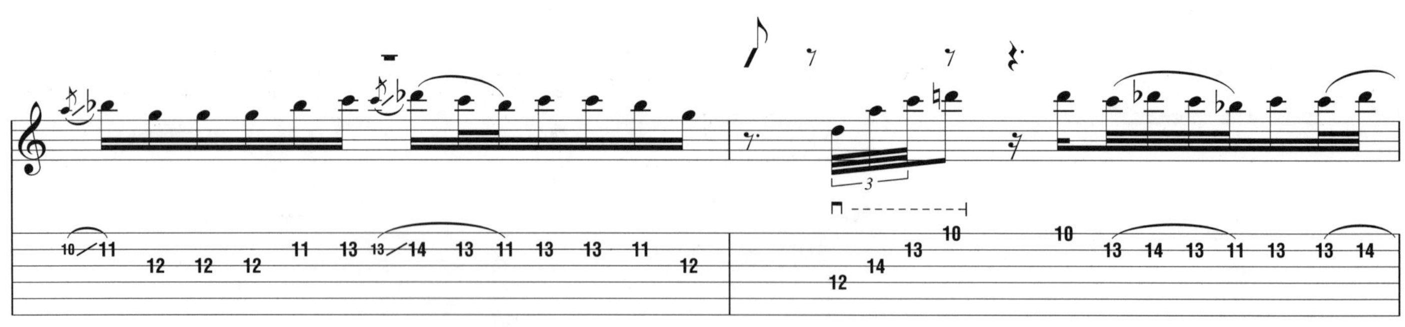
10 11 12 12 12 11 13 13 14 13 11 13 13 11 12
12 14 13 10 10 13 14 13 11 13 13 14

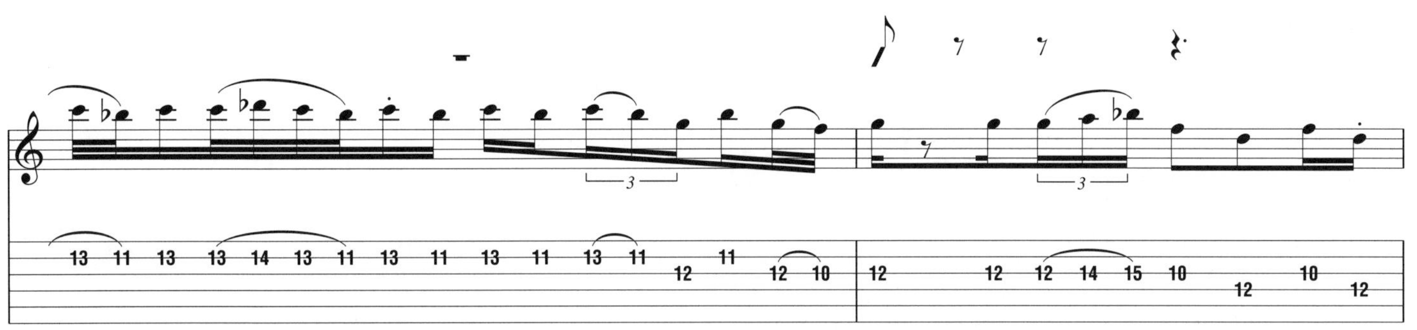

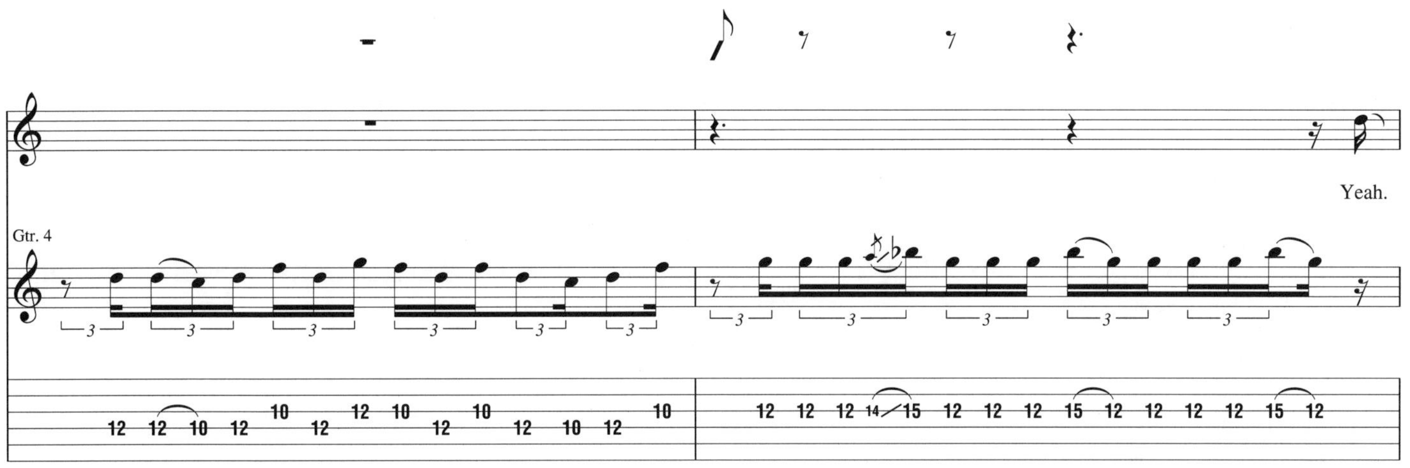
Gtr. 4
Yeah.

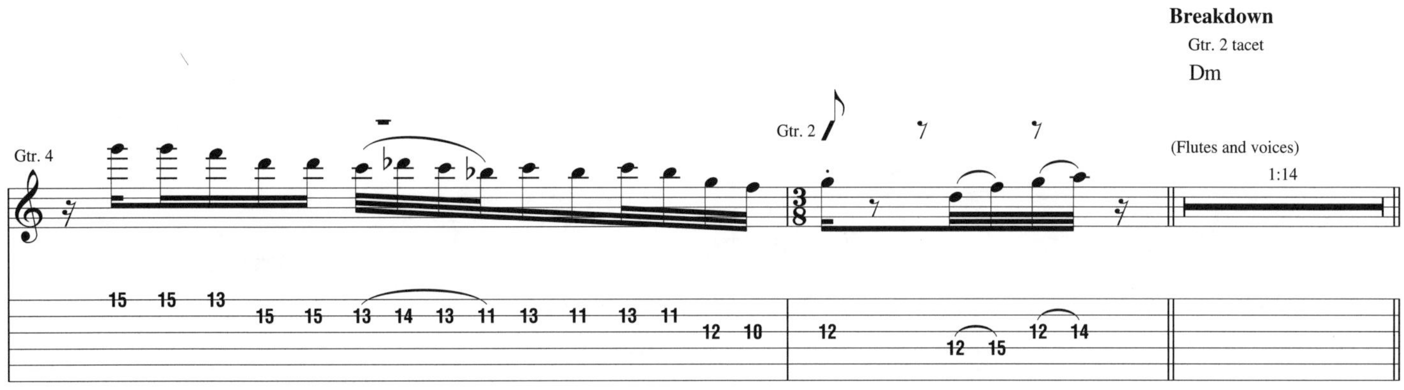
Breakdown
Gtr. 2 tacet
Dm
Gtr. 4
Gtr. 2
(Flutes and voices)
1:14

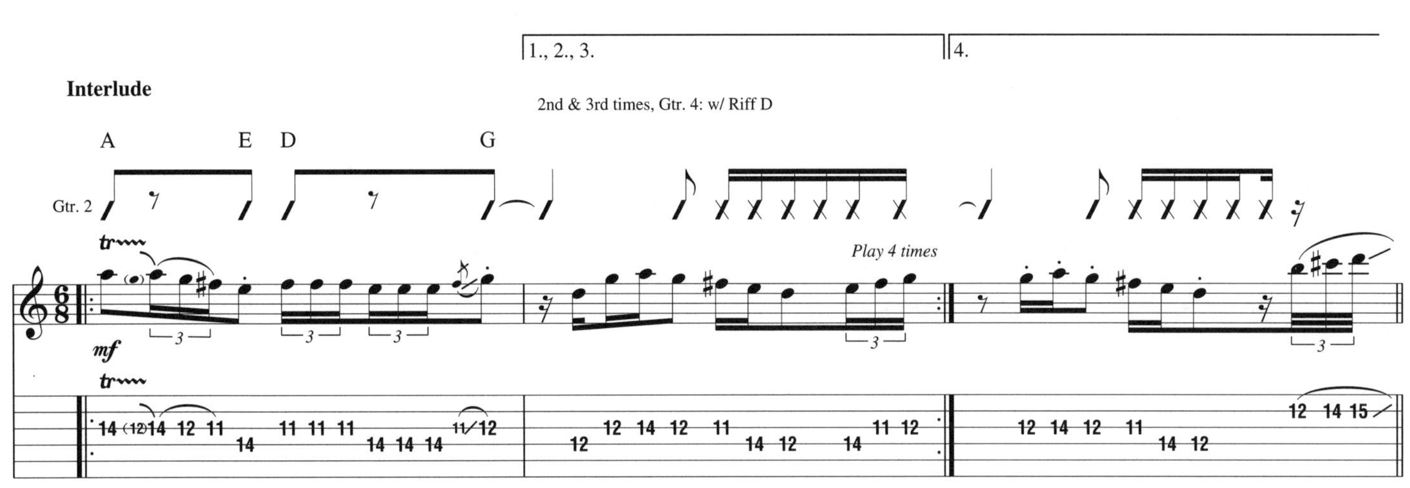
Interlude
1., 2., 3.
4.
2nd & 3rd times, Gtr. 4: w/ Riff D
A
E
D
G
Gtr. 2
Play 4 times
mf

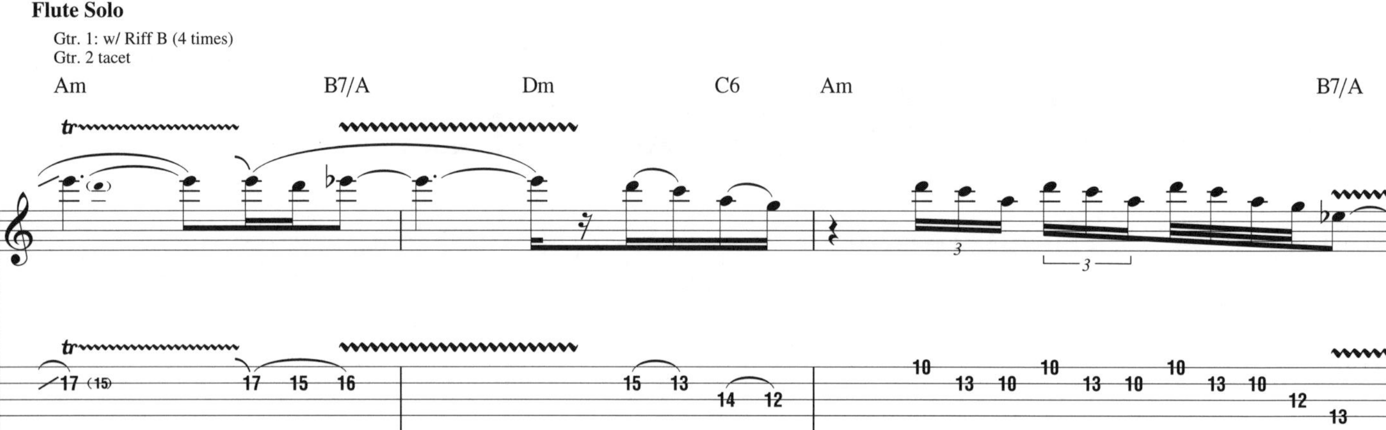
Flute Solo
Gtr. 1: w/ Riff B (4 times)
Gtr. 2 tacet
Am
B7/A
Dm
C6
Am
B7/A
tr

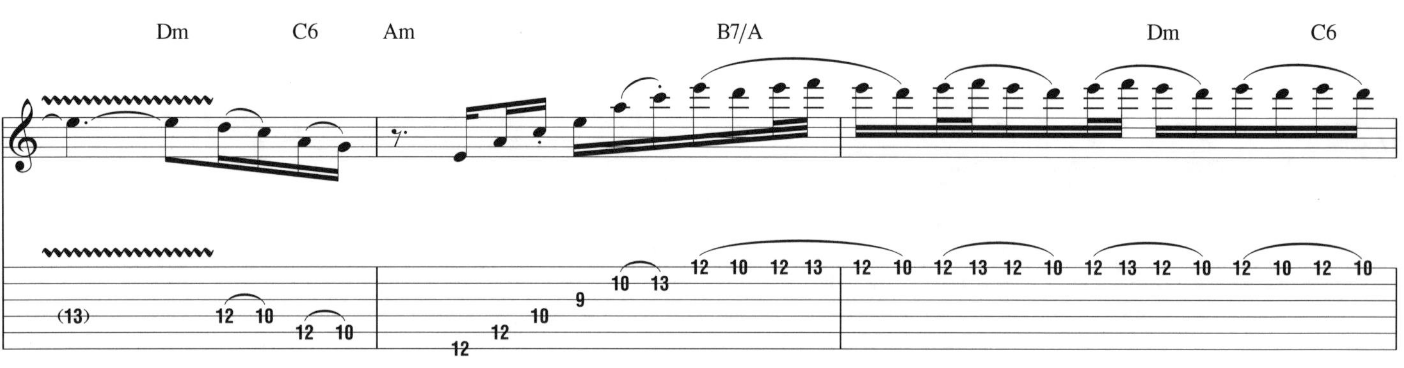
Dm
C6
Am
B7/A
Dm
C6

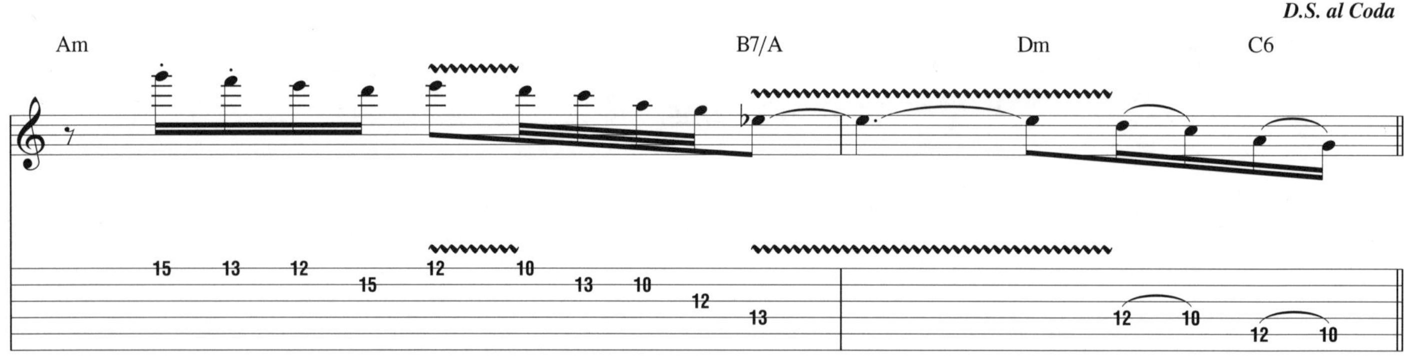
D.S. al Coda
Am
B7/A
Dm
C6

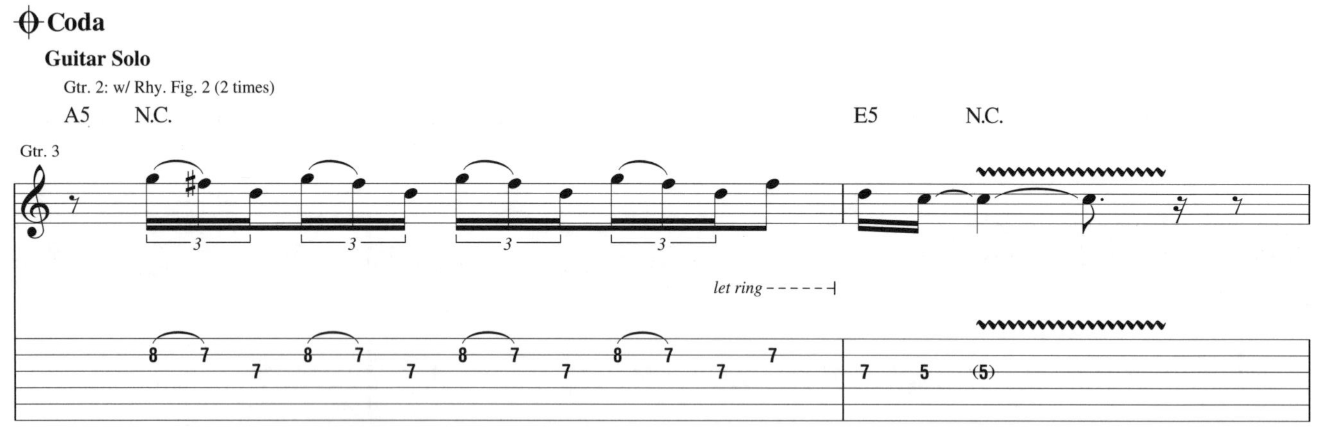
Coda
Guitar Solo
Gtr. 2: w/ Rhy. Fig. 2 (2 times)
A5
N.C.
E5
N.C.
Gtr. 3
let ring

D5
N.C.
F5
C5
G5

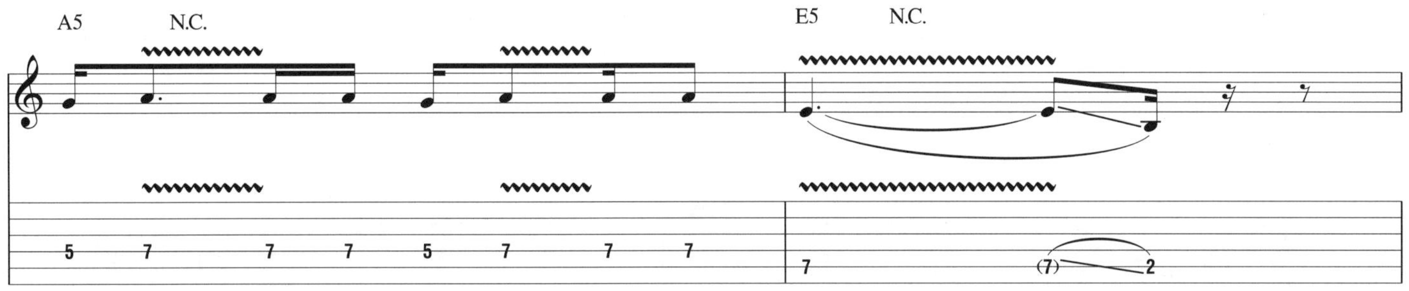

A5
N.C.
E5
N.C.

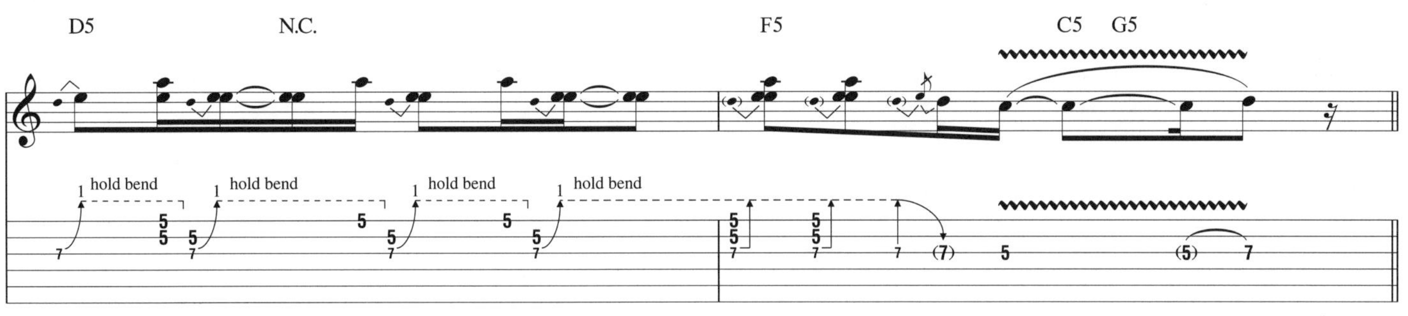

D5
N.C.
F5
C5
G5
hold bend
hold bend
hold bend
hold bend

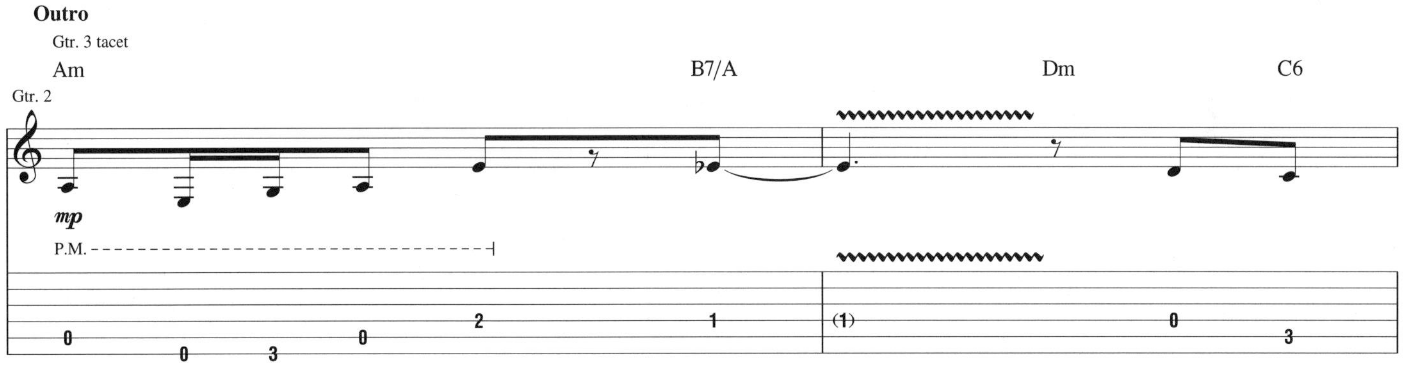

Outro
Gtr. 3 tacet
Am
B7/A
Dm
C6
Gtr. 2
mp
P.M.

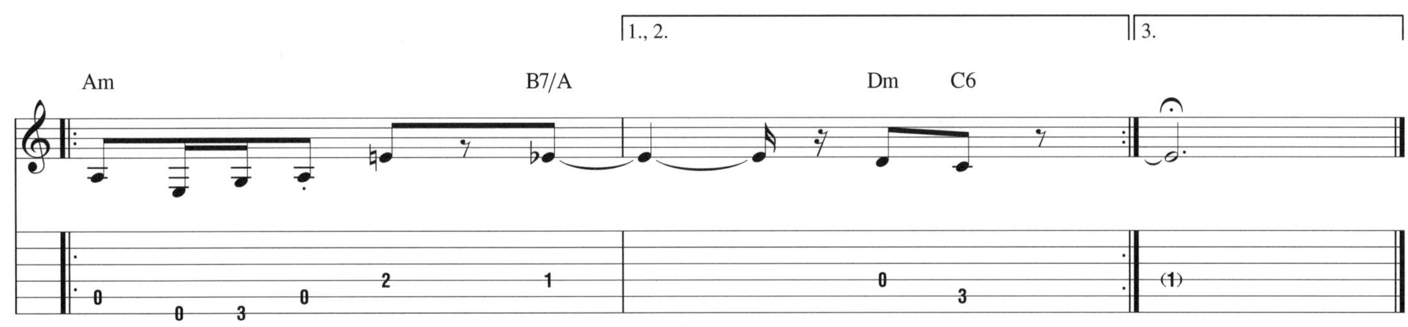

1., 2.
3.
Am
B7/A
Dm
C6

Hymn #43

Words and Music by Ian Anderson

Verse

Moderately ♩ = 82

2nd time, Gtr. 4: w/ Fill 1

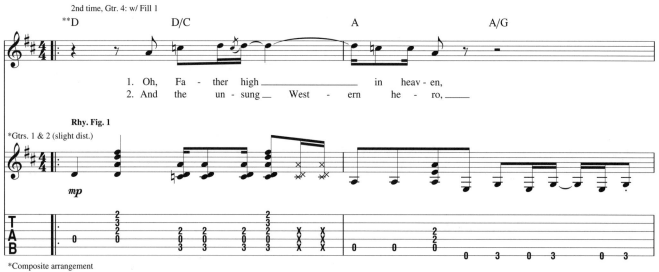

**D D/C A A/G

1. Oh, Fa - ther high in heav - en,
2. And the un - sung West - ern he - ro,

Rhy. Fig. 1

*Gtrs. 1 & 2 (slight dist.)

mp

*Composite arrangement

**Chord symbols reflect overall harmony.

D D/C G
smile down up - on your son, yeah, hey,
he killed an In - di - an or three, yeah, hey,
P.M.

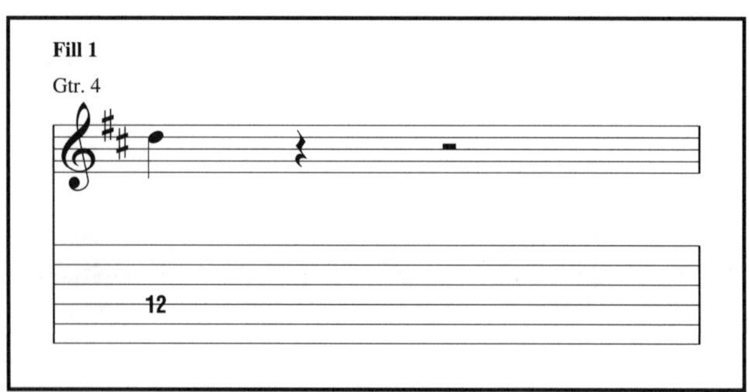

Fill 1
Gtr. 4
12

D
D/C
G/B
B♭maj7
who's bus - y with his mon - ey games;
and when he made his name in Hol - ly - wood,
End Rhy. Fig. 1

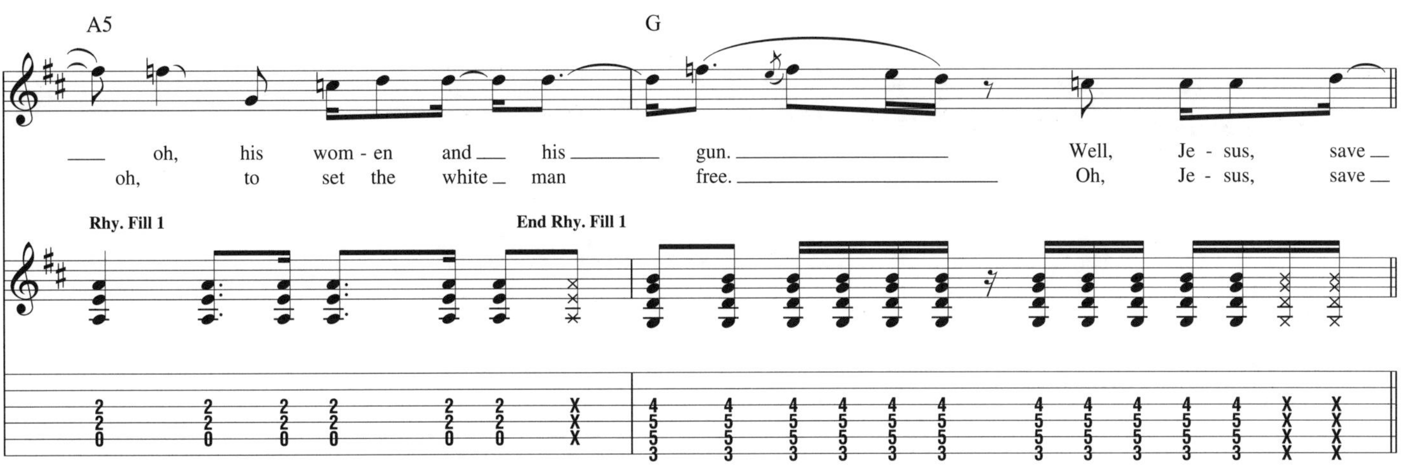
A5
G
oh, his wom - en and his gun.
Well, Je - sus, save
oh, to set the white man free.
Oh, Je - sus, save
Rhy. Fill 1
End Rhy. Fill 1

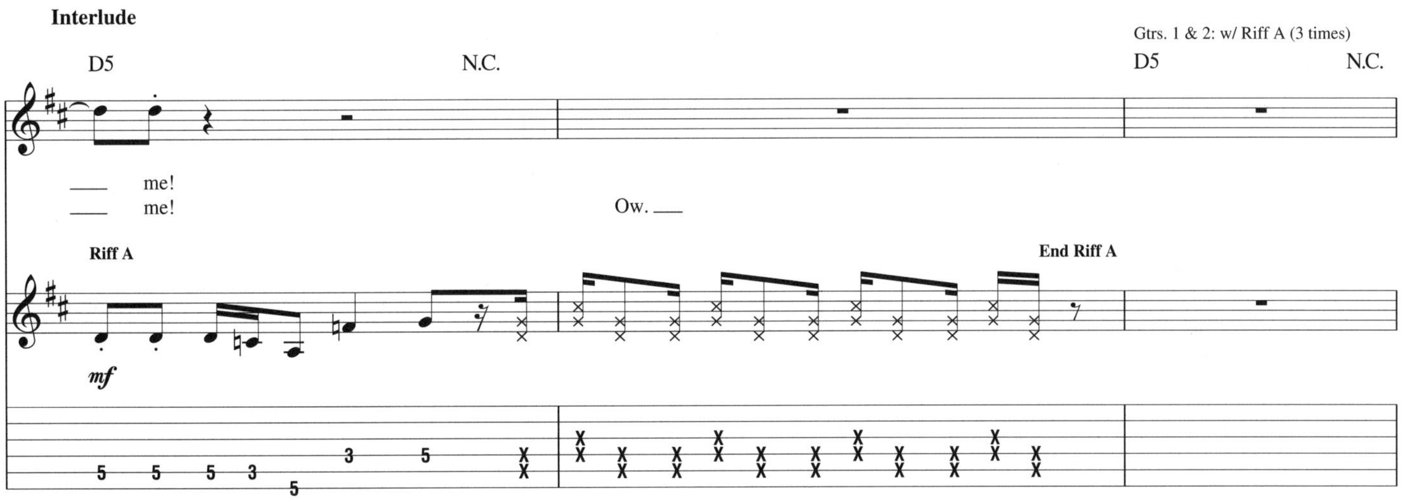
Interlude
D5
N.C.
Gtrs. 1 & 2: w/ Riff A (3 times)
D5
N.C.
me!
me!
Ow.
Riff A
End Riff A
mf

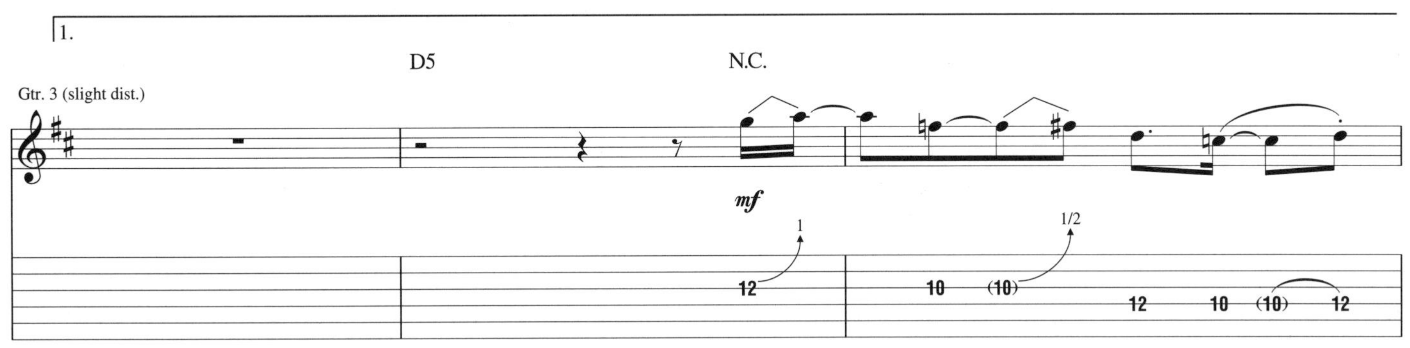
1.
Gtr. 3 (slight dist.)
D5
N.C.
mf
1
1/2

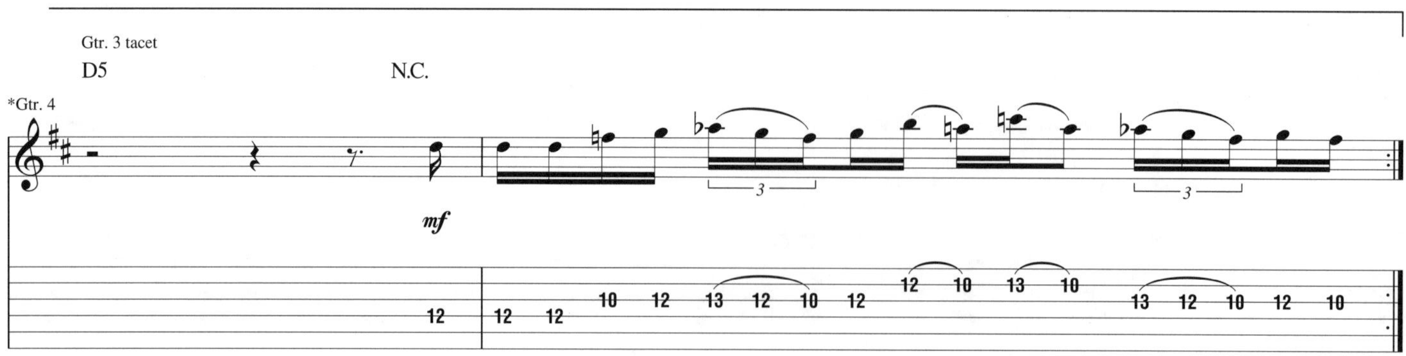

*Flute arr. for gtr.

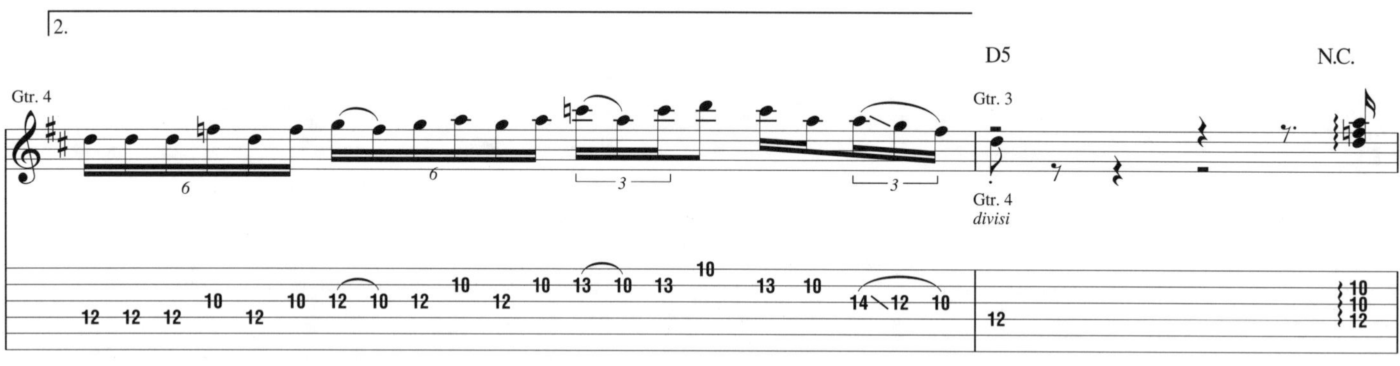

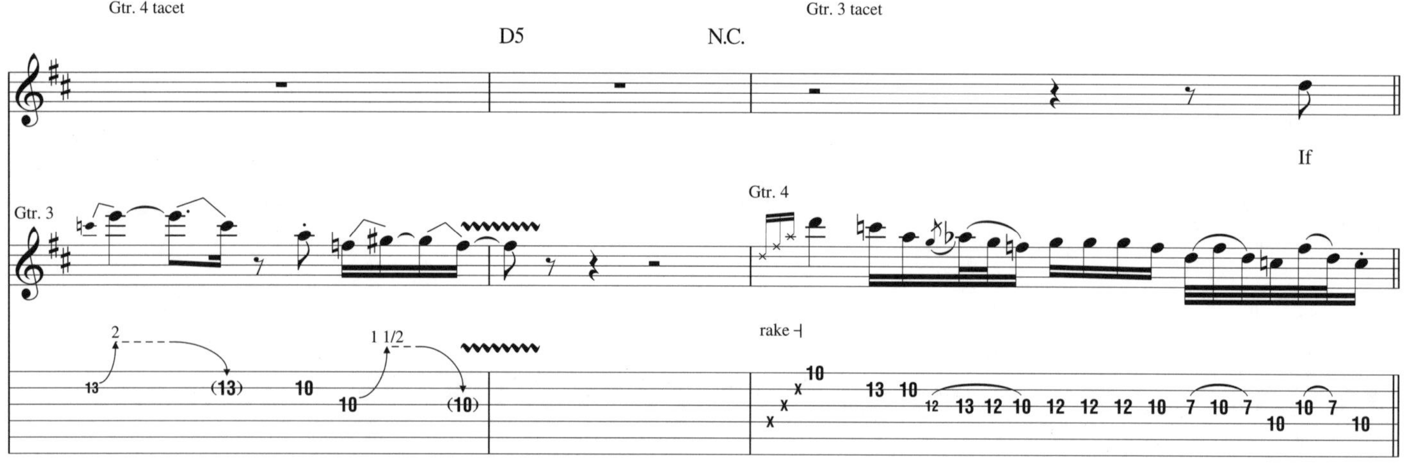

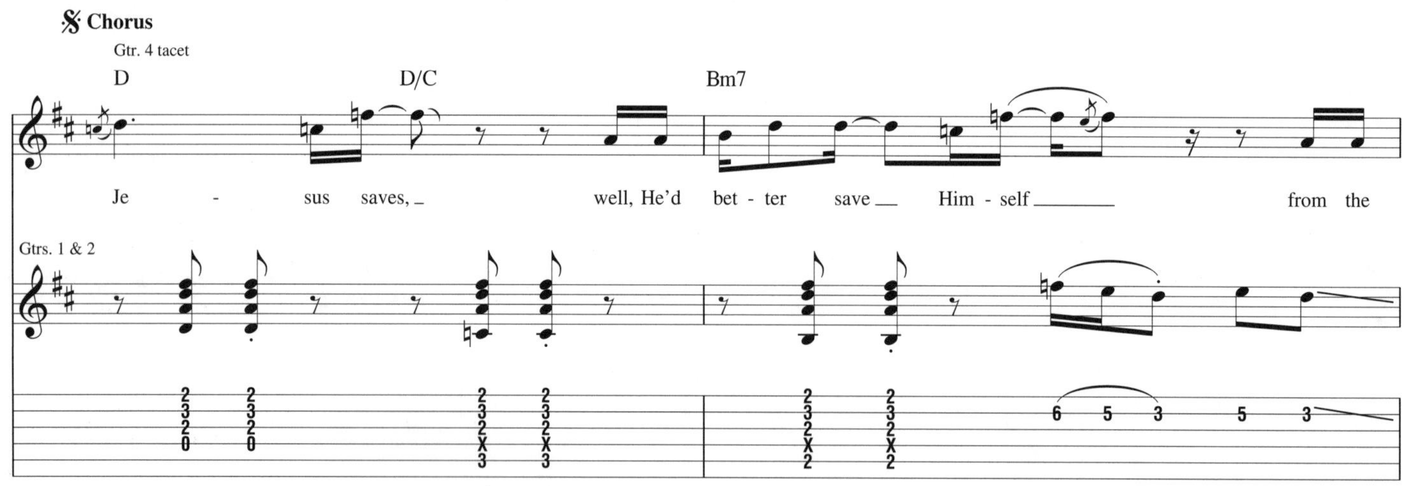

To Coda ⊕

Guitar Solo

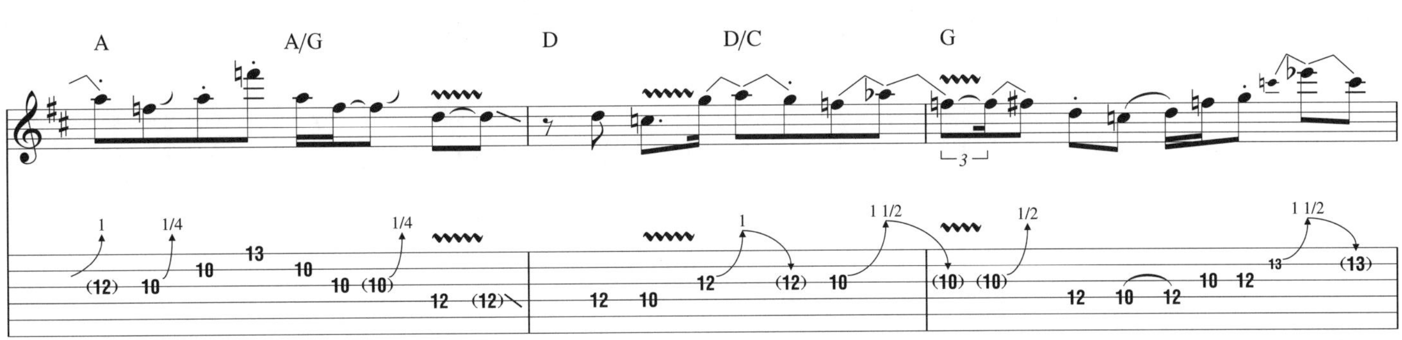

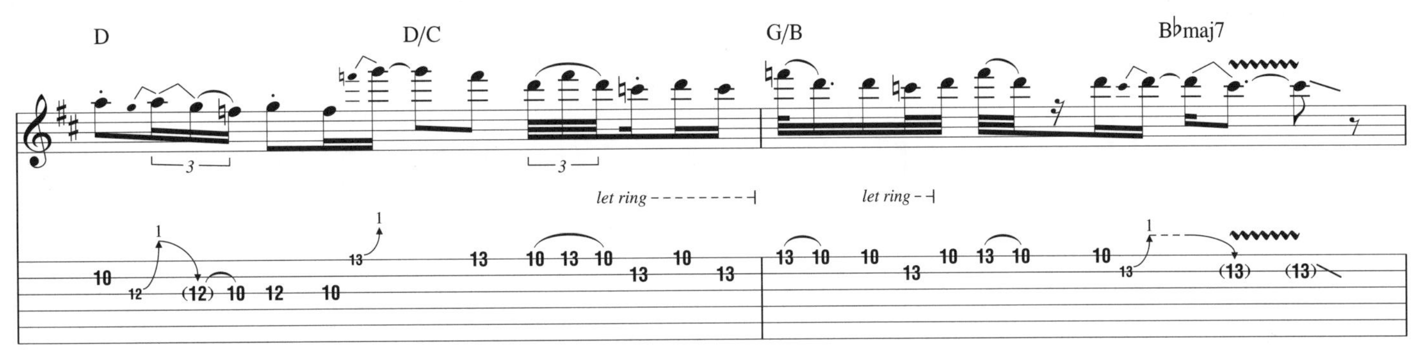

D.S. al Coda

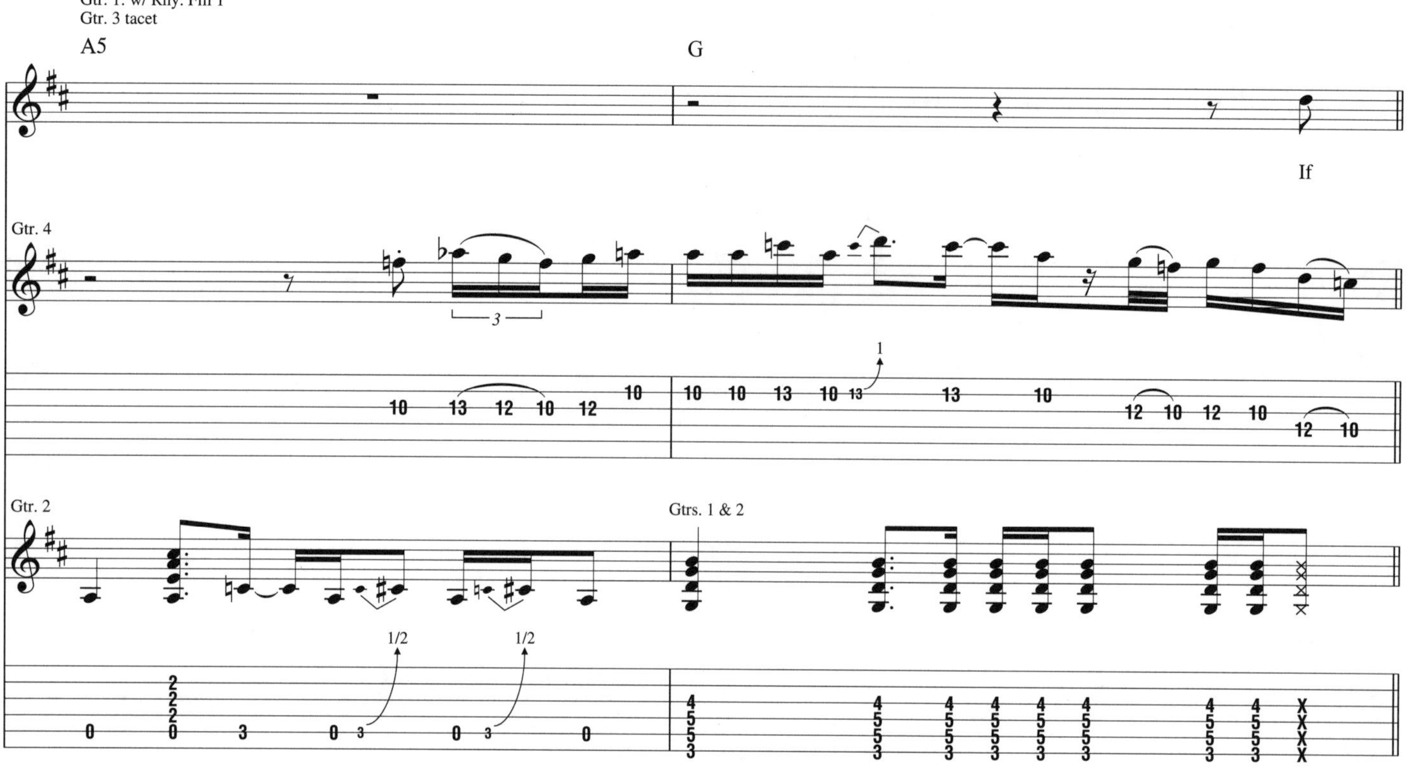

Interlude

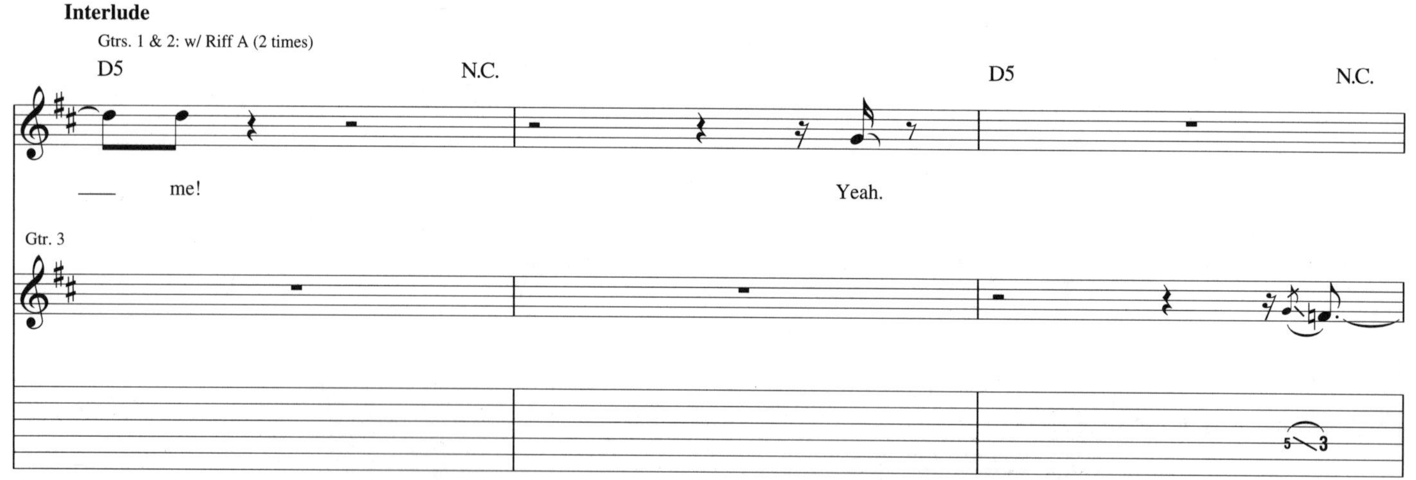

Verse

Gtrs. 1 & 2: w/ Rhy. Fig. 1
Gtr. 3 tacet
D
D/C
A
A/G
3. Ah, well, I saw Him in the cit - y,
grad. bend
1/2
(3)
X X 3 5 3 5

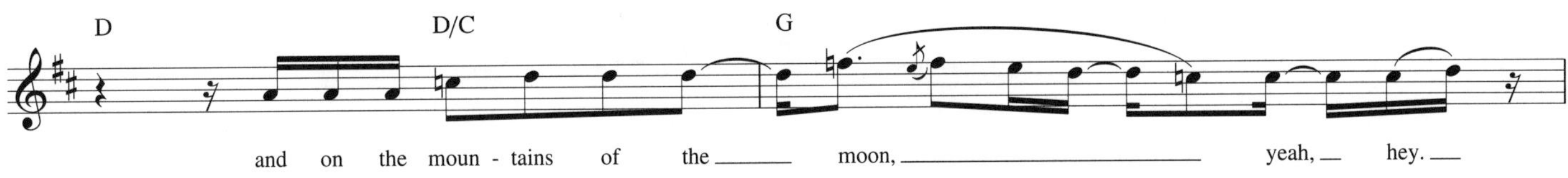
D
D/C
G
and on the moun - tains of the moon, yeah, hey.

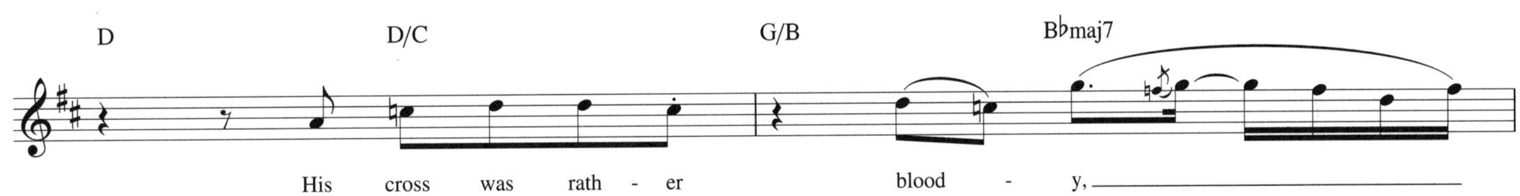
D
D/C
G/B
B♭maj7
His cross was rath - er blood - y,

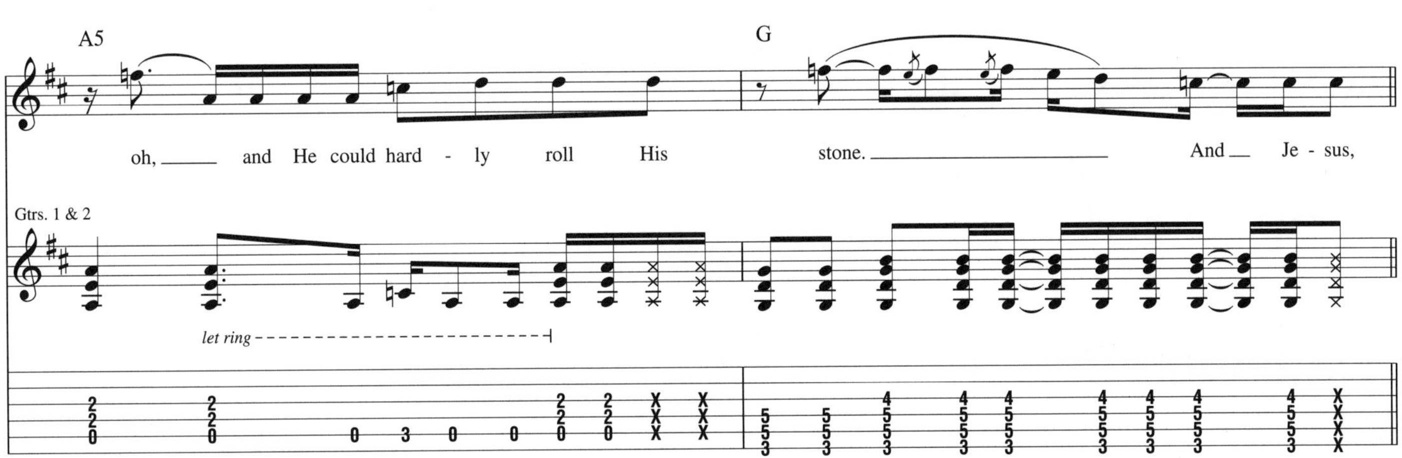
A5
G
oh, and He could hard - ly roll His stone. And Je - sus,
Gtrs. 1 & 2
let ring

Outro

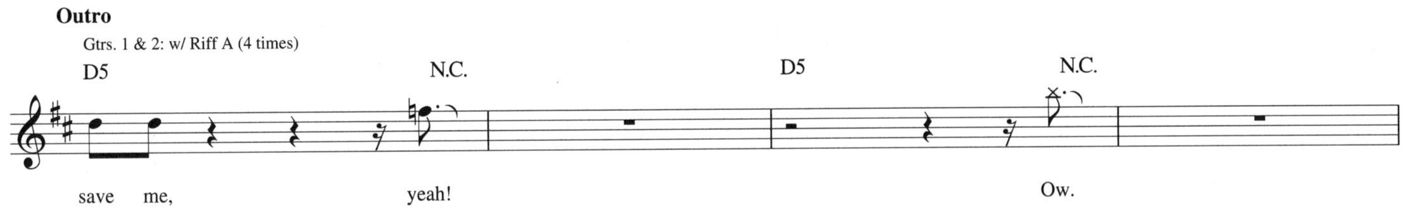
Gtrs. 1 & 2: w/ Riff A (4 times)
D5
N.C.
D5
N.C.
save me, yeah! Ow.

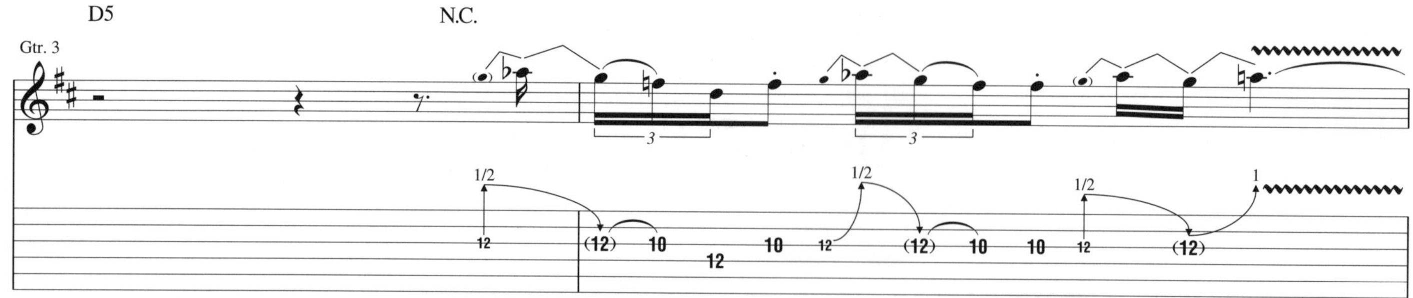

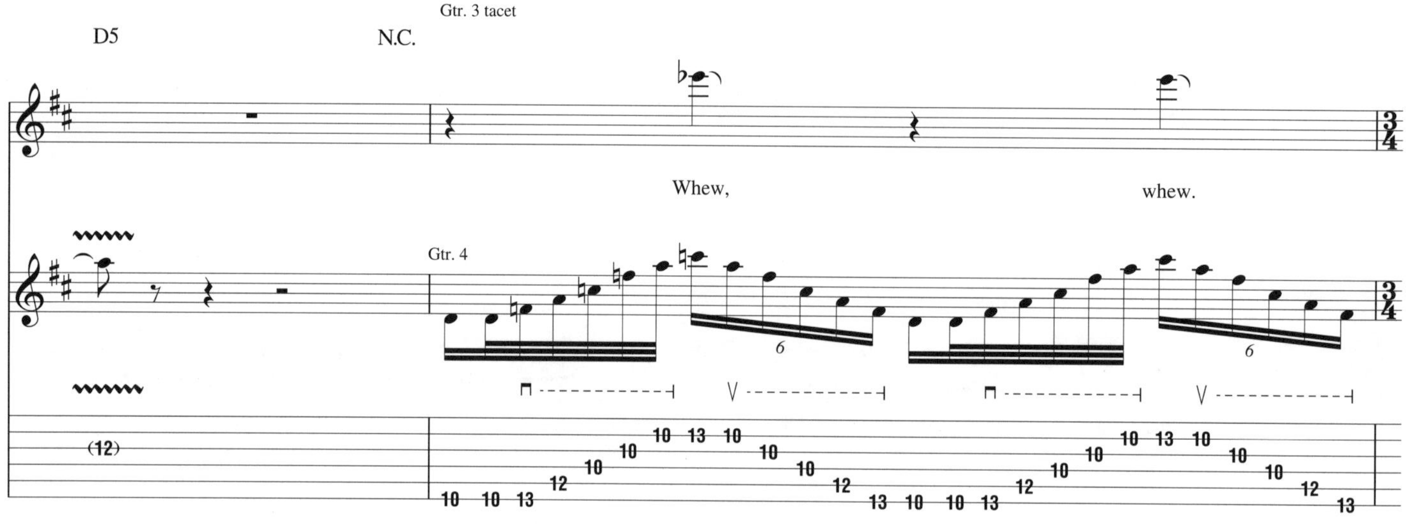

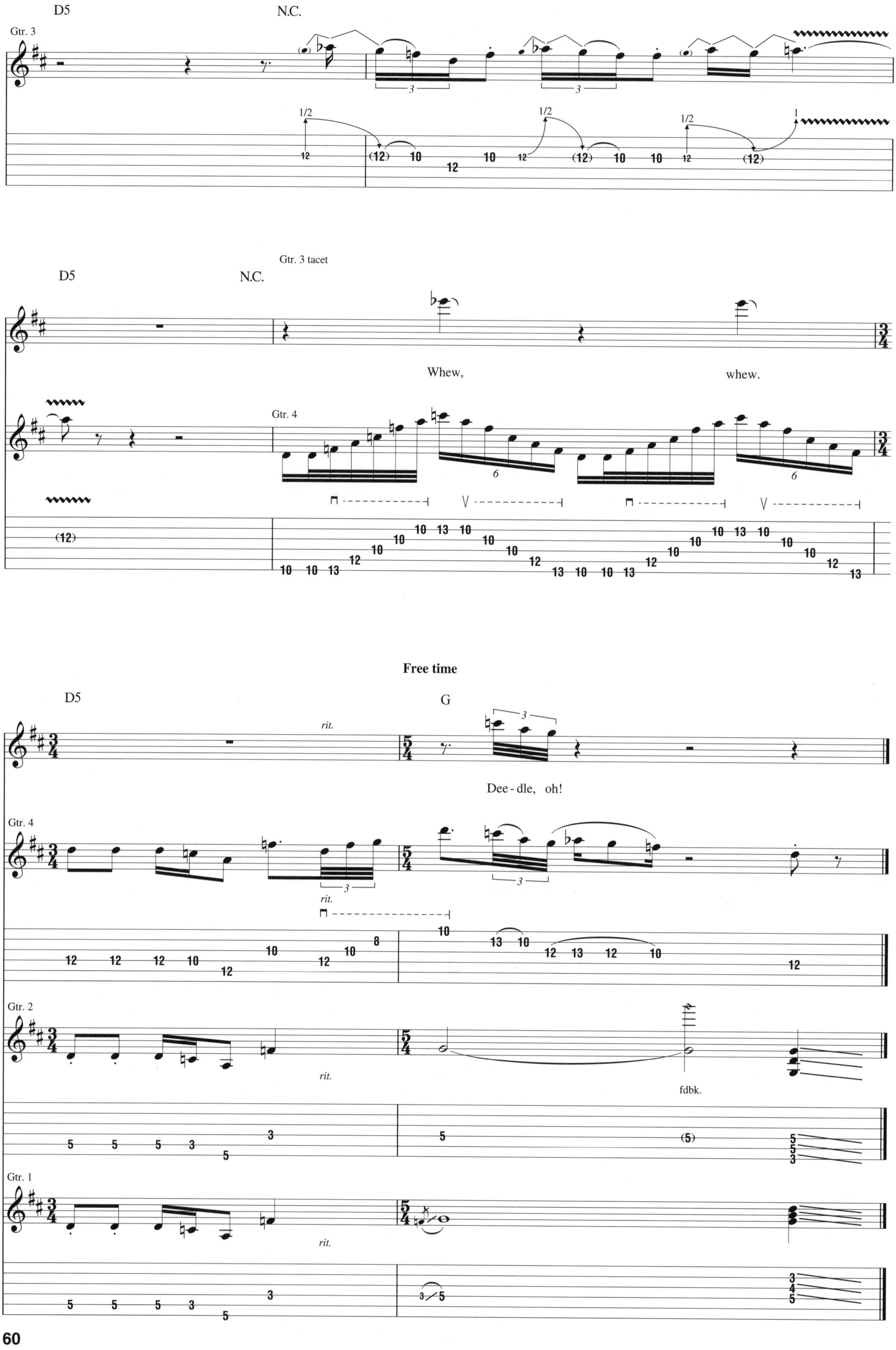

Free time

D5 G

rit.

Dee-dle, oh!

Gtr. 4

rit.

Gtr. 2

rit.

fdbk.

Gtr. 1

rit.

Slipstream

Words and Music by Ian Anderson

*Symbols in parentheses represent chord names respective to capoed guitar. Symbols above reflect actual sounding chords. Capoed fret is "0" in tab. Chord symbols reflect basic harmony.

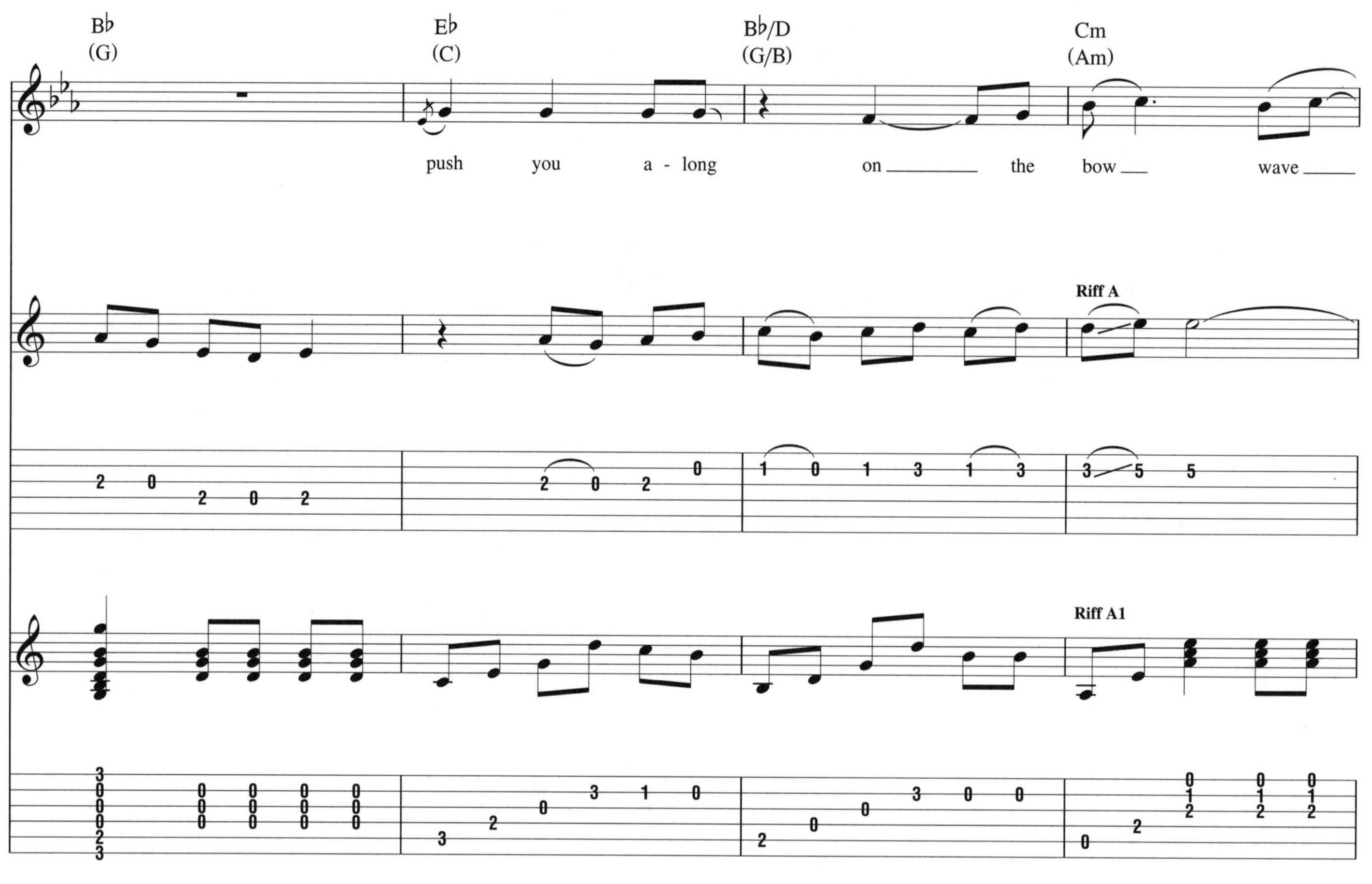
B♭
(G)
E♭
(C)
B♭/D
(G/B)
Cm
(Am)
push you a - long on the bow wave
Riff A
Riff A1

B♭
(G)
Cm
(Am)
of their spir - it - less, un - dy - ing selves.
End Riff A
End Riff A1

B♭
(G)
E♭
(C)
B♭/D
(G/B)
And you press on God's wait - er your

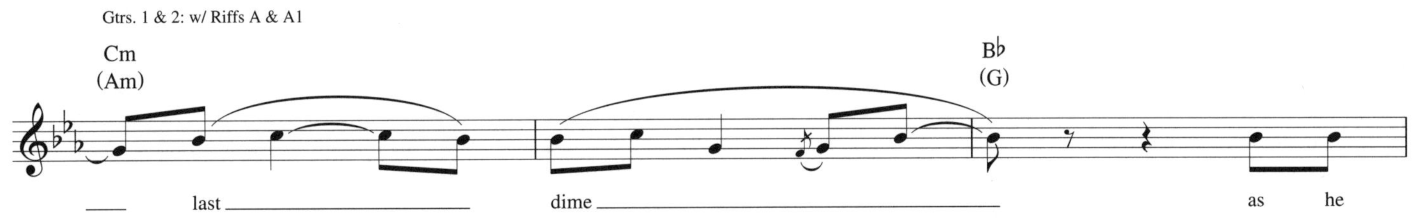
Gtrs. 1 & 2: w/ Riffs A & A1
Cm
(Am)
B♭
(G)
last dime as he

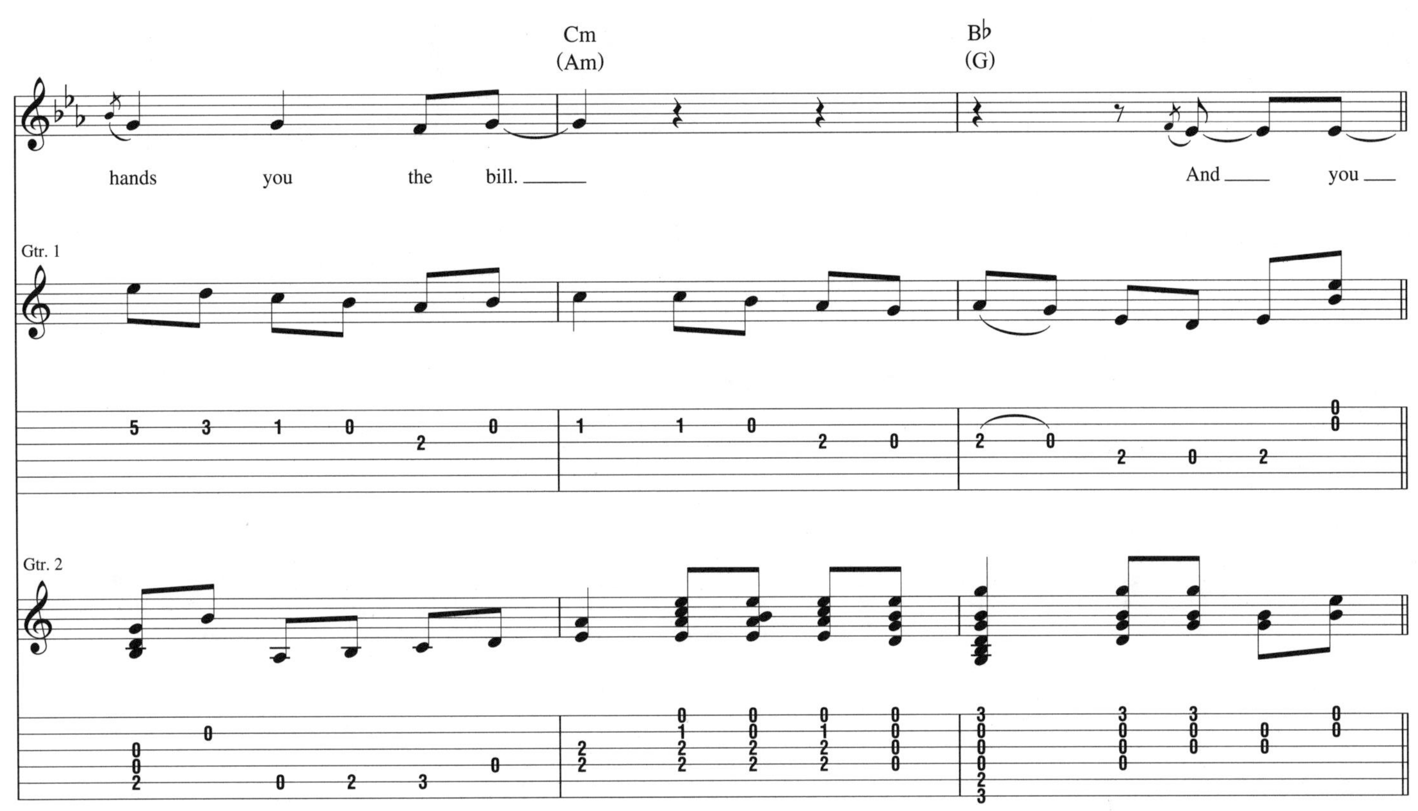
Cm
(Am)
B♭
(G)
hands you the bill. And you
Gtr. 1
Gtr. 2

Chorus

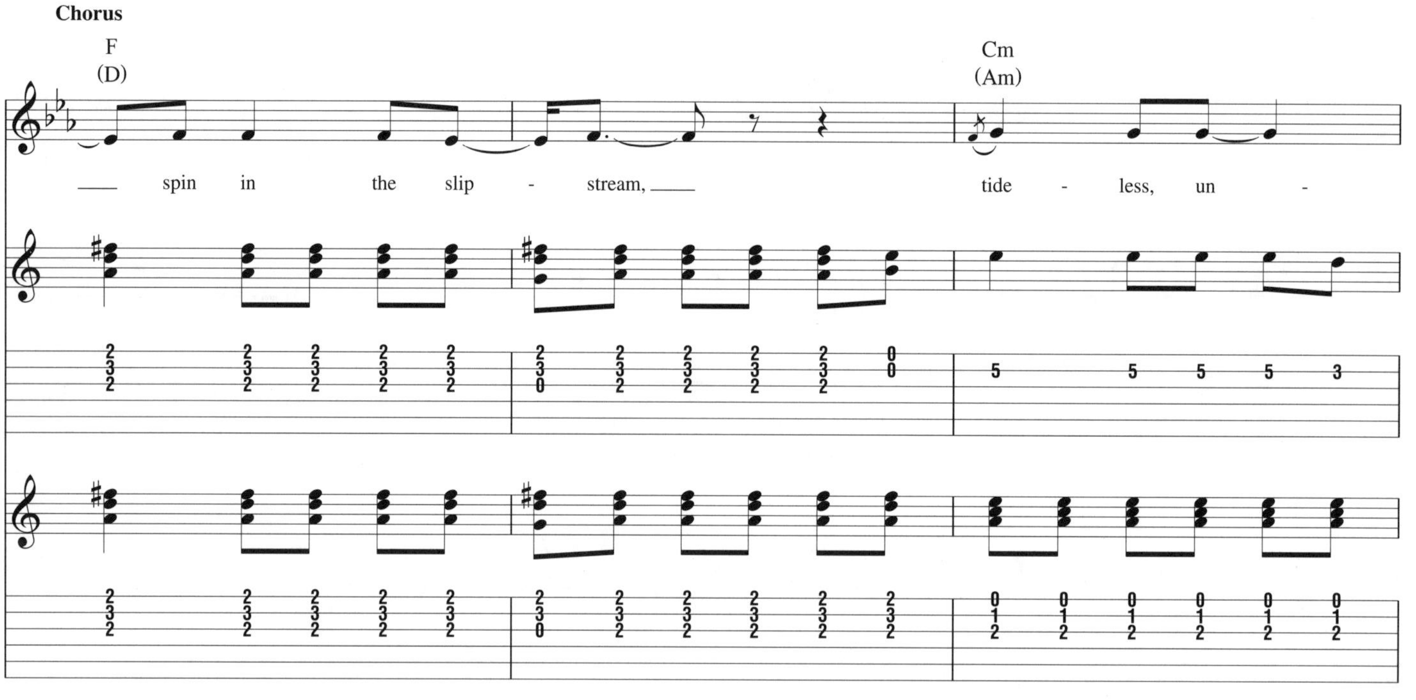

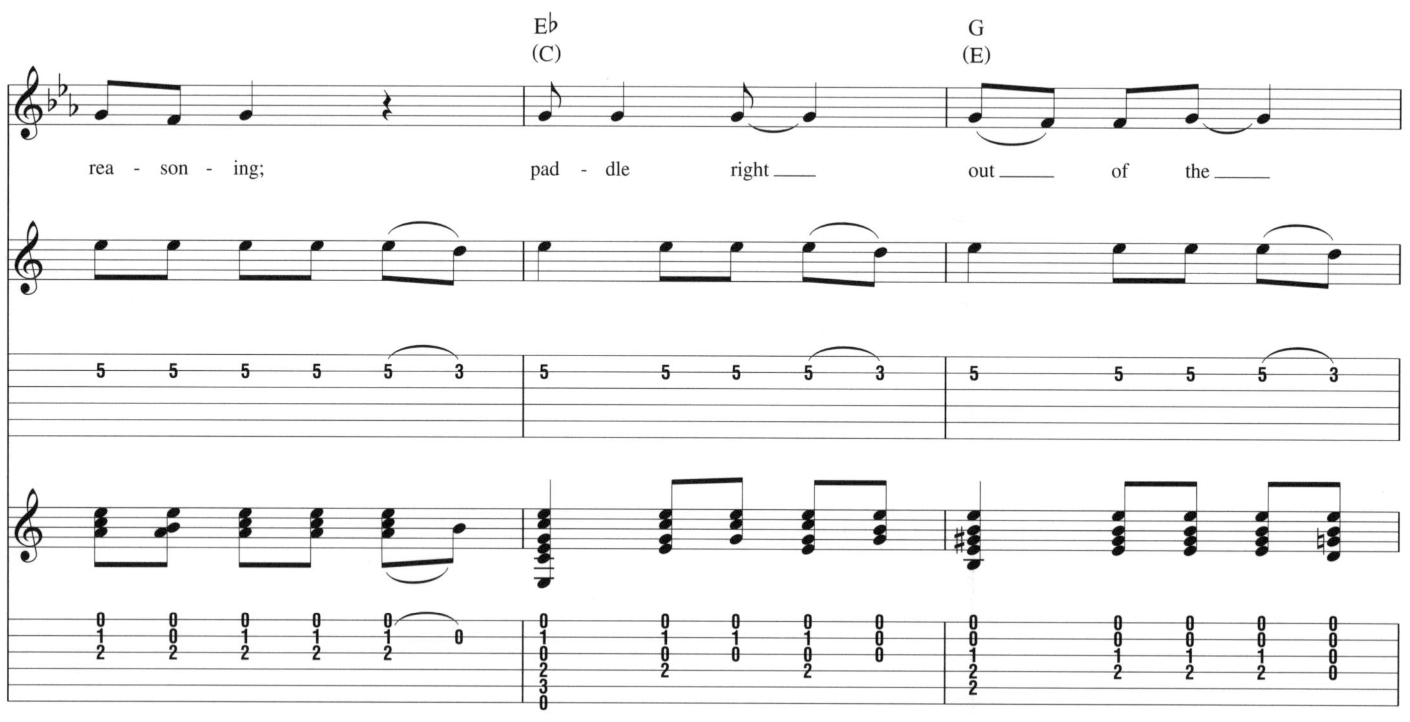

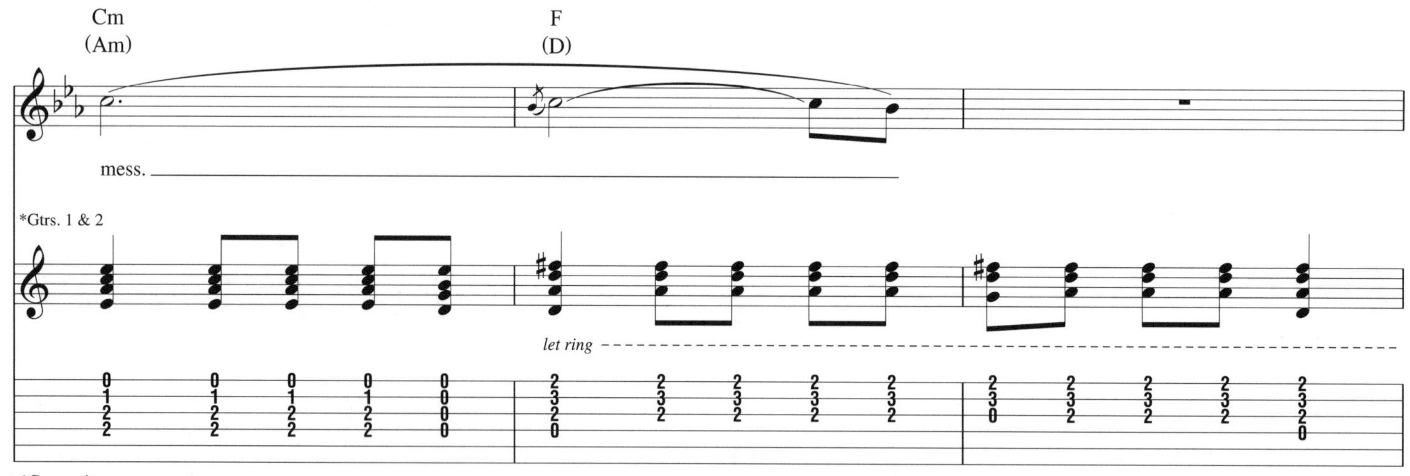

*Composite arrangement

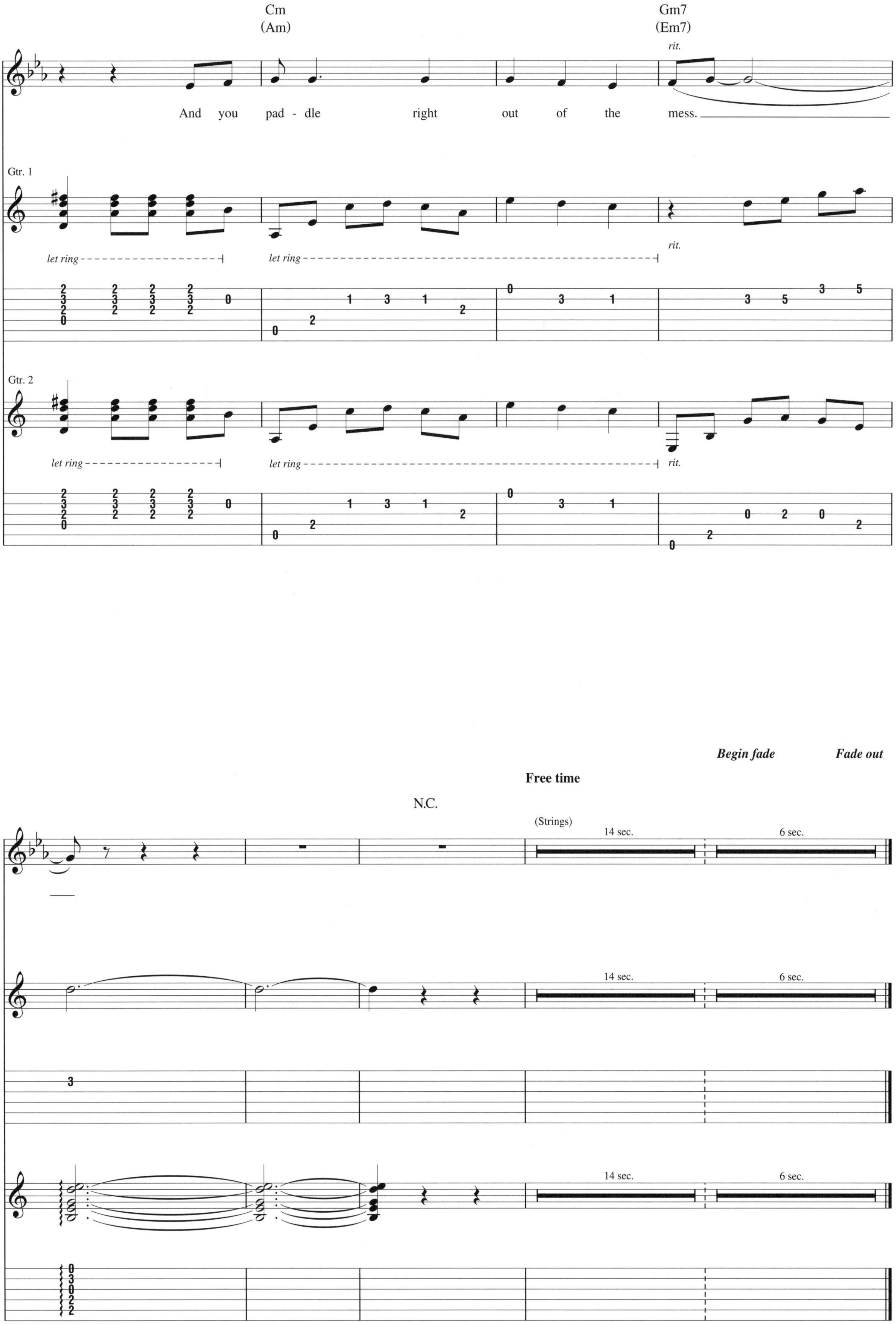

Begin fade *Fade out*

Free time

N.C.

(Strings)

14 sec. 6 sec.

14 sec. 6 sec.

14 sec. 6 sec.

Locomotive Breath

Words and Music by Ian Anderson

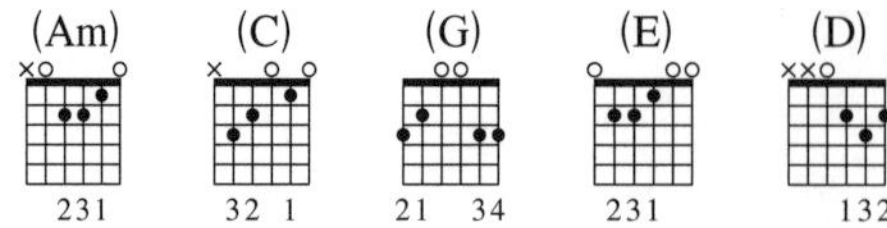

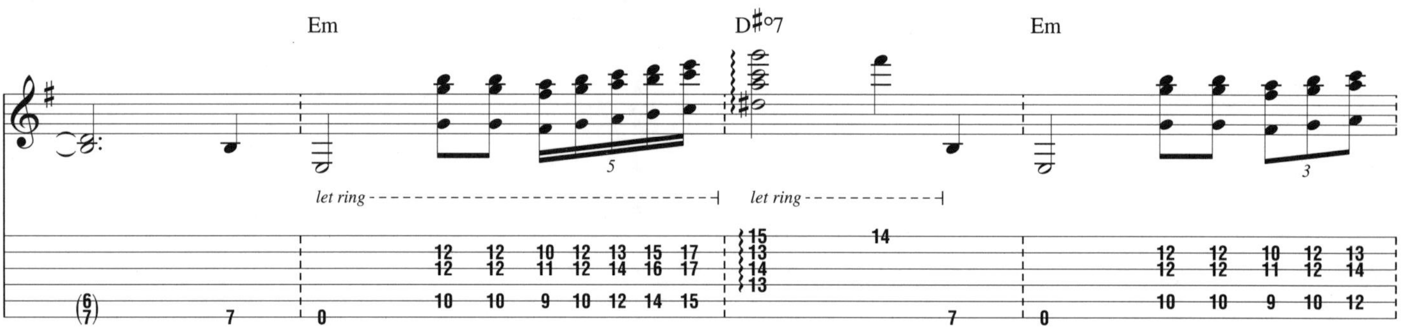

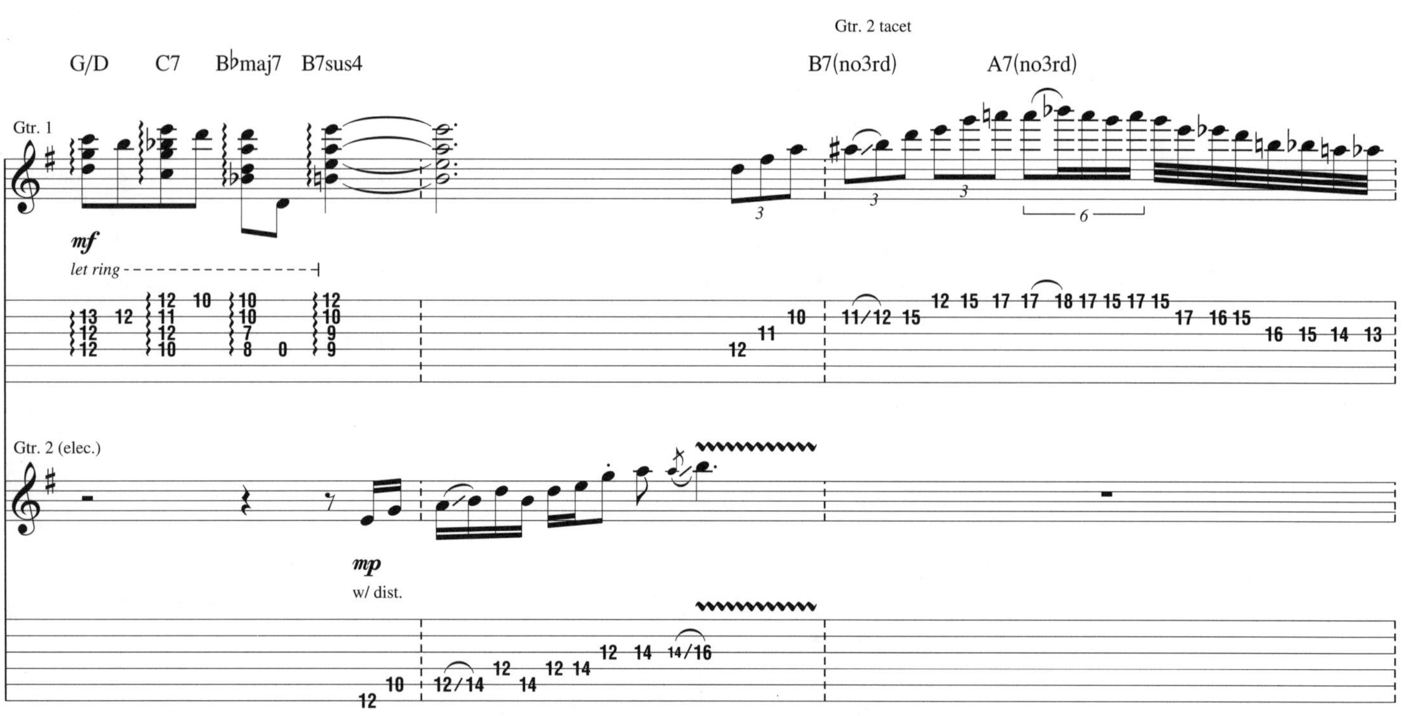

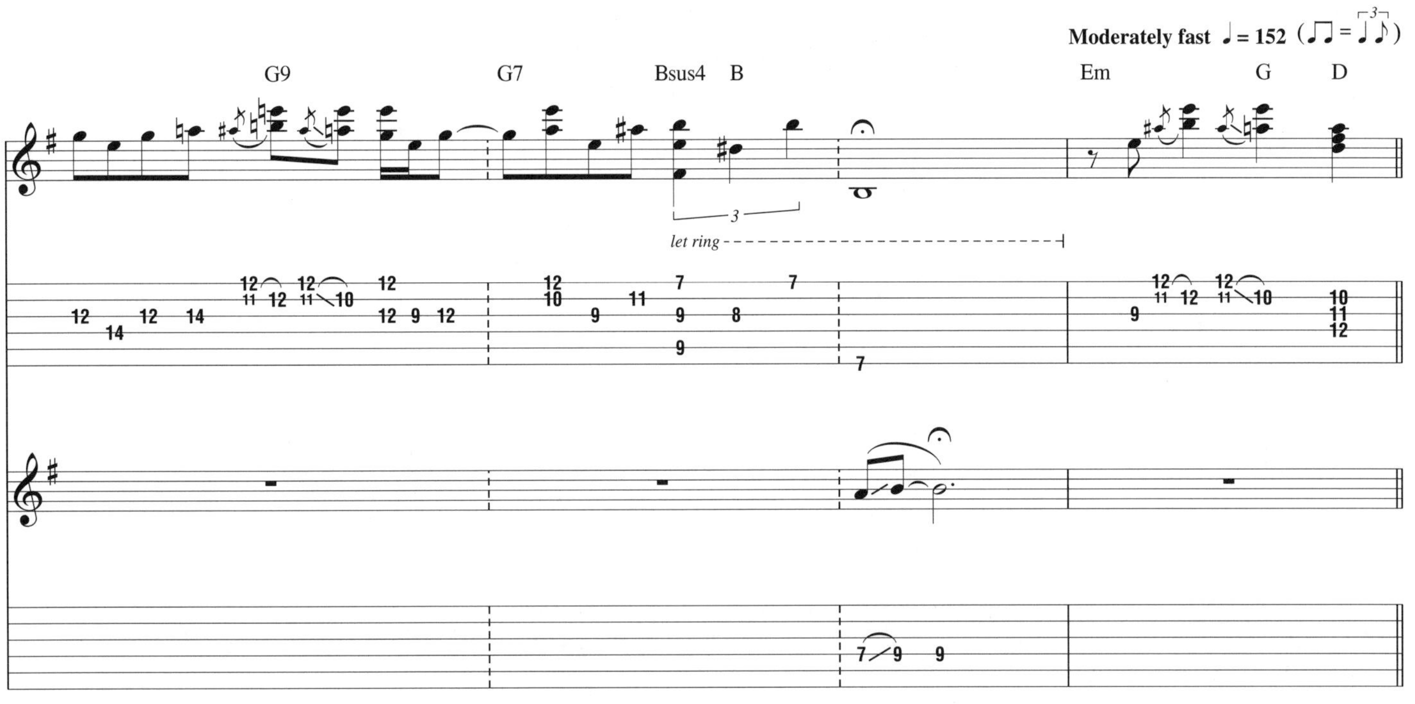
Moderately fast ♩ = 152
G9
G7
Bsus4 B
Em
G
D
let ring

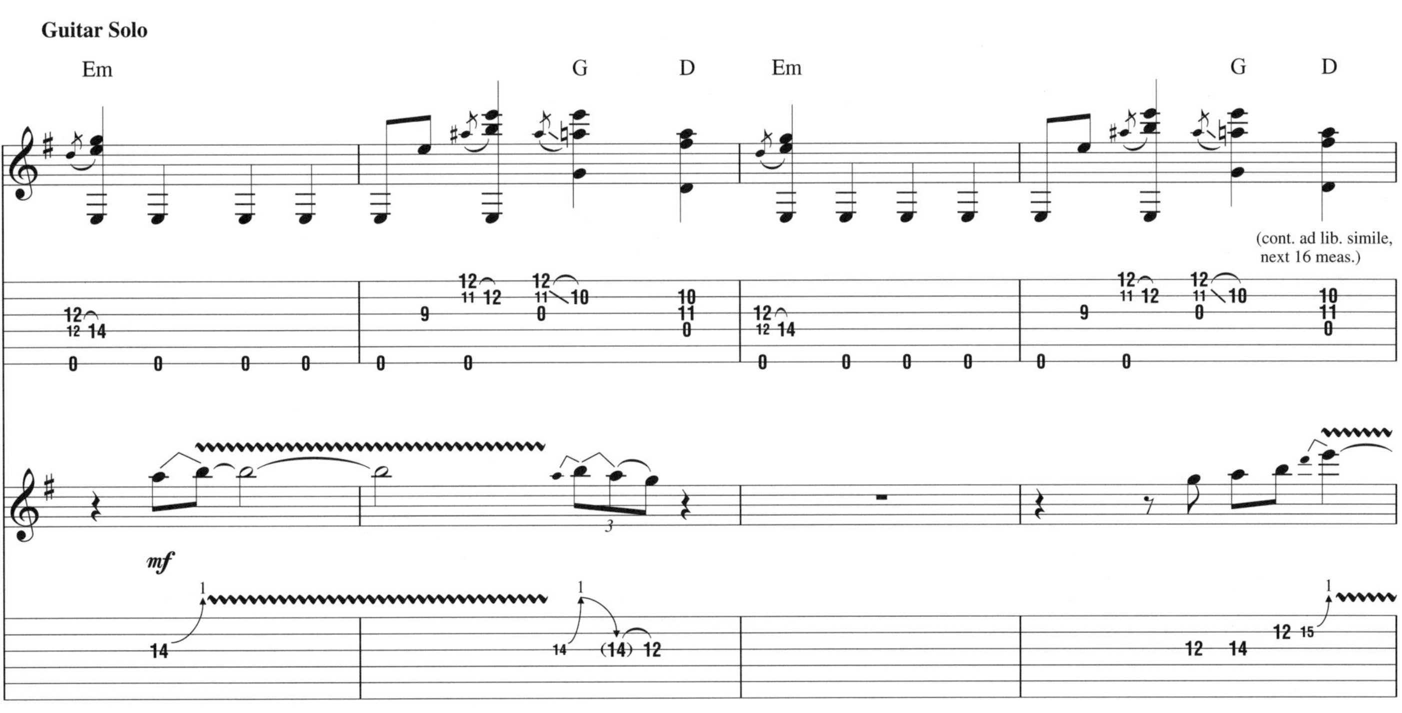
Guitar Solo
Em
G
D
Em
G
D
mf
(cont. ad lib. simile, next 16 meas.)

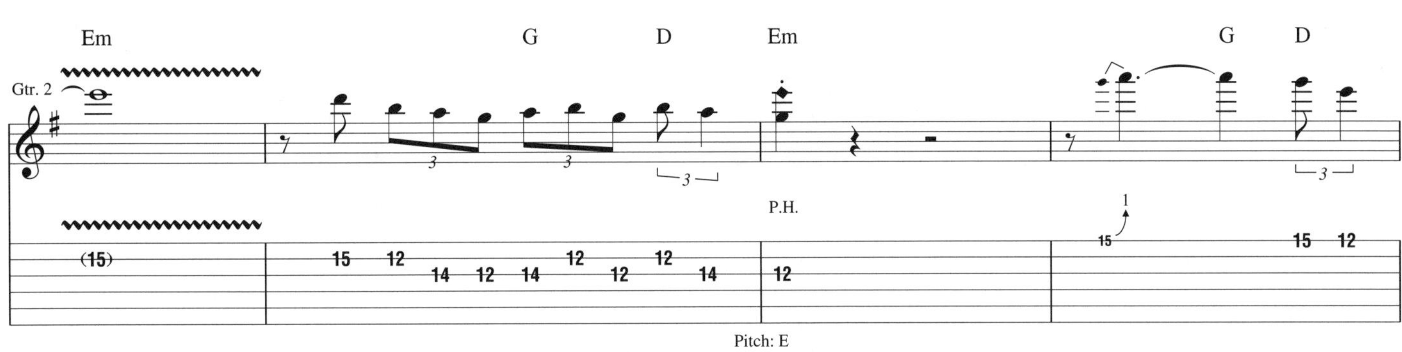
Em
G
D
Em
G
D
Gtr. 2
P.H.
Pitch: E

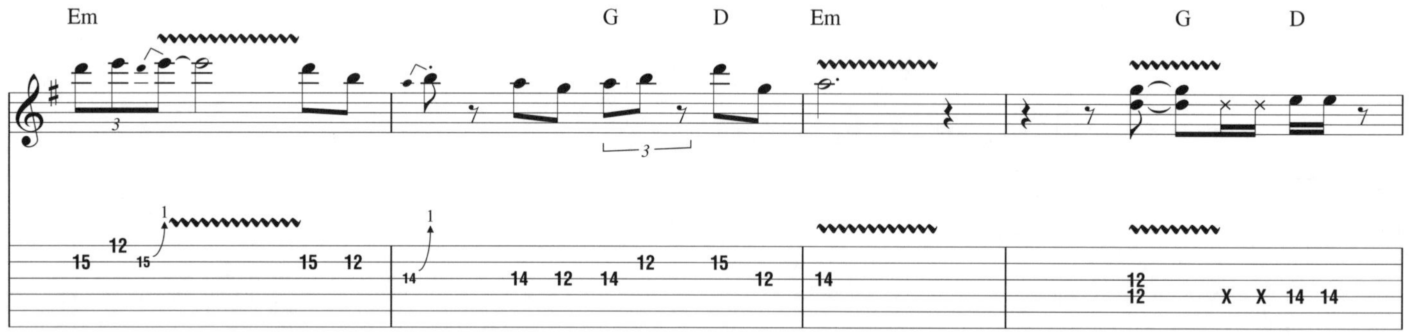
Em
G
D
Em
G
D

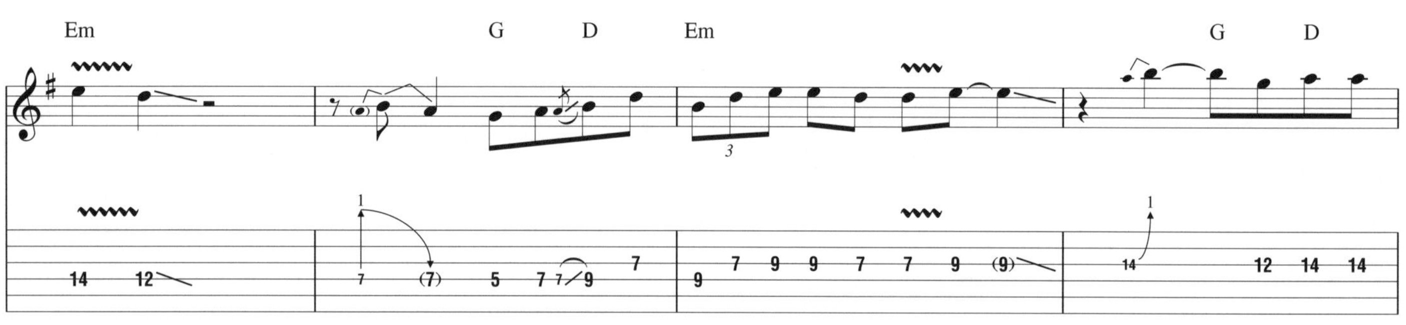
Em
G
D
Em
G
D

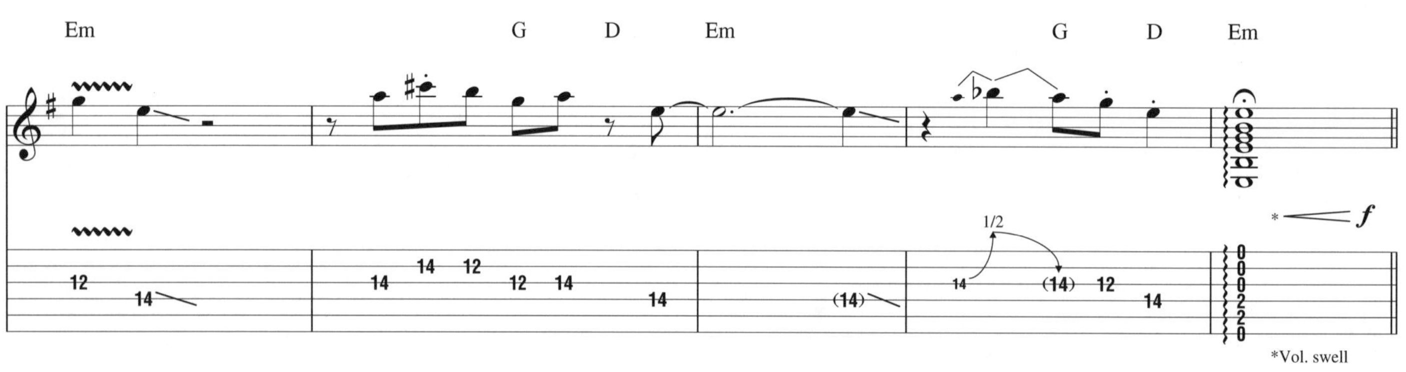
Em
G
D
Em
G
D
Em
*Vol. swell

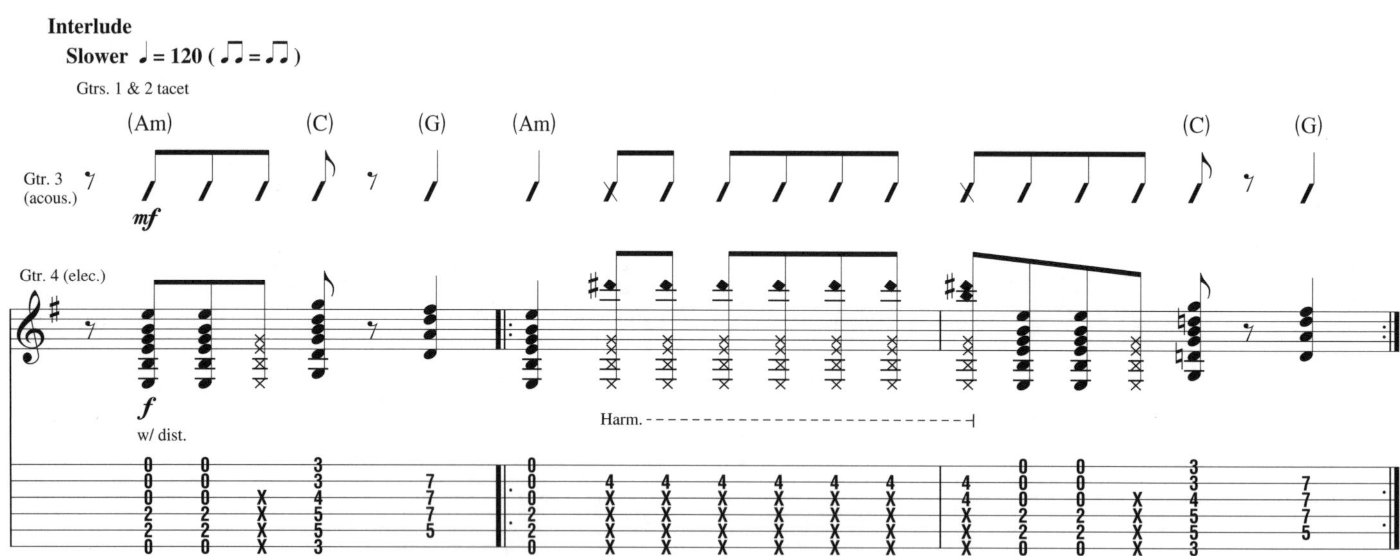
Interlude
Slower ♩= 120
Gtrs. 1 & 2 tacet
(Am)
(C)
(G)
(Am)
(C)
(G)
Gtr. 3 (acous.)
mf
Gtr. 4 (elec.)
f
w/ dist.
Harm.

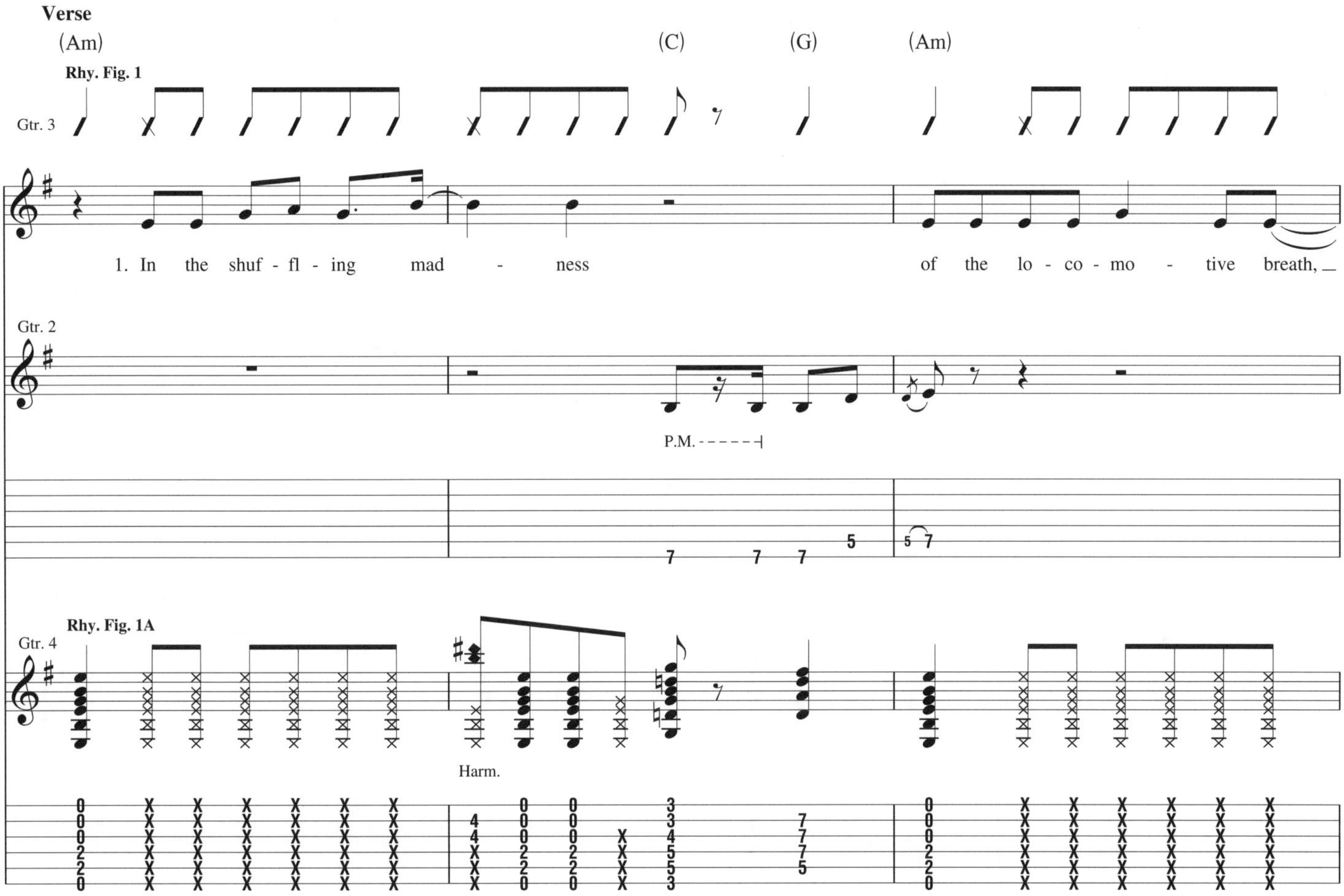

Verse

(Am) (C) (G) (Am)

Rhy. Fig. 1

Gtr. 3

1. In the shuf - fl - ing mad - ness of the lo - co - mo - tive breath, __

Gtr. 2

P.M.

Rhy. Fig. 1A

Gtr. 4

Harm.

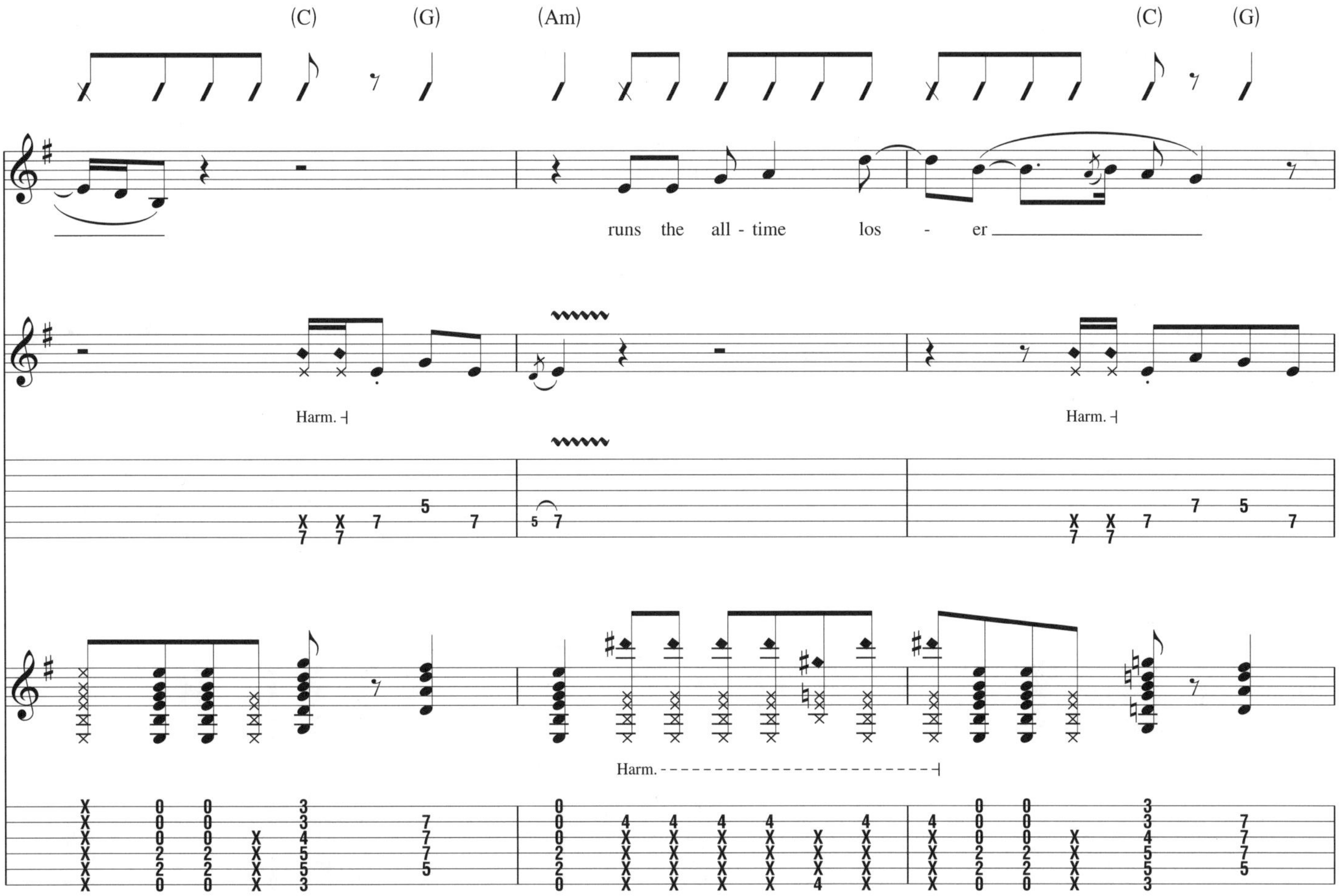

(C) (G) (Am) (C) (G)

runs the all - time los - er __________

Harm.

Harm.

Harm.

(E) (G) (Am)

head - long to ___ his death. Oh, ___ he feels the pis - ton scrap-

Harm. Harm.

(C) (G) (Am) (C) (G)

- ing, steam ___ break - ing on ___ his brow. ___ Old

Harm. Harm. Harm. Harm.

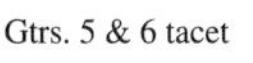

(C) (D) (E)

Gtr. 3

Char - lie stole the han - dle, and the train, it won't stop

Fill 1 End Fill 1

Gtr. 5 (elec.)

mf

w/ dist.

Fill 1A End Fill 1A

Gtr. 6 (elec.)

mf

w/ dist.

Gtr. 2

Gtr. 4

Harm.

(G) (Am)

go - ing. No way to slow down.

Gtr. 2

Harm.

Gtr. 4

Harm.

(C) (G) (Am) (C) (G)

End Rhy. Fig. 1

Oh!

Harm.

Harm.

End Rhy. Fig. 1A

Harm.

Harm.

Harm.

Verse

*Symbols in parentheses represent chord names respective to capoed guitar. Symbols above reflect actual sounding chords.

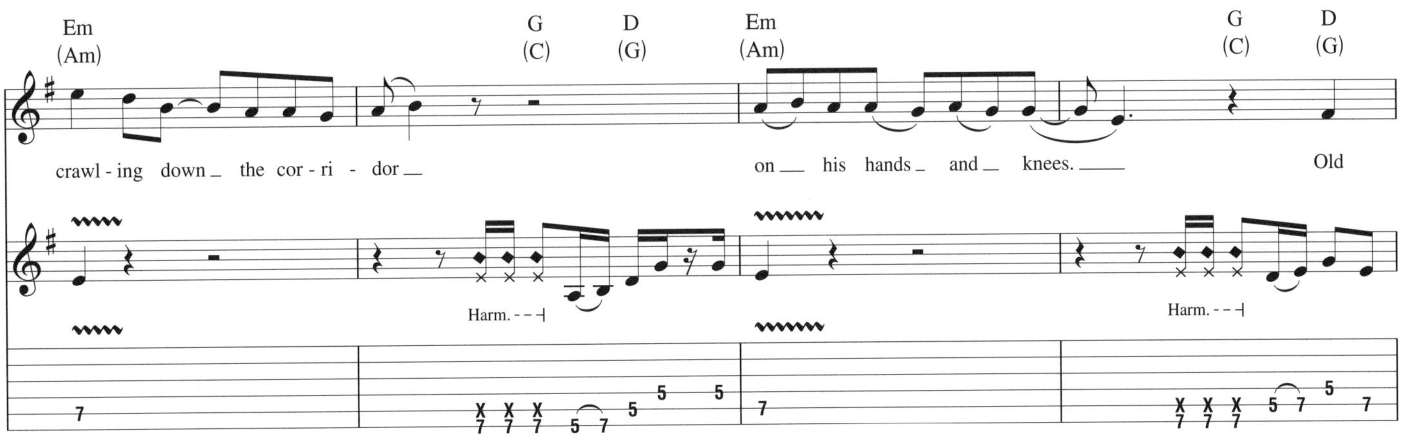

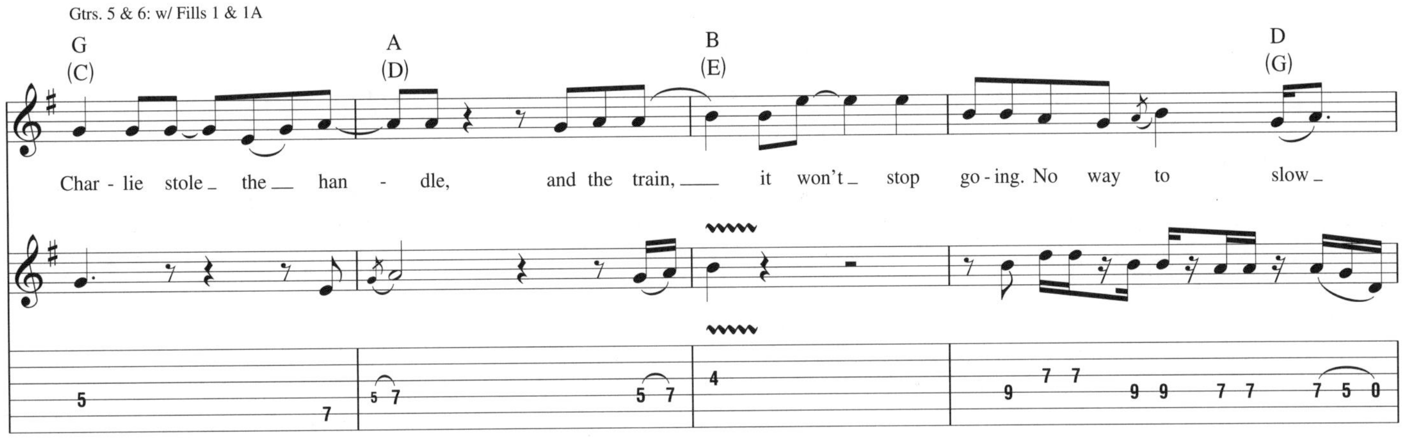

Flute Solo

Gtrs. 3 & 4: w/ Rhy. Figs. 1 & 1A

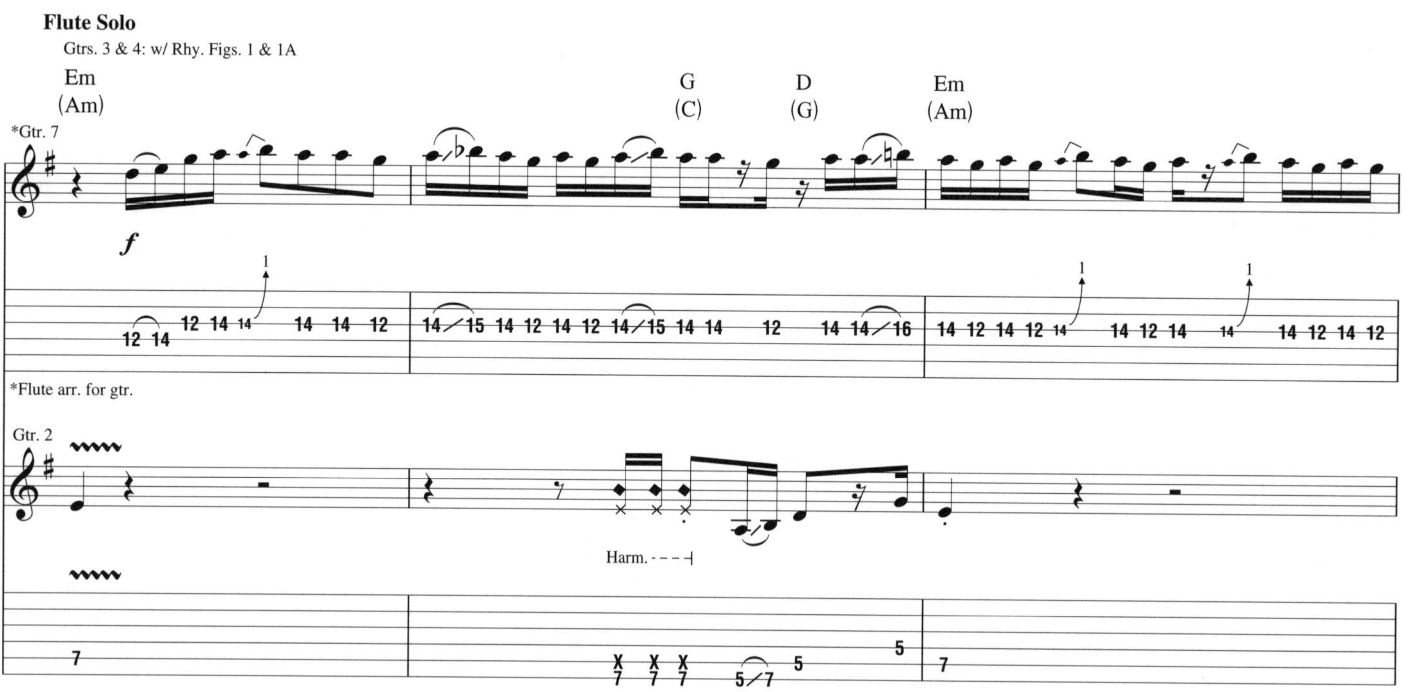

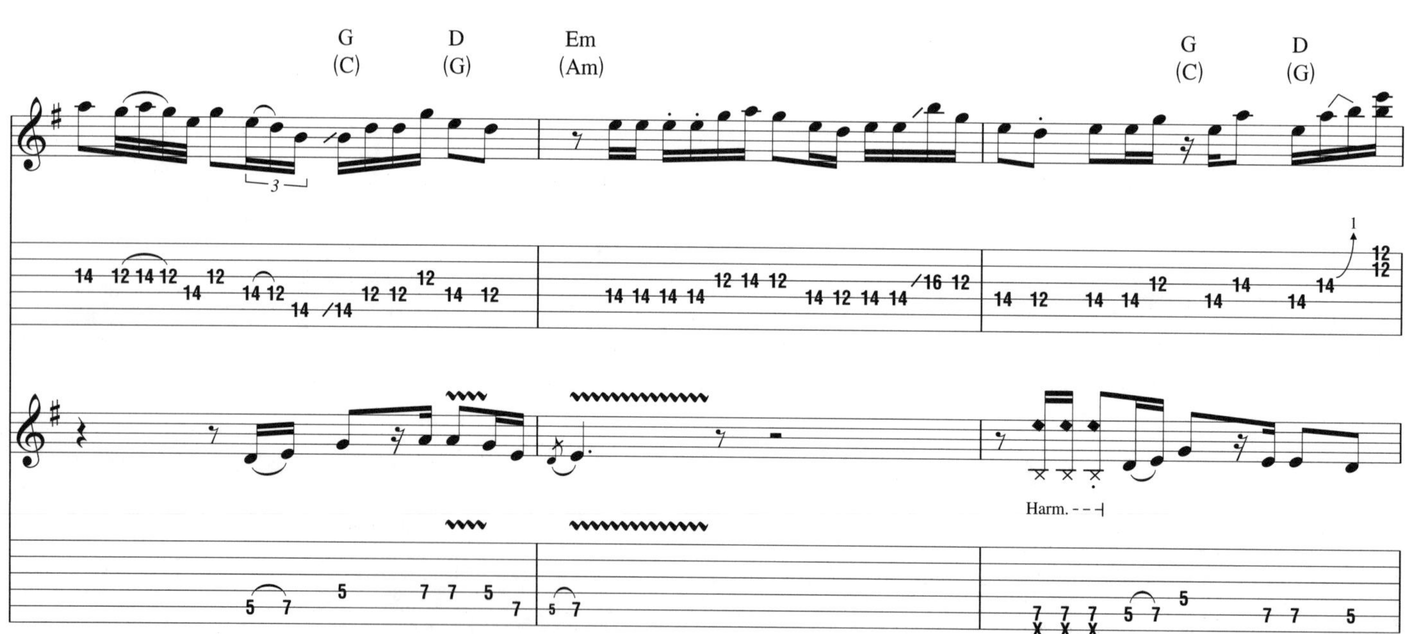

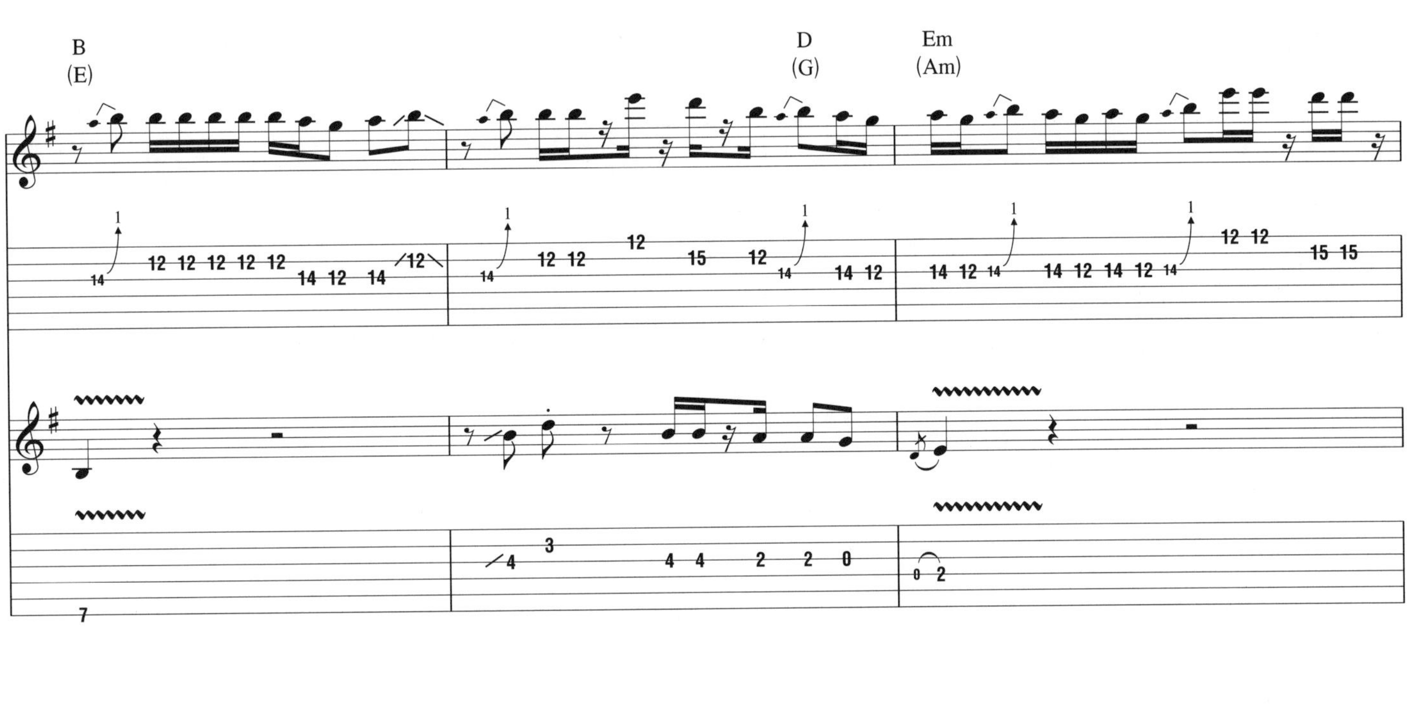
B
(E)
D
(G)
Em
(Am)

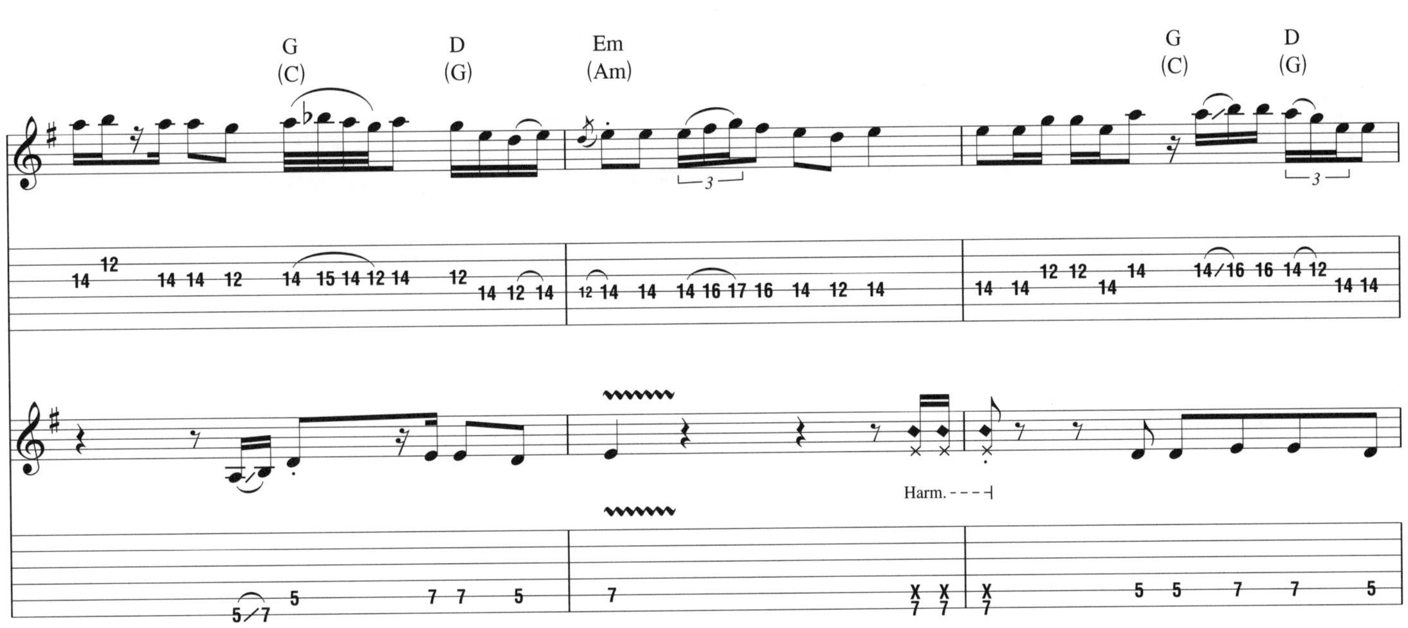
G
(C)
D
(G)
Em
(Am)
G
(C)
D
(G)
Harm.

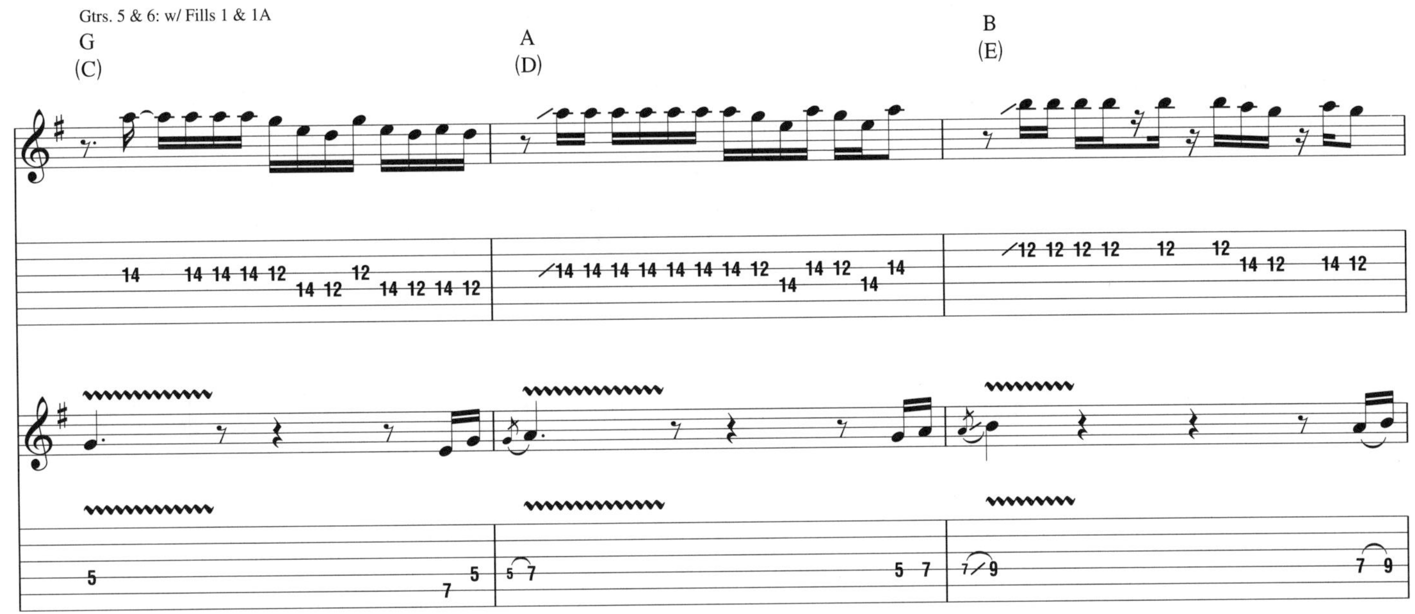
Gtrs. 5 & 6: w/ Fills 1 & 1A
G
(C)
A
(D)
B
(E)

D
(G)
Em
(Am)
G
(C)
D
(G)
P.M.

Em
(Am)
G
(C)
D
(G)
1/2
Harm.

Verse
Gtrs. 3 & 4: w/ Rhy. Figs. 1 & 1A (1st 12 meas.)
Gtr. 7 tacet
Em
(Am)
G
(C)
D
(G)
Em
(Am)
G
(C)
D
(G)
3. He hears the si-lence howl - ing,
catch-es an - gels as they fall.
Gtr. 2
Harm.

Em
(Am)
G
(C)
D
(G)
B
(E)
D
(G)
And the all-time win - ner
has got him by the balls.
Oh, he
P.M.
picks up Gid - 'on's Bi - ble,
o - pen at page one.
I thank
Harm.
Gtrs. 5 & 6: w/ Fills 1 & 1A
Gtr. 3
God he stole the han - dle,
and the train, it won't stop
go - ing. No way to slow
Gtr. 2
Gtr. 4

Gtrs. 3 & 4: w/ Rhy. Figs. 1 & 1A (last 4 meas.)
Em (Am) G (C) D (G) Em (Am) G (C) D (G)
down. Ow! No way to slow down. No. way to slow
Gtr. 2

Outro

Gtrs. 3 & 4: w/ Rhy. Figs. 1 & 1A (1st 2 meas., till fade)
Em (Am) G (C) D (G) Em (Am)
down. No way to slow down. Ow!
P.M.
Harm.

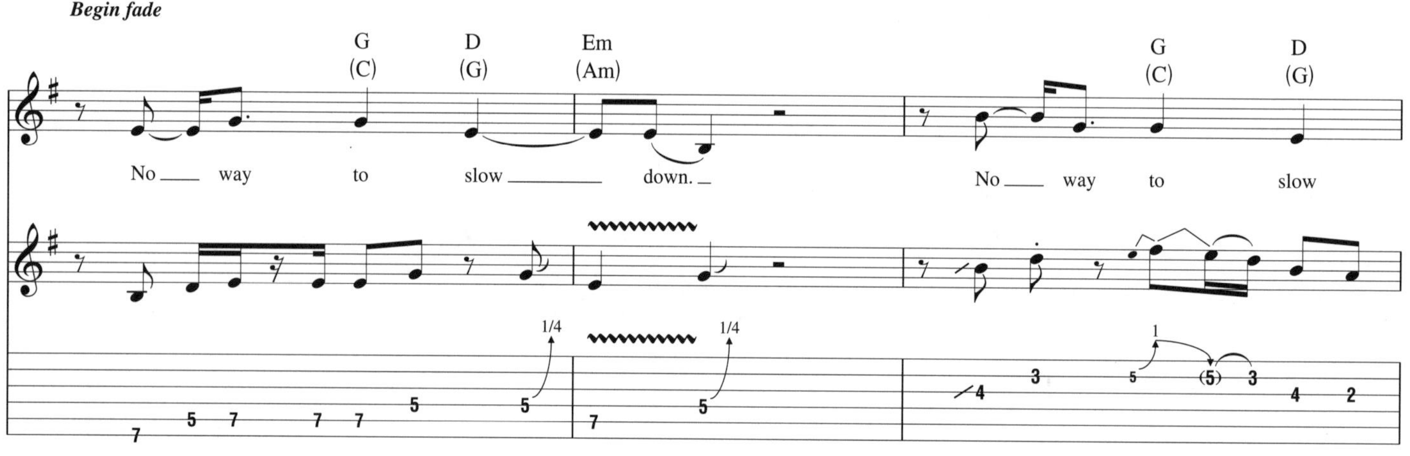
Begin fade
G (C) D (G) Em (Am) G (C) D (G)
No way to slow down. No way to slow
1/4
1/4
1

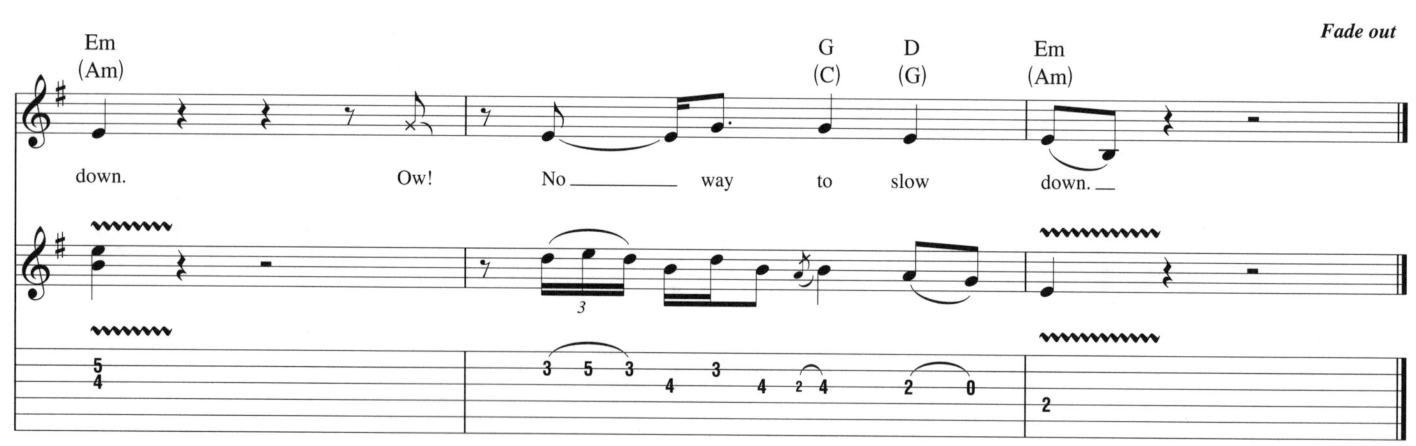
Fade out
Em (Am) G (C) D (G) Em (Am)
down. Ow! No way to slow down.
3

Wind Up

Words and Music by Ian Anderson

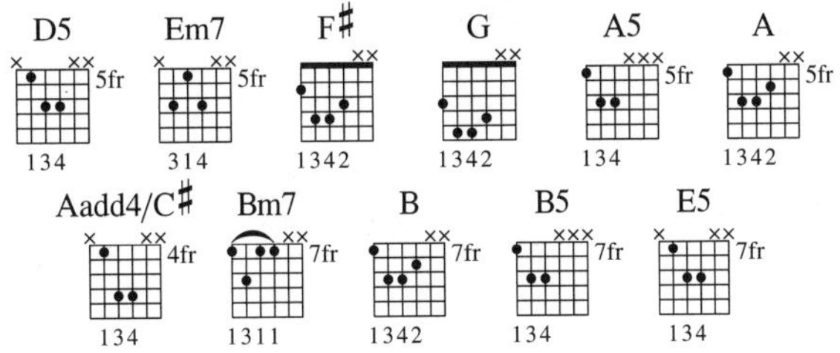

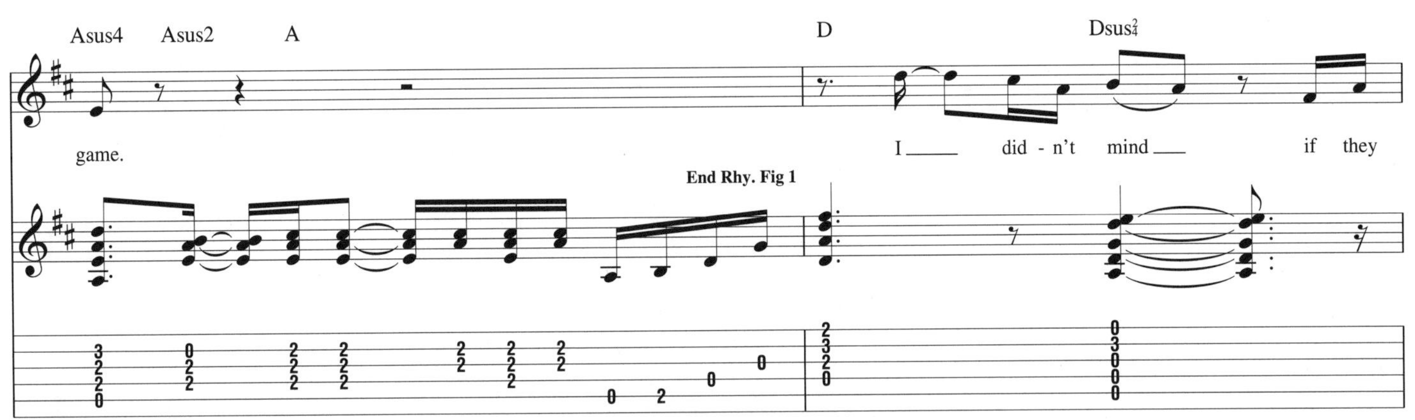

Gtr. 2: w/ Rhy. Fig. 1
D
F♯
G
D
Asus4 Asus2 A
groomed me for suc-cess, uh huh, or if they said_ that I was just a fool.
2. So I

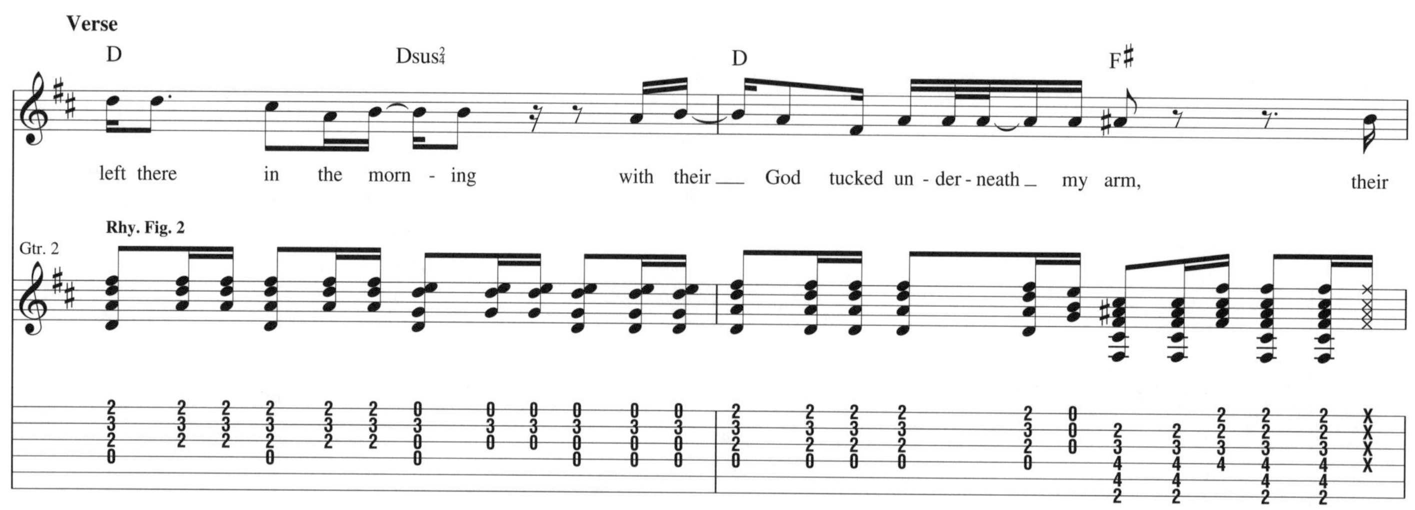
Verse
D
Dsus2/4
D
F♯
left there in the morn - ing with their_ God tucked un-der-neath_ my arm, their
Rhy. Fig. 2
Gtr. 2

G
D
Asus4
Asus2
A
half-assed smiles_ and the book_ of rules.
And I
End Rhy. Fig. 2

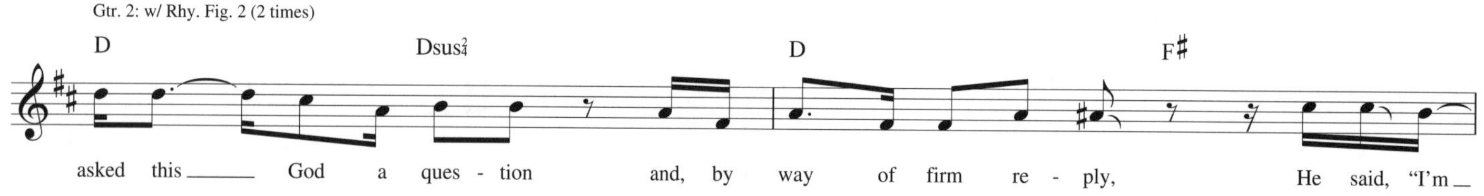
Gtr. 2: w/ Rhy. Fig. 2 (2 times)
D
Dsus2/4
D
F♯
asked this_ God a ques - tion and, by way of firm re - ply, He said, "I'm_

G
D
Asus4
Asus2
A
_ not the kind you have_ to wind up on_ Sun - days."
So

D
Dsus4/2
D
F♯
3
to my old head-mas-ter and to an-y-one who cares, be-

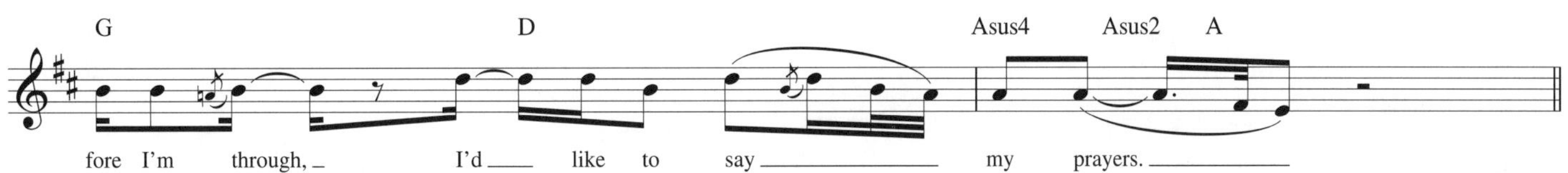
G
D
Asus4
Asus2
A
fore I'm through, I'd like to say my prayers.

Verse

D5
Em7
D5
F♯
Rhy. Fig. 3A
Gtr. 4 (elec.)
mf
w/ slight dist.
3. I don't be-lieve you, you had the whole damn thing all wrong, He's
Rhy. Fig. 3
Gtr. 3 (elec.)
mf
w/ slight dist.
let ring

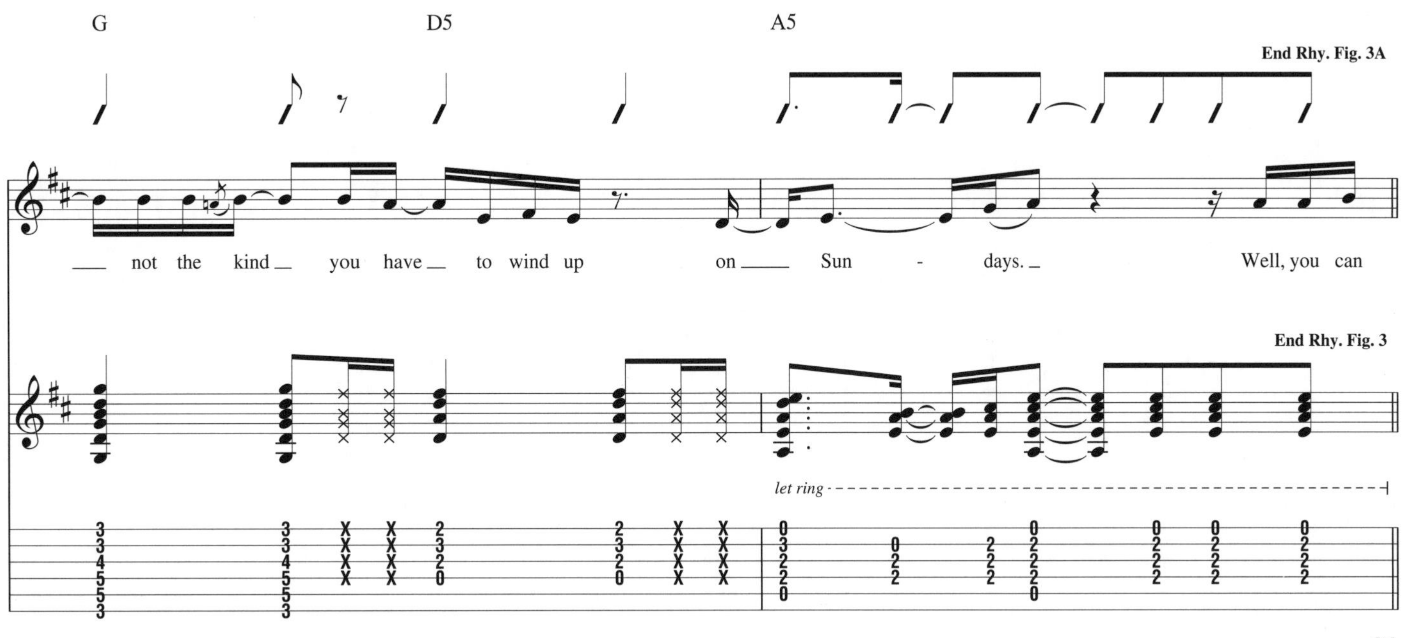
G
D5
A5
End Rhy. Fig. 3A
not the kind you have to wind up on Sun-days. Well, you can
End Rhy. Fig. 3
let ring

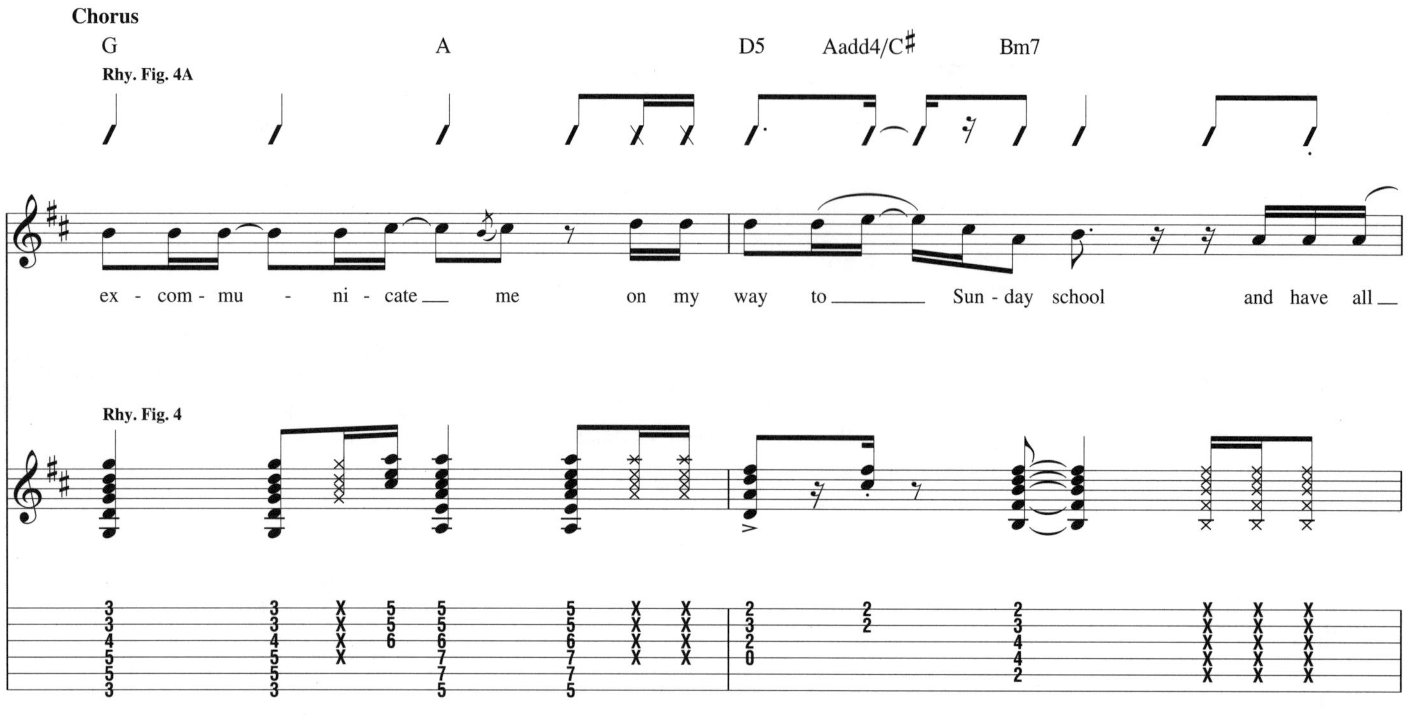

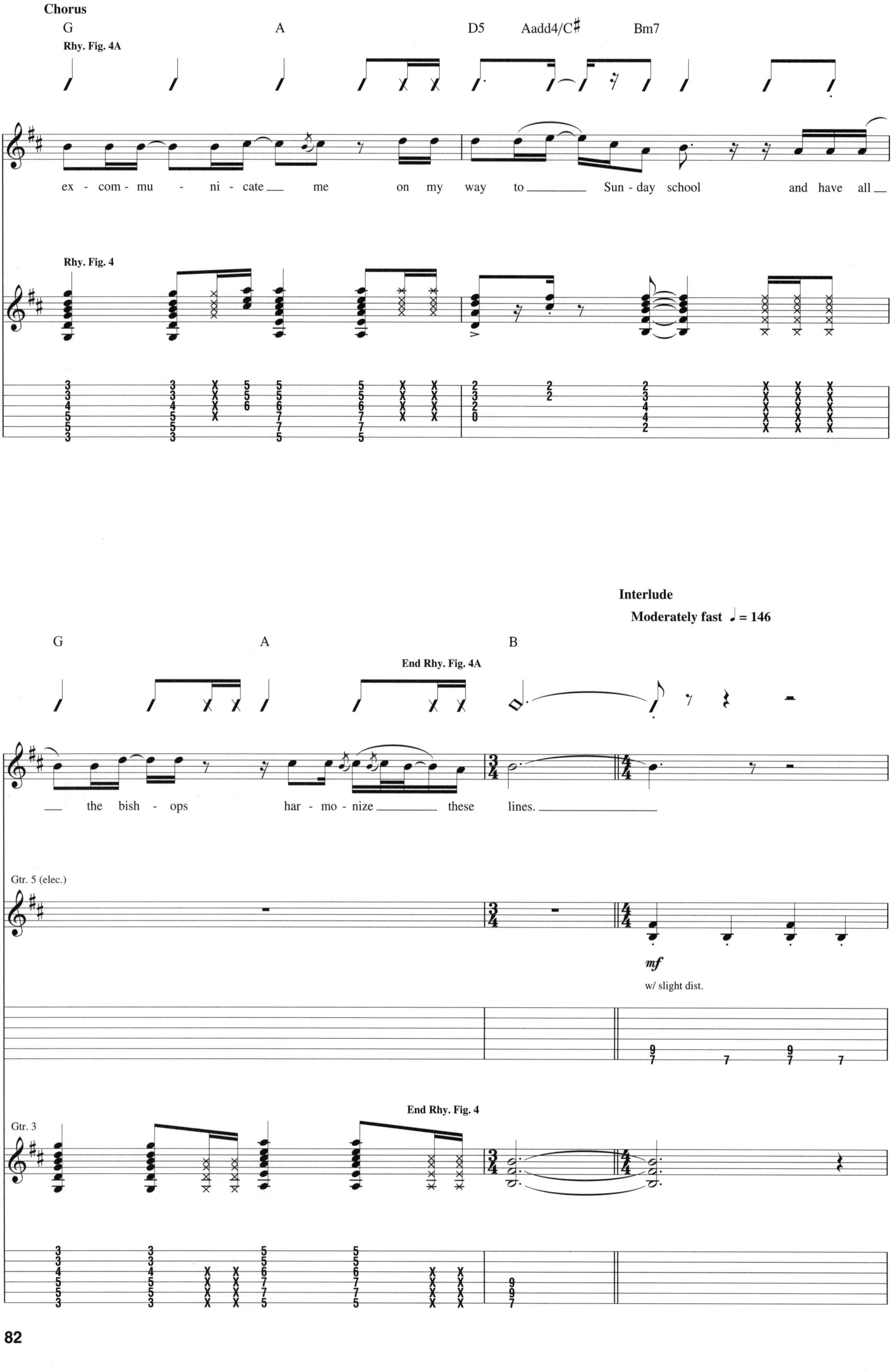

Chorus
G
A
D5
Aadd4/C♯
Bm7
Rhy. Fig. 4A
ex - com - mu - ni - cate me on my way to Sun - day school and have all
Rhy. Fig. 4
Interlude
Moderately fast ♩ = 146
G
A
B
End Rhy. Fig. 4A
the bish - ops har - mo - nize these lines.
Gtr. 5 (elec.)
mf
w/ slight dist.
Gtr. 3
End Rhy. Fig. 4

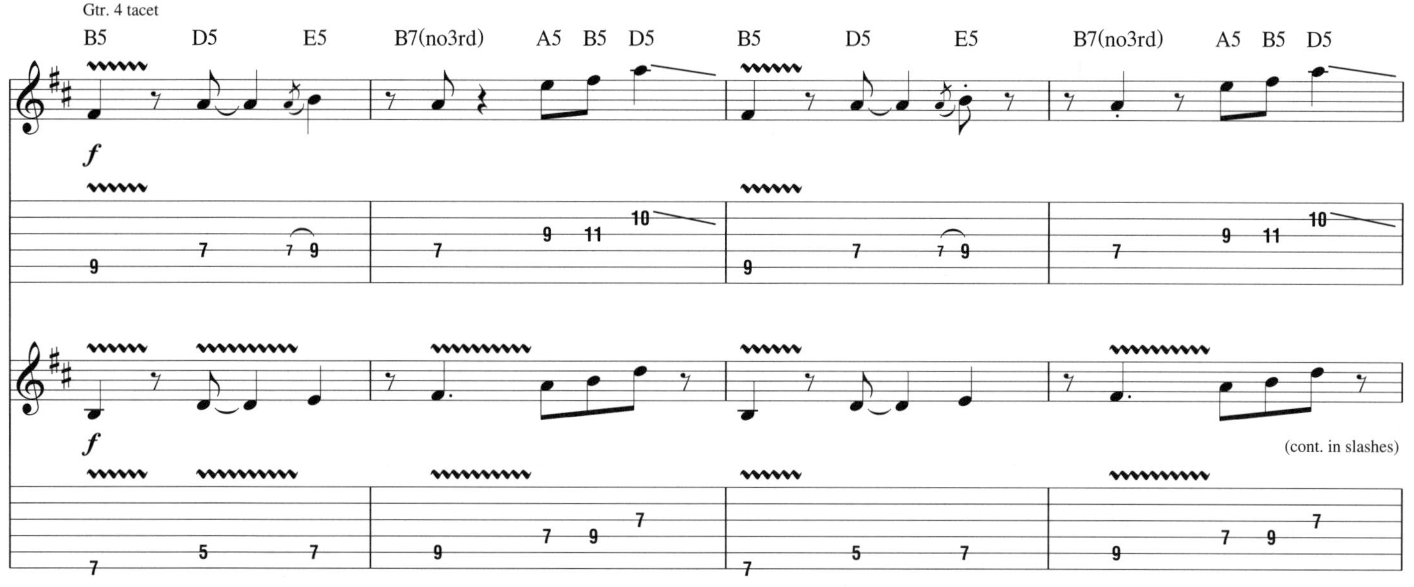
Gtr. 4 tacet
B5 D5 E5 B7(no3rd) A5 B5 D5 B5 D5 E5 B7(no3rd) A5 B5 D5
(cont. in slashes)

B5 A5 B5 E5 D5 A5 B5 E5 B5 E5 D5 A5
Gtr. 3
Gtr. 5
(cont. in notation)

Verse
A5 B5 A5 B5 E5 D5 B5 A5 B5 A5 B5
4. How do you dare to tell me that I'm my Fa -
5. When I was young and they packed me off to school
Gtr. 5
Riff A1
End Riff A1
Riff B1
Gtr. 3
Riff A
End Riff A
Riff B

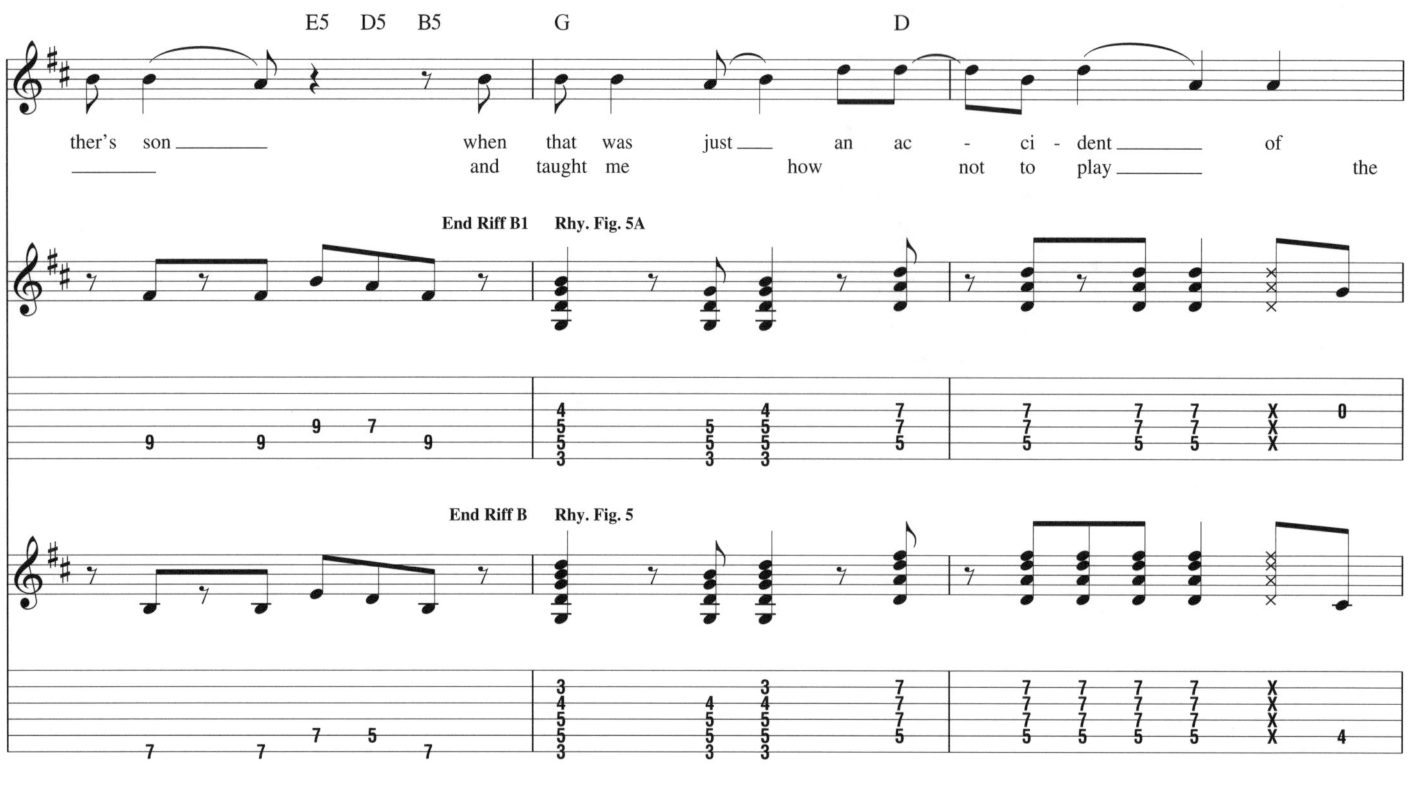
E5 D5 B5 G D
ther's son when that was just an ac - ci - dent of
and taught me how not to play the
End Riff B1
Rhy. Fig. 5A
End Riff B
Rhy. Fig. 5

F♯ F♯7 F♯ A5 B5 A5 B5 E5 D5 B5
Birth, yeah. I'd rath - er look a - round me, com -
game. I did - n't mind if they
End Rhy. Fig. 5A
End Rhy. Fig. 5

Gtrs. 3 & 5: w/ Riffs B & B1
Gtrs. 3 & 5: w/ Rhy. Figs. 5 & 5A
A5 B5 A5 B5 E5 D5 B5 G D
pose a bet - ter song, 'cause that's the hon - est
groomed me for suc - cess or if they said that

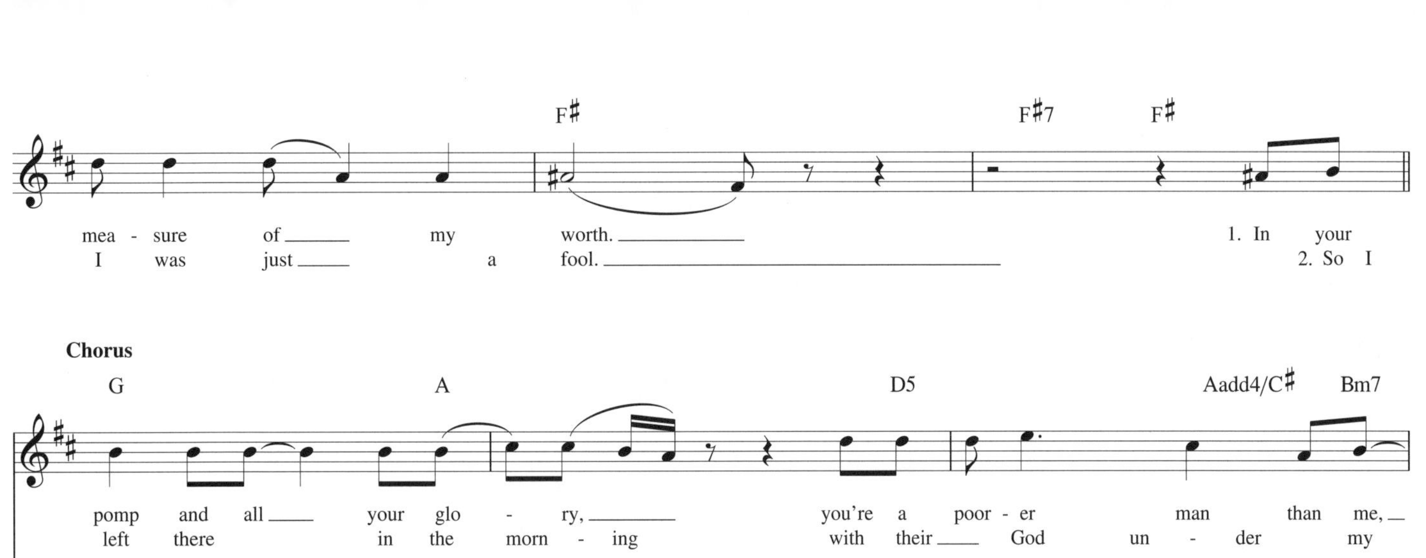
F♯
F♯7
F♯
mea - sure of my worth.
1. In your
I was just a fool.
2. So I

Chorus

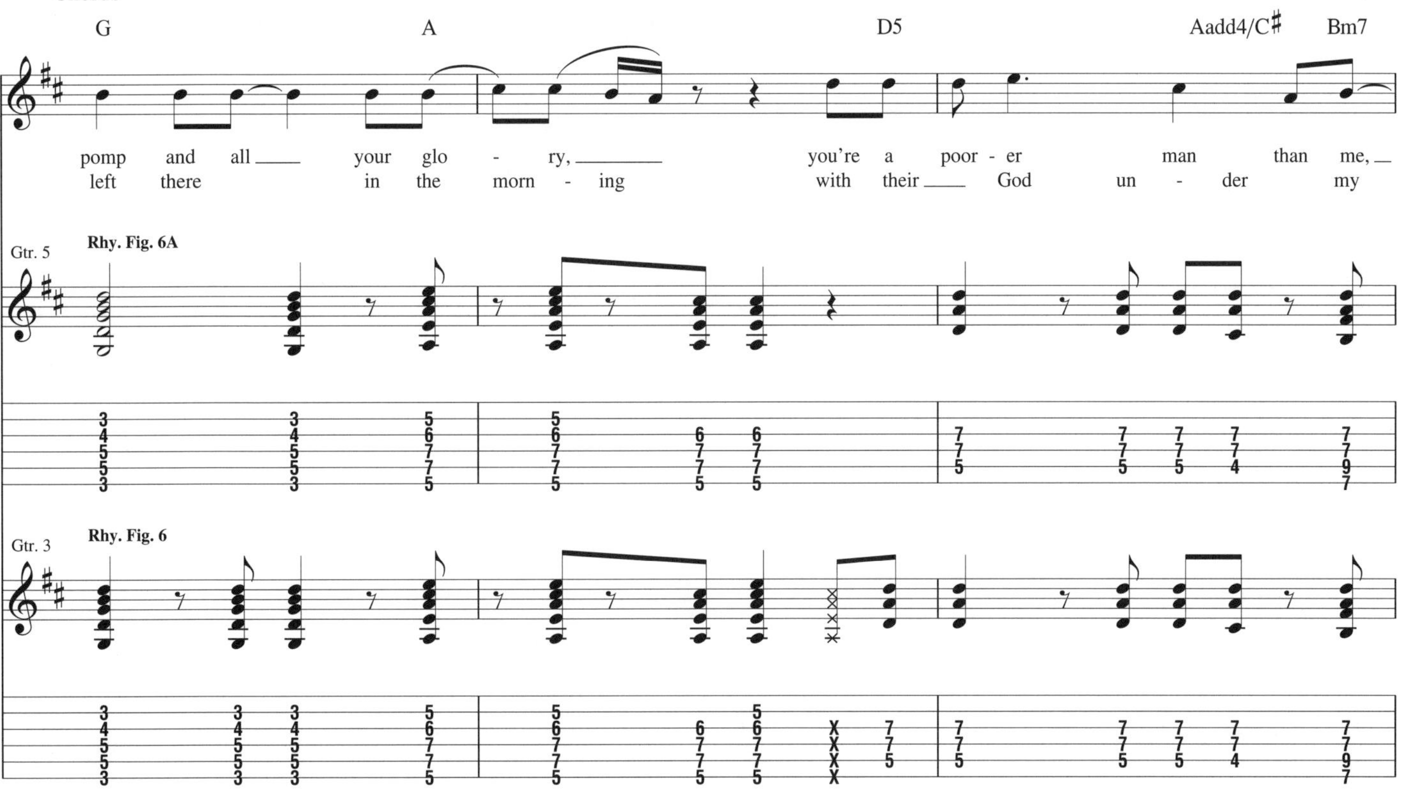
G
A
D5
Aadd4/C♯
Bm7
pomp and all your glo - ry, you're a poor - er man than me,
left there in the morn - ing with their God un - der my
Gtr. 5
Rhy. Fig. 6A
Gtr. 3
Rhy. Fig. 6

To Coda
G
A
B5
as you lick the boots of death born out of fear.
arm, their half-assed smiles and the book of
Gtr. 5
End Rhy. Fig. 6A
P.M.
P.M.
Gtr. 3
End Rhy. Fig. 6
P.M.

D.S. al Coda

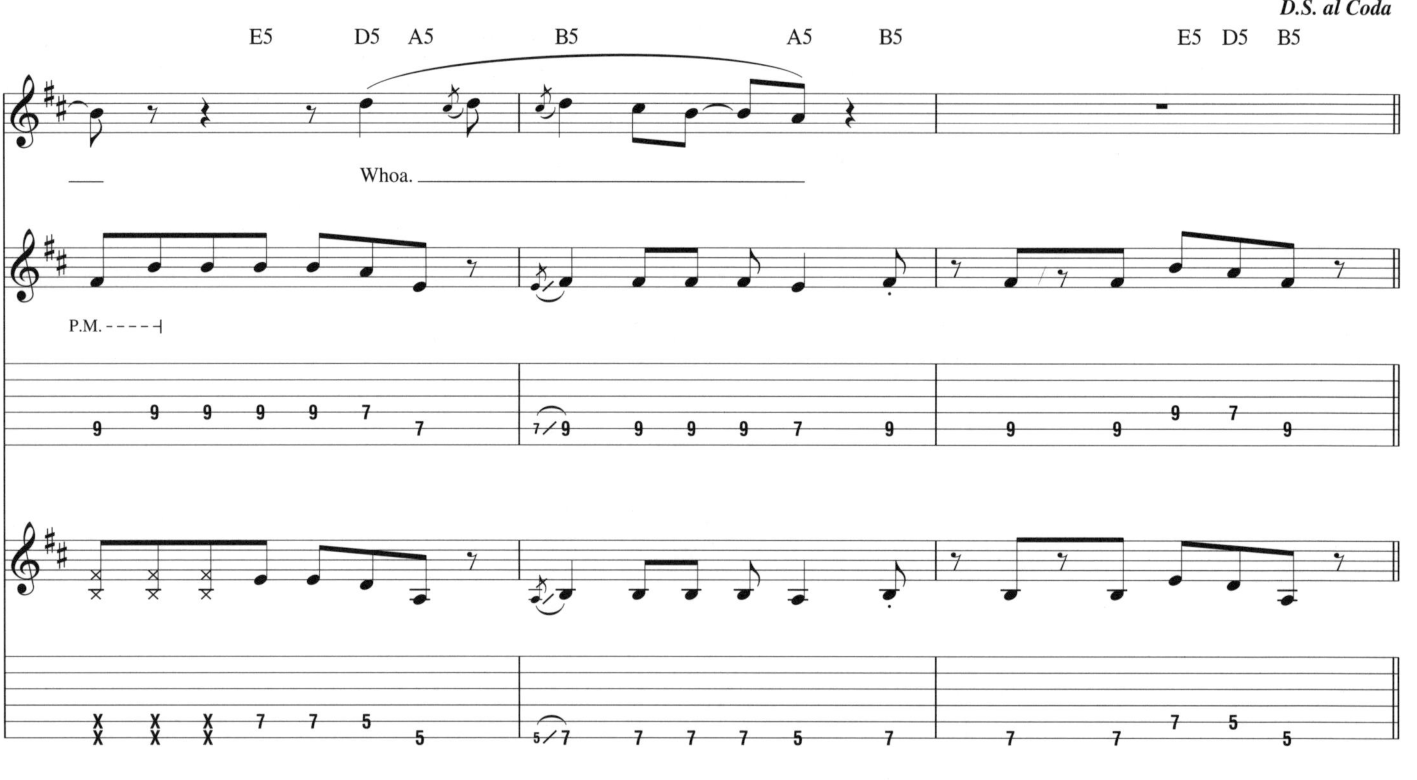
E5
D5
A5
B5
A5
B5
E5
D5
B5
Whoa.
P.M.

Coda

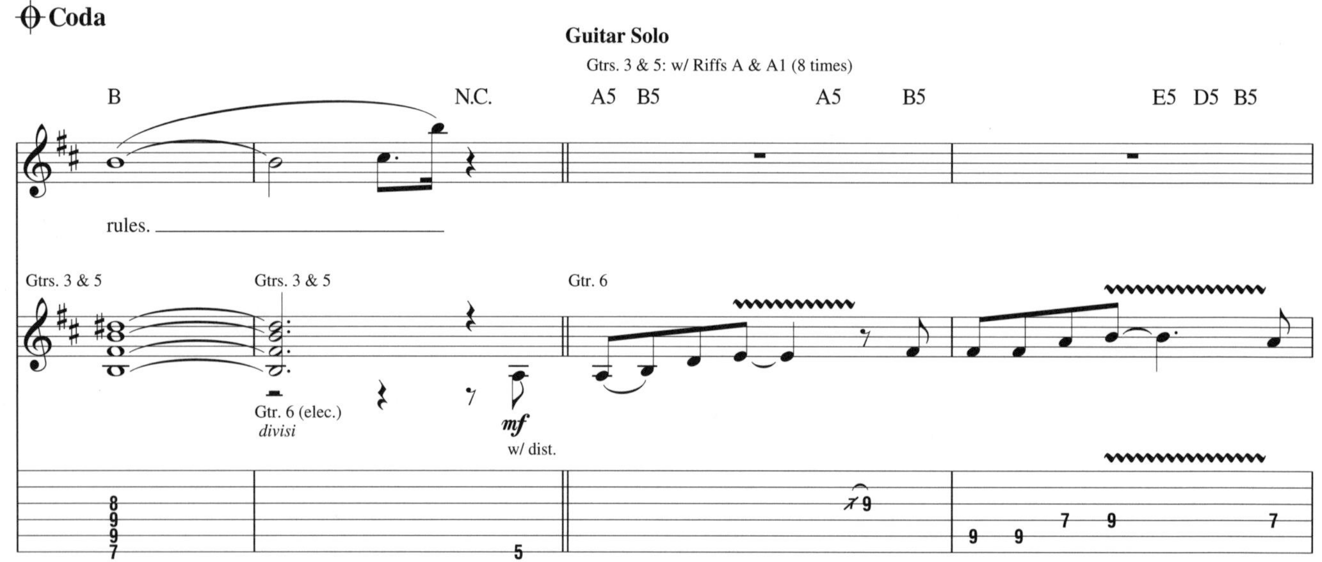
Guitar Solo
Gtrs. 3 & 5: w/ Riffs A & A1 (8 times)
B
N.C.
A5
B5
A5
B5
E5
D5
B5
rules.
Gtrs. 3 & 5
Gtrs. 3 & 5
Gtr. 6
Gtr. 6 (elec.)
divisi
mf
w/ dist.

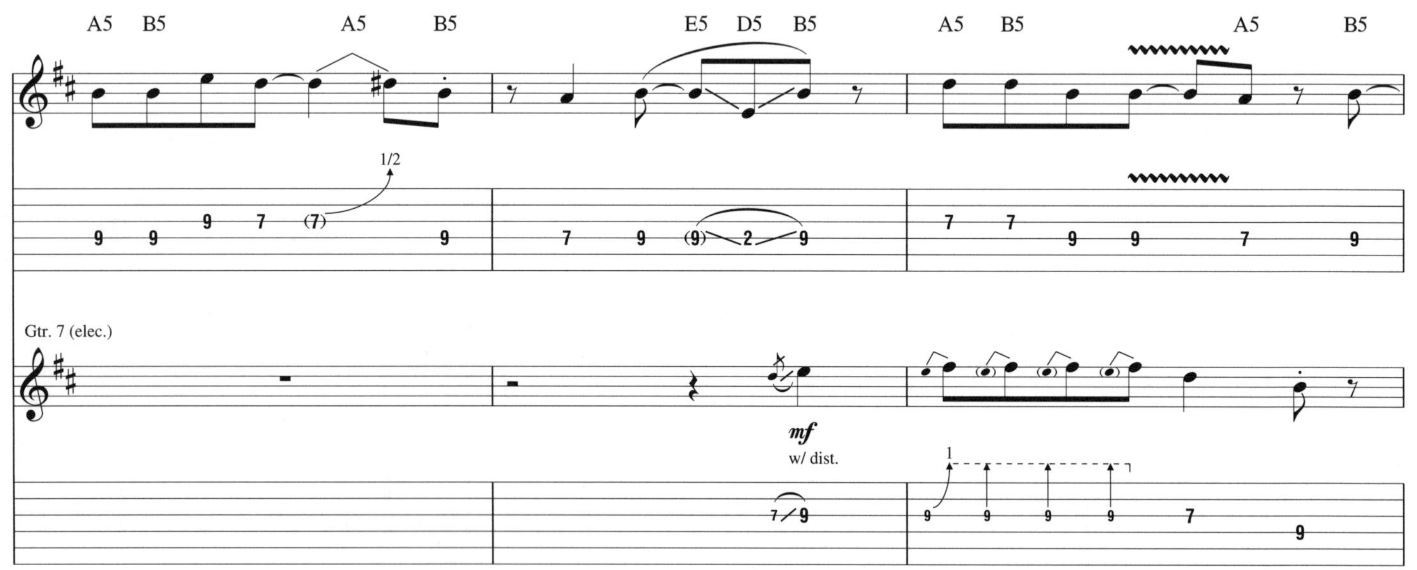
A5
B5
A5
B5
E5
D5
B5
A5
B5
A5
B5
1/2
Gtr. 7 (elec.)
mf
w/ dist.

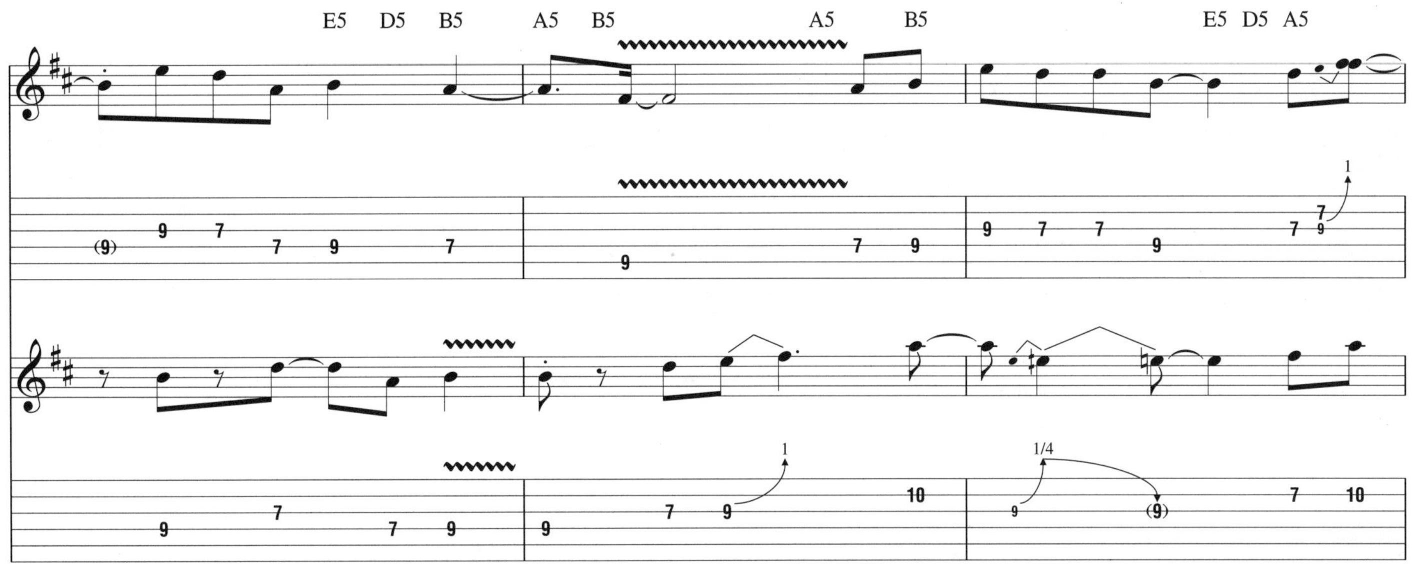
E5 D5 B5 A5 B5 A5 B5 E5 D5 A5

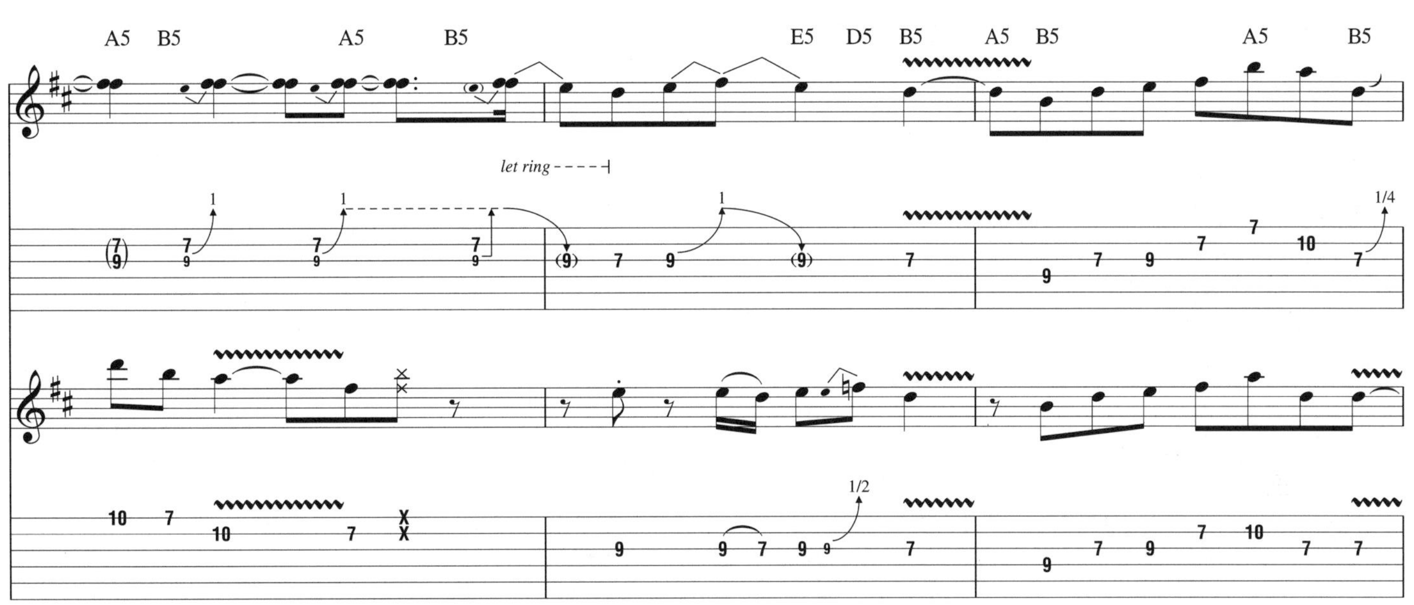
A5 B5 A5 B5 E5 D5 B5 A5 B5 A5 B5
let ring

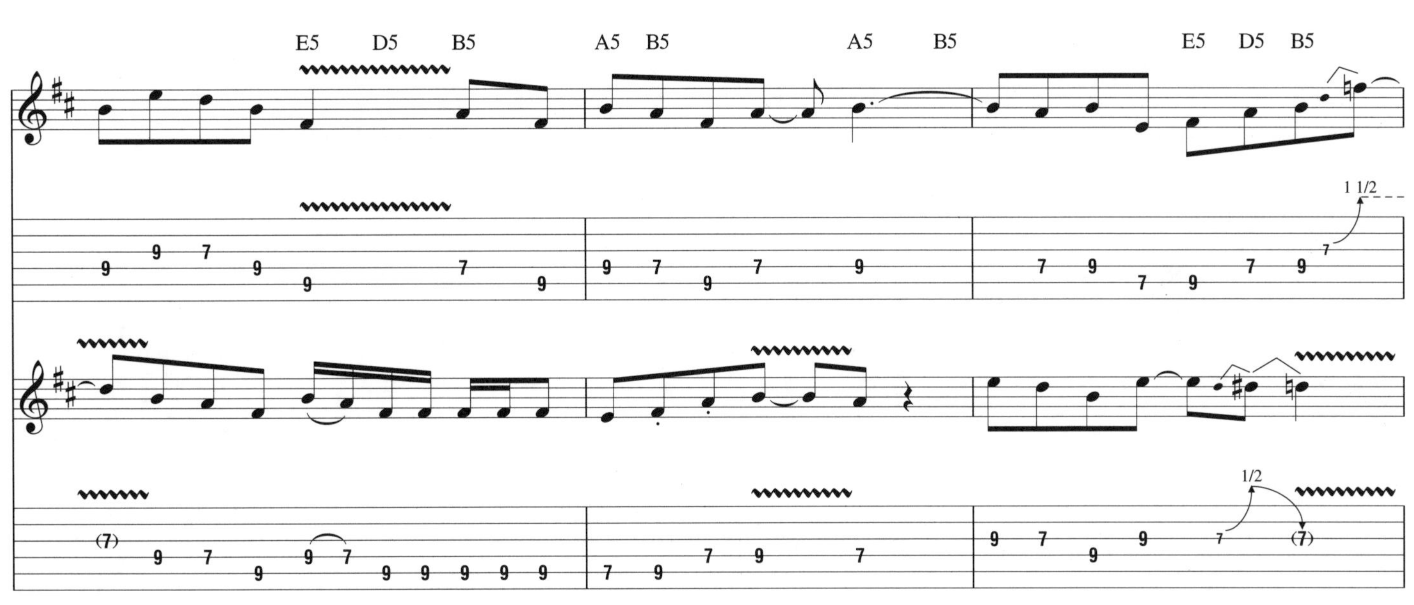
E5 D5 B5 A5 B5 A5 B5 E5 D5 B5

Chorus
Gtrs. 3 & 5: w/ Rhy. Figs. 6 & 6A
Gtrs. 6 & 7 tacet
A5 B5 A5 B5 E5 D5 B5 G A
Well, you can ex - com - mu - ni - cate
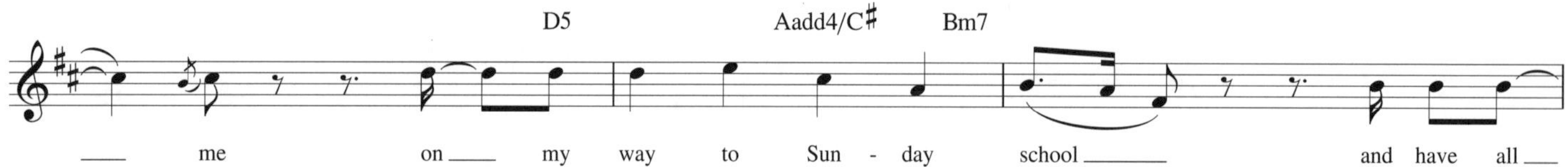
D5 Aadd4/C♯ Bm7
me on my way to Sun - day school and have all

Gtrs. 3 & 5 tacet
G A B5 N.C.
the bish - ops har - mo - nize these lines.
Gtrs. 3 & 5
P.M.
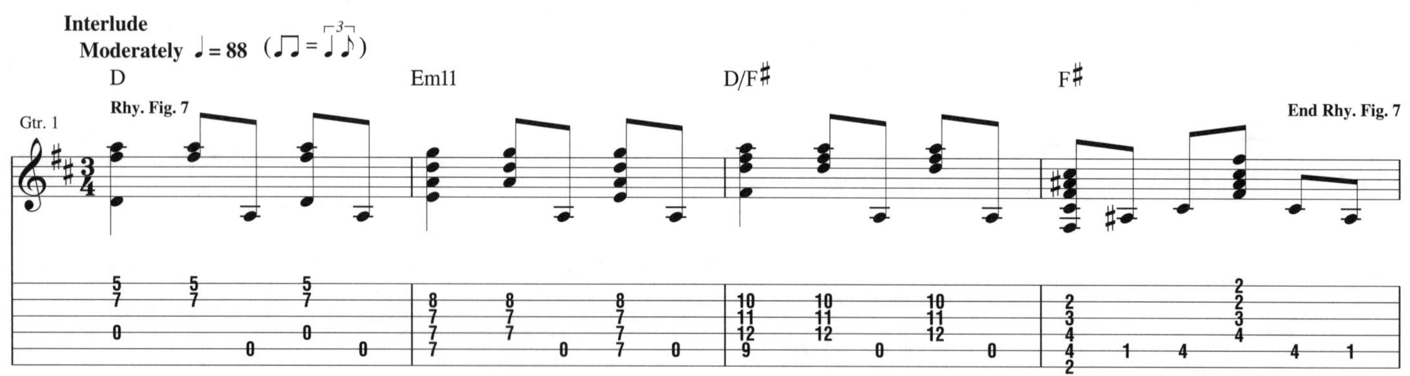
Interlude
Moderately ♩ = 88
D Em11 D/F♯ F♯
Gtr. 1
Rhy. Fig. 7
End Rhy. Fig. 7

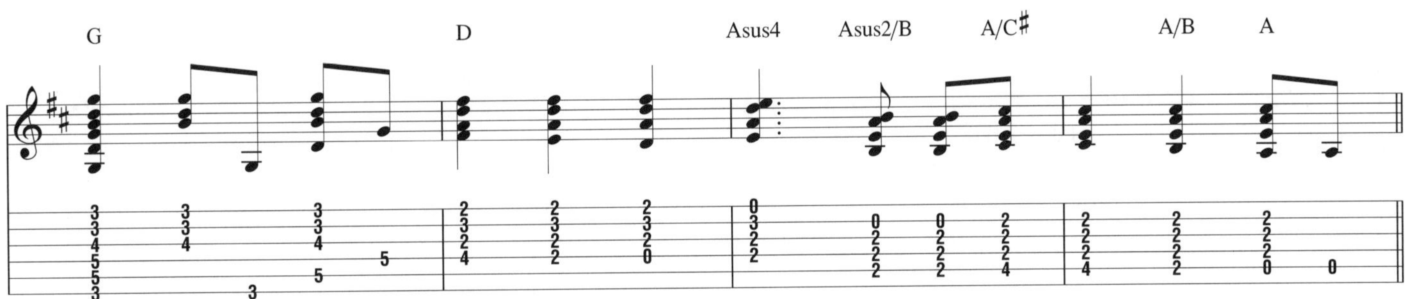
G
D
Asus4
Asus2/B
A/C♯
A/B
A

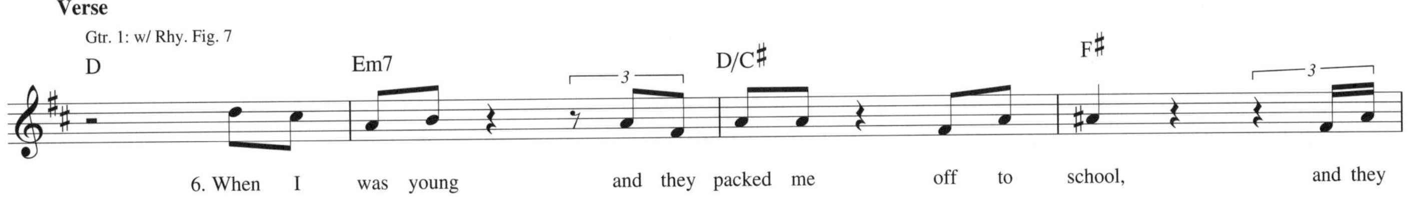
Verse
Gtr. 1: w/ Rhy. Fig. 7
D
Em7
D/C♯
F♯
6. When I was young and they packed me off to school, and they

G
D
Asus4
Asus2/B
A/C♯
taught me how not to play the game. Laughed: Mm, hmm.
Gtr. 1
let ring

Verse

Moderately slow ♩ = 62
Gtr. 1 tacet
Gtr. 3: w/ Rhy. Fig. 3 (2 times)
D
Dsus2/4
D
F♯
7. I did - n't mind if they groomed me for suc - cess, uh, or

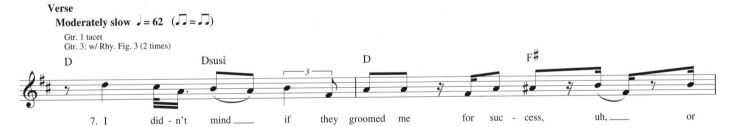

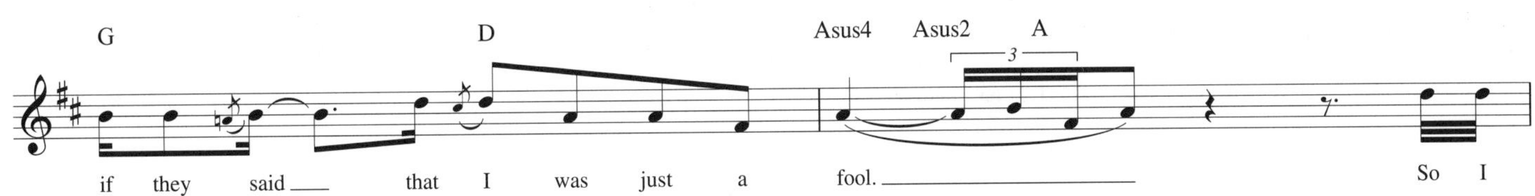
G
D
Asus4
Asus2
A
if they said that I was just a fool. So I

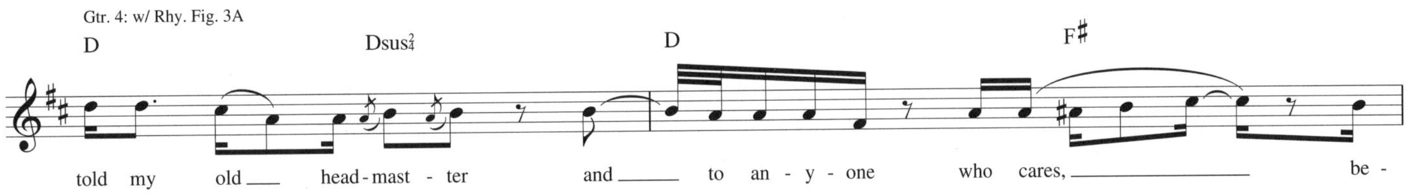
Gtr. 4: w/ Rhy. Fig. 3A
D
Dsus2/4
D
F♯
told my old head - mast - ter and to an - y - one who cares, be -

G
D
Asus4
Asus2
A
fore I'm through I'd like to say my prayers. Well, you can

Chorus

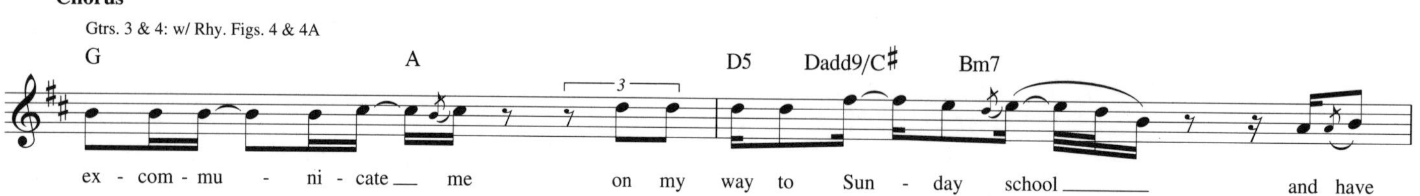
Gtrs. 3 & 4: w/ Rhy. Figs. 4 & 4A
G
A
D5
Dadd9/C♯
Bm7
ex - com - mu - ni - cate me on my way to Sun - day school and have

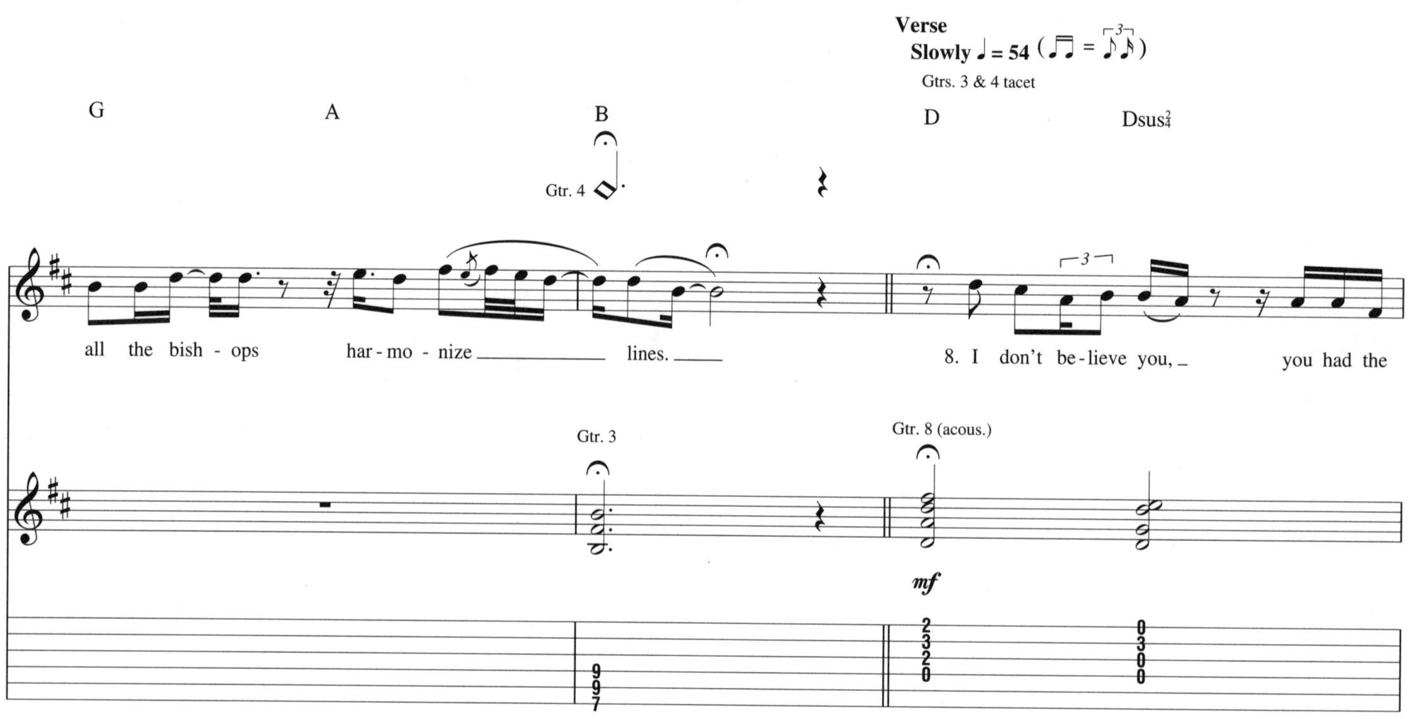
Verse
Slowly ♩ = 54
Gtrs. 3 & 4 tacet
G
A
B
D
Dsus2/4
Gtr. 4
all the bish - ops har - mo - nize lines.
8. I don't be - lieve you, you had the
Gtr. 3
Gtr. 8 (acous.)
mf

D
F♯
G
D
Asus4
Asus2
A
N.C.
whole damn thing all wrong. Uh, he's not the kind you have to wind up on Sun - day. (Laughed:) Uh, huh.

*Sung as even sixteenth notes.

**Played as even sixteenth notes.

Lick Your Fingers Clean

Words and Music by Ian Anderson

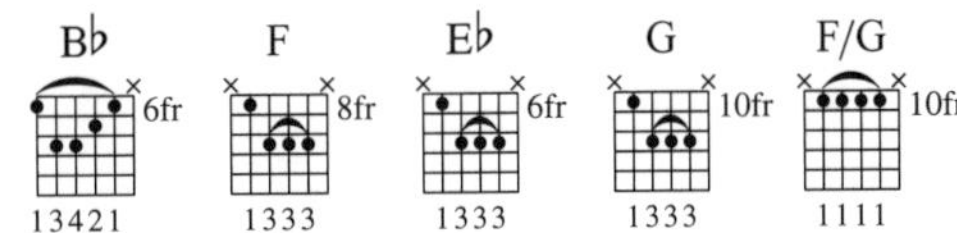

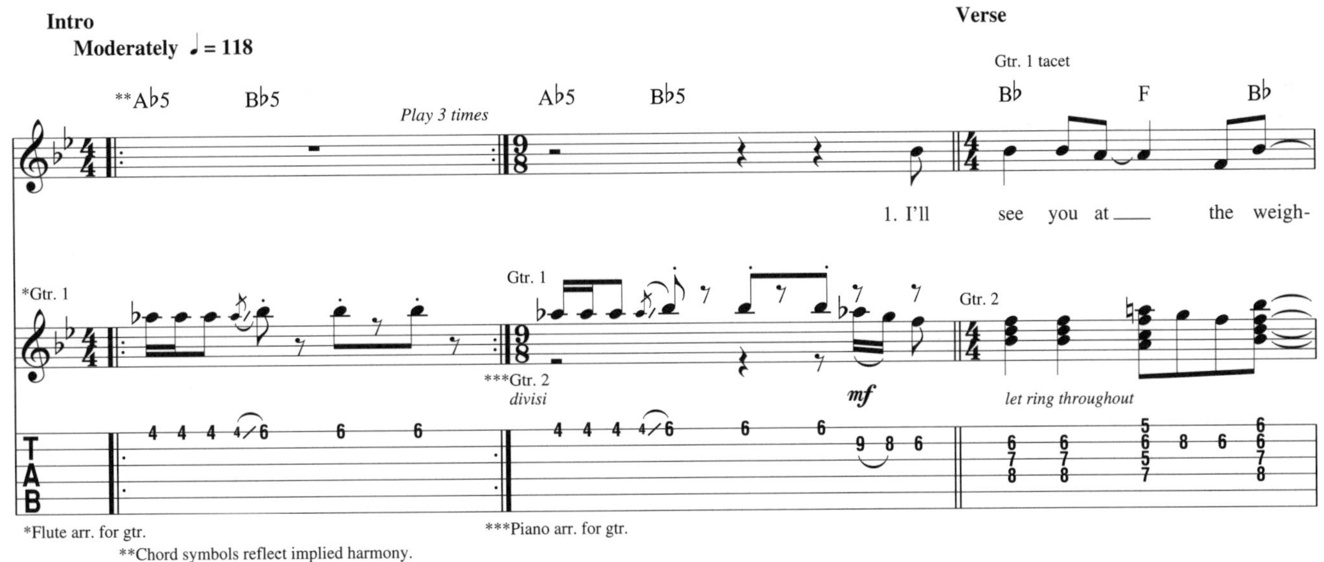

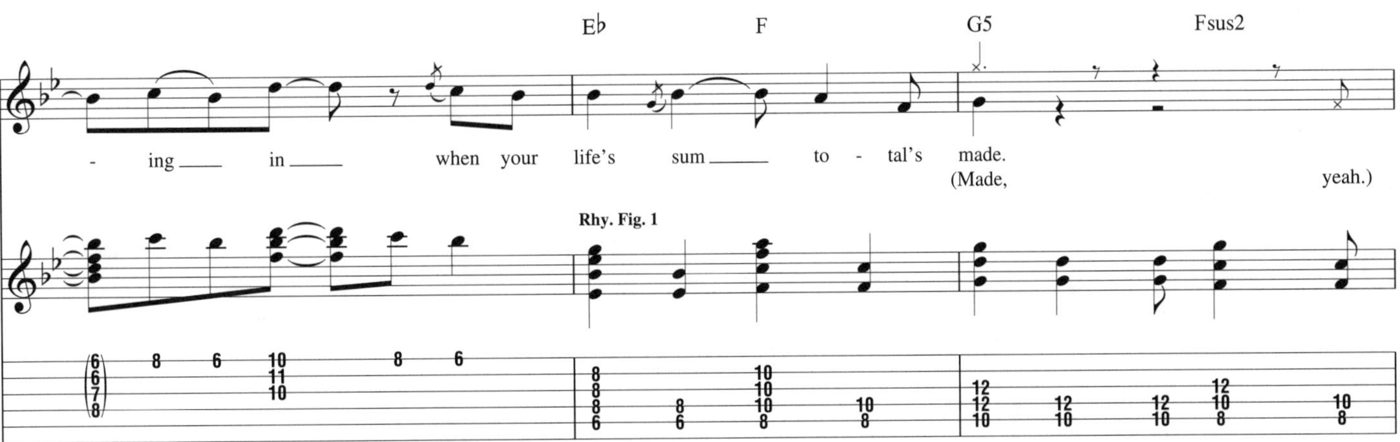

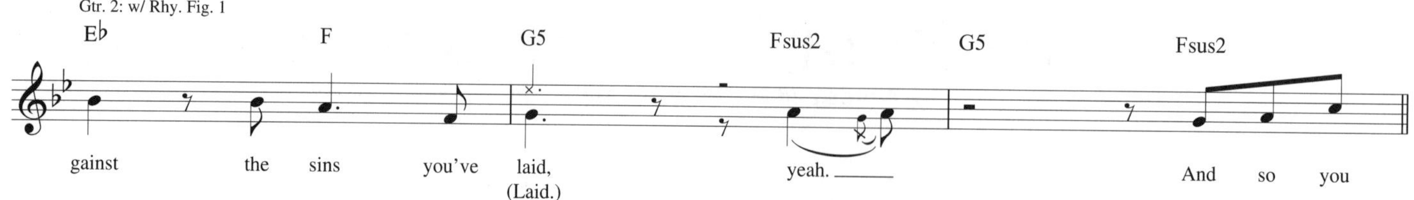
Gtr. 2: w/ Rhy. Fig. 1
E♭
F
G5
Fsus2
G5
Fsus2
gainst the sins you've laid,
(Laid.)
yeah.
And so you

Chorus
2nd time, Gtr. 1 tacet
C5
B♭
G
F
G
B♭
E♭
(1.) place your fi - nal bur - den on your hard - pressed next of kin.
(2., 3.) say you real - ly should make the deal as he of - fers 'round the hat.
*Gtrs. 3 & 4 (slight dist.)
mf
*Composite arrangement

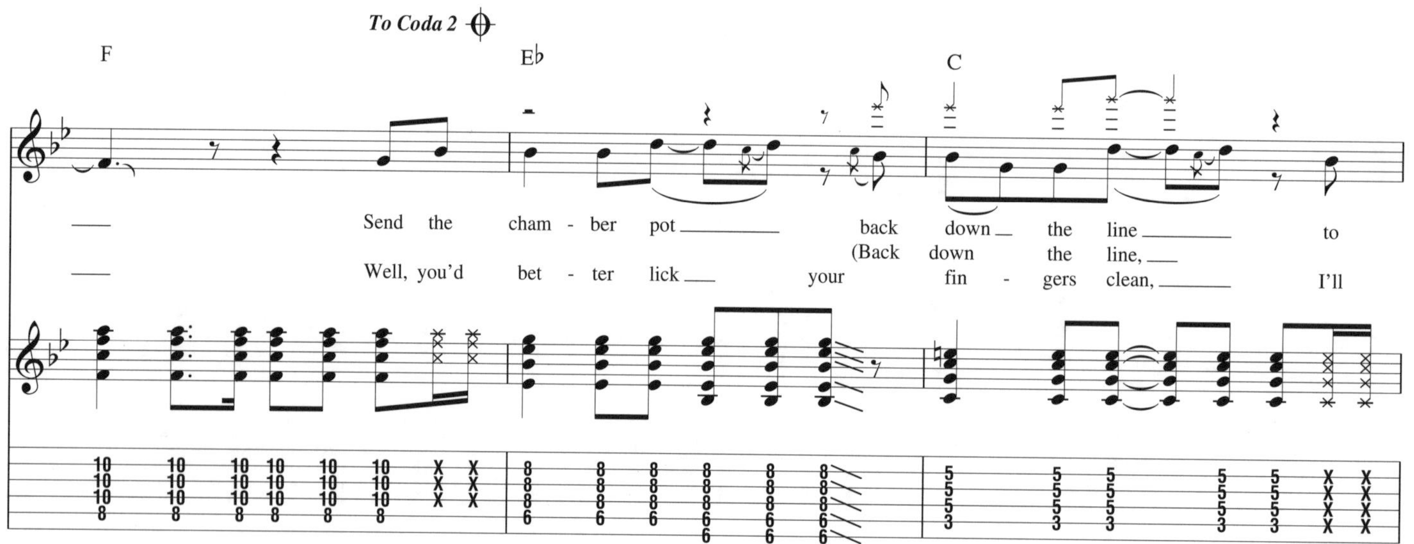
To Coda 2
F
E♭
C
Send the cham - ber pot back down the line to
(Back down the line,
Well, you'd bet - ter lick your fin - gers clean, I'll

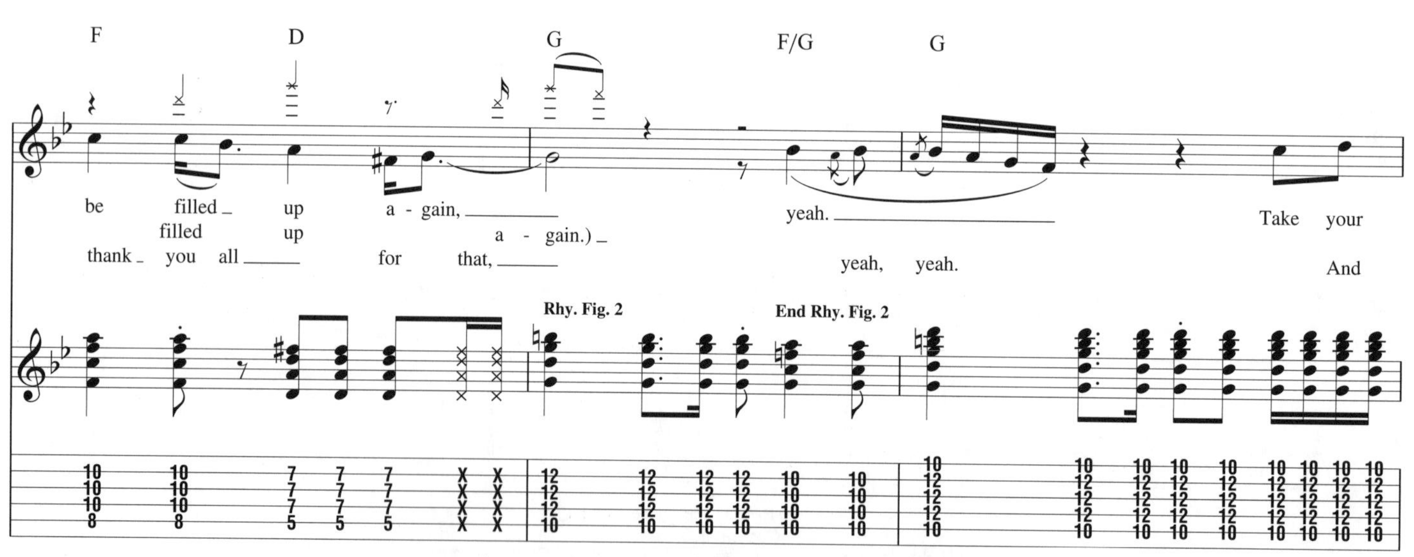
F
D
G
F/G
G
be filled up a - gain, yeah. Take your
filled up a - gain.)
thank you all for that, yeah, yeah. And
Rhy. Fig. 2
End Rhy. Fig. 2

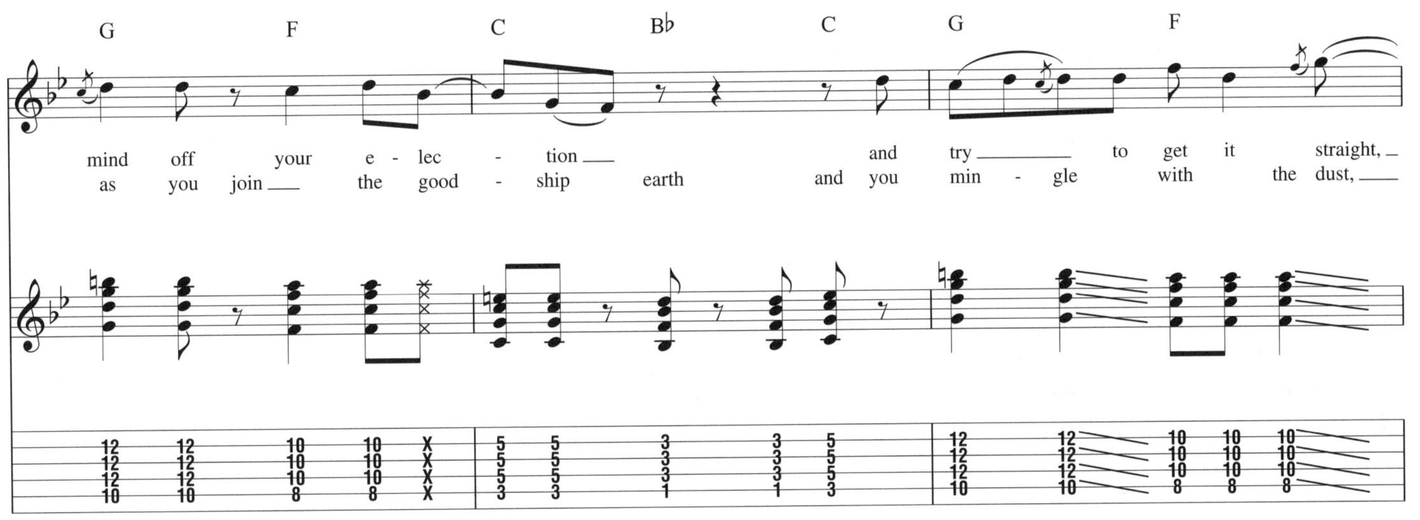
G F C B♭ C G F
mind off your e - lec - tion and try to get it straight,
as you join the good - ship earth and you min - gle with the dust,

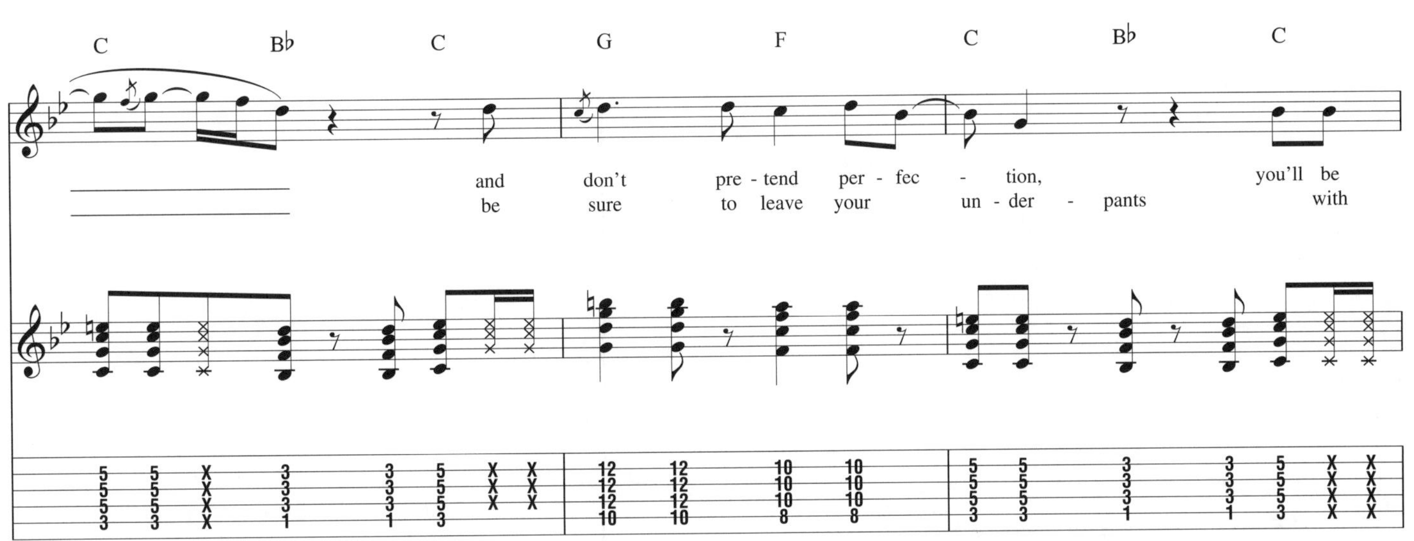
C B♭ C G F C B♭ C
and don't pre - tend per - fec - tion, you'll be
be sure to leave your un - der - pants with

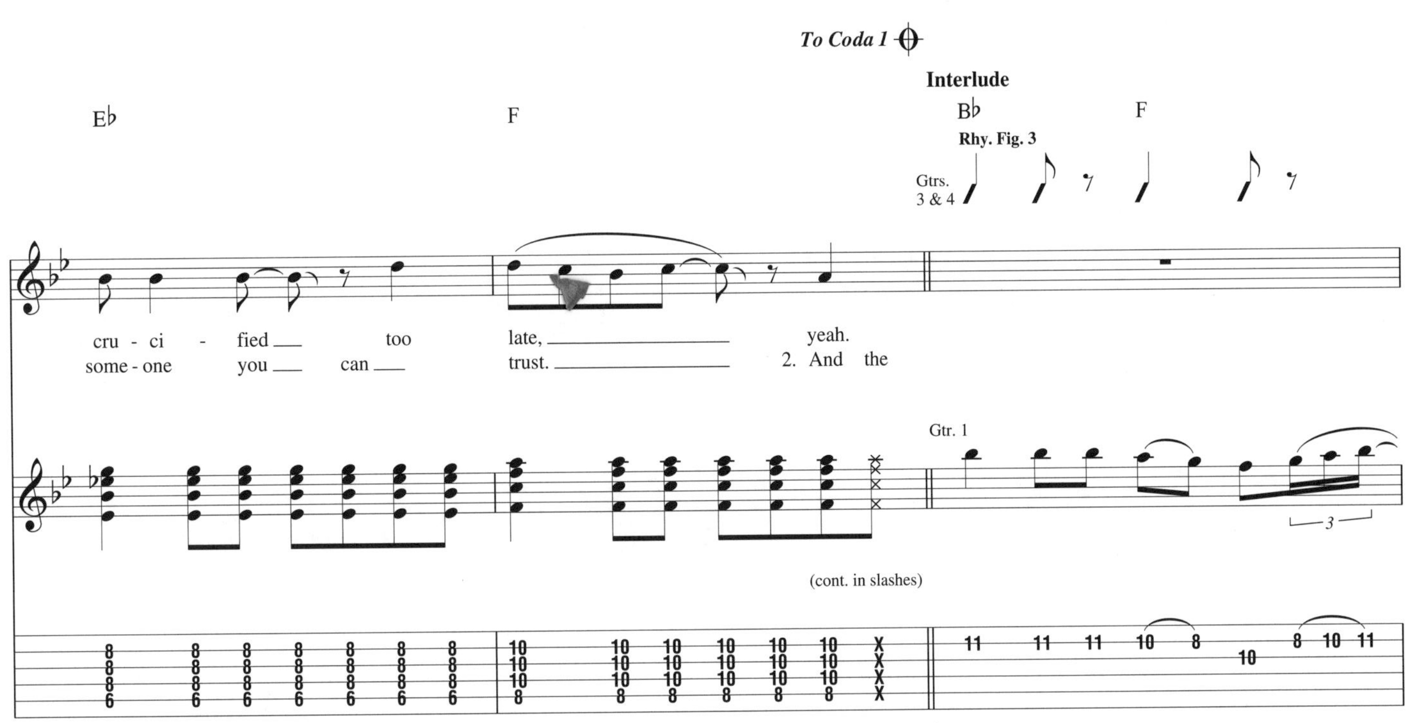
To Coda 1
Interlude
E♭ F B♭ F
Rhy. Fig. 3
Gtrs. 3 & 4
cru - ci - fied too late, yeah.
some - one you can trust. 2. And the
Gtr. 1
(cont. in slashes)

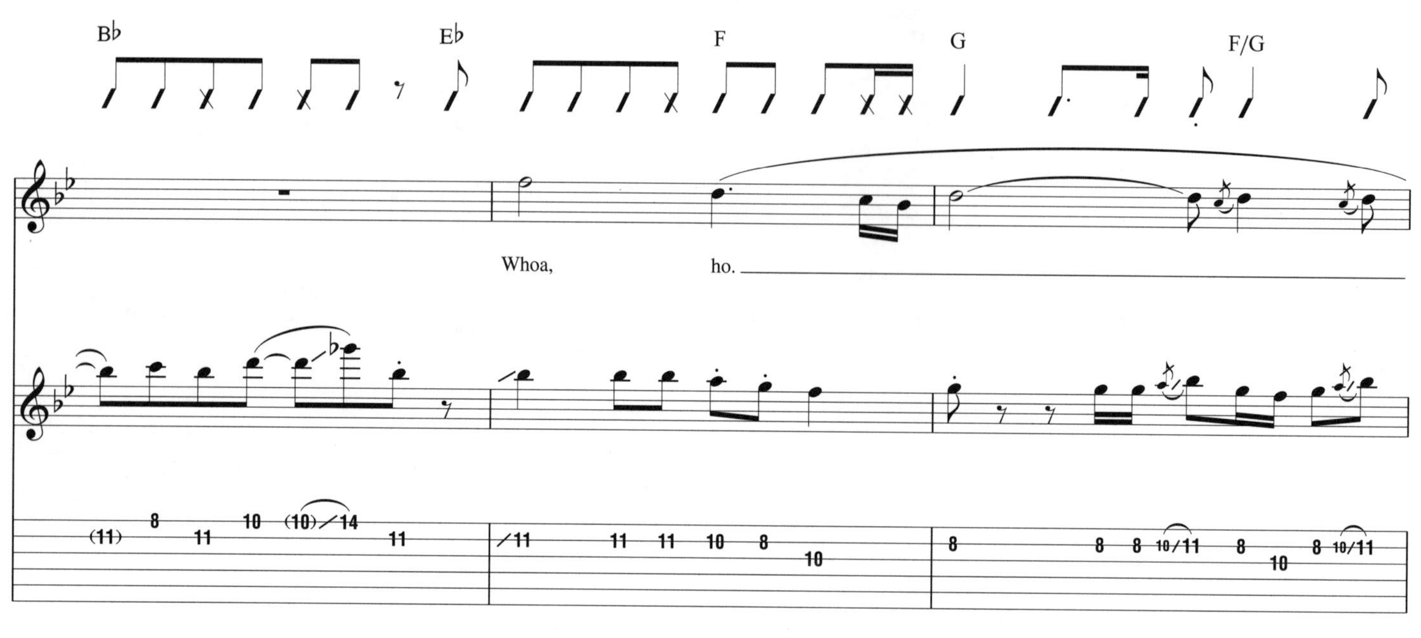
B♭
E♭
F
G
F/G
Whoa,
ho.
(11)
8
11
10
(10)
14
11
11
11
11
10
8
10
8
8
8
10/11
8
10
8
10/11

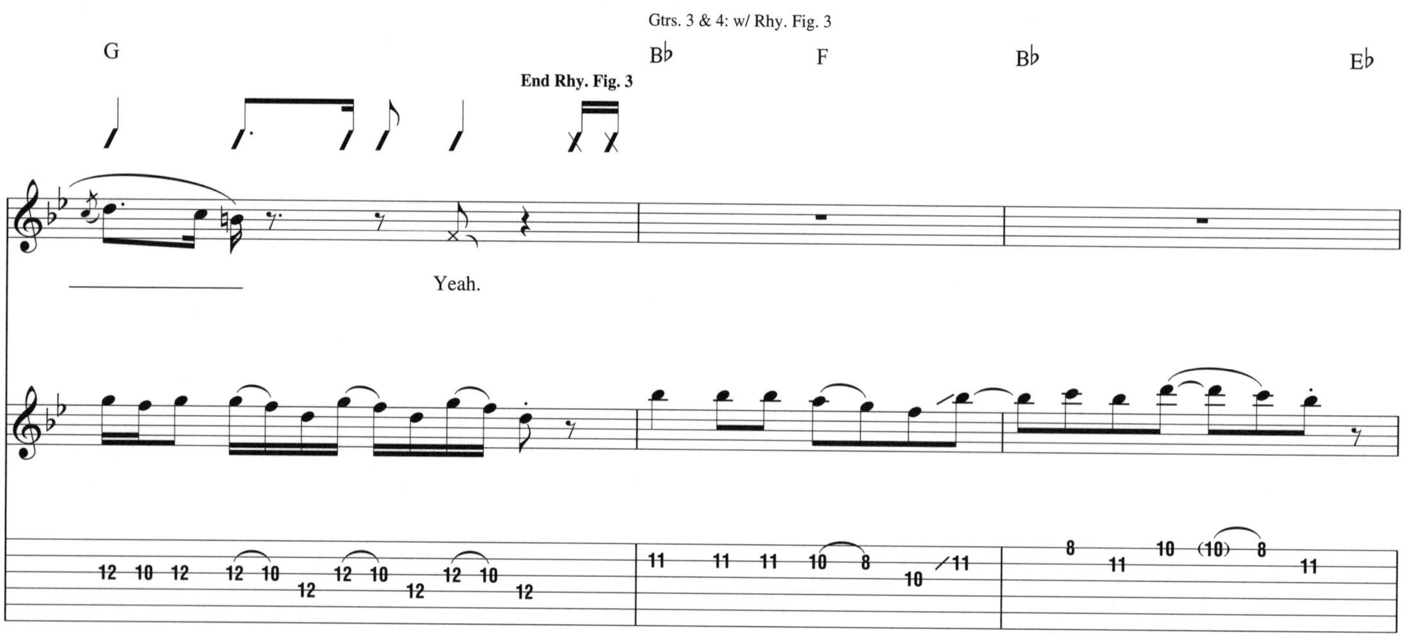
Gtrs. 3 & 4: w/ Rhy. Fig. 3
G
End Rhy. Fig. 3
B♭
F
B♭
E♭
Yeah.
12
10
12
12
10
12
12
10
12
12
10
12
11
11
11
10
8
10
11
8
11
10
(10)
8
11

D.S. al Coda 1
F
G
F/G
G
Whoa,
ho.
And he'll
Gtr. 1
11
11
8
8
10
8
8
9/10
13
11
12
10/11
12
10
12
10
12
10
12
12
10
12

Gtrs. 3 & 4: w/ Rhy. Fig. 3 (2 times)
B♭ F B♭ E♭ F
hard head - ed so - cial work - er who bathes his hands in

G F/G G B♭ F
blood, yeah, will wel - come you with arms
(Blood.)
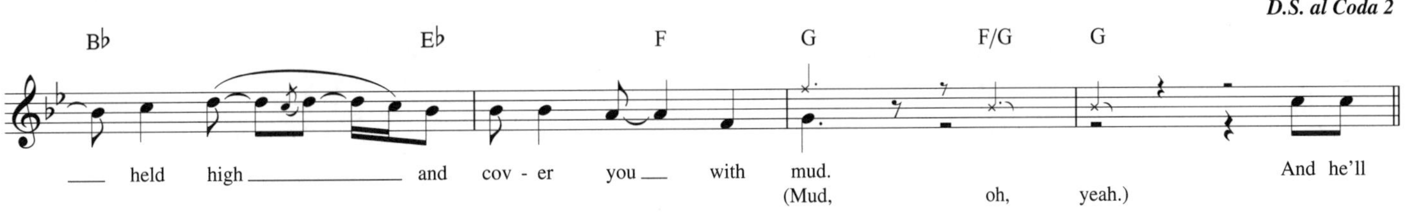
D.S. al Coda 2
B♭ E♭ F G F/G G
held high and cov - er you with mud. And he'll
(Mud, oh, yeah.)

Coda 2
E♭ C
rit.
bet - ter lick, ah, your fin - gers clean, well, I'll
Gtrs. 3 & 4
rit.
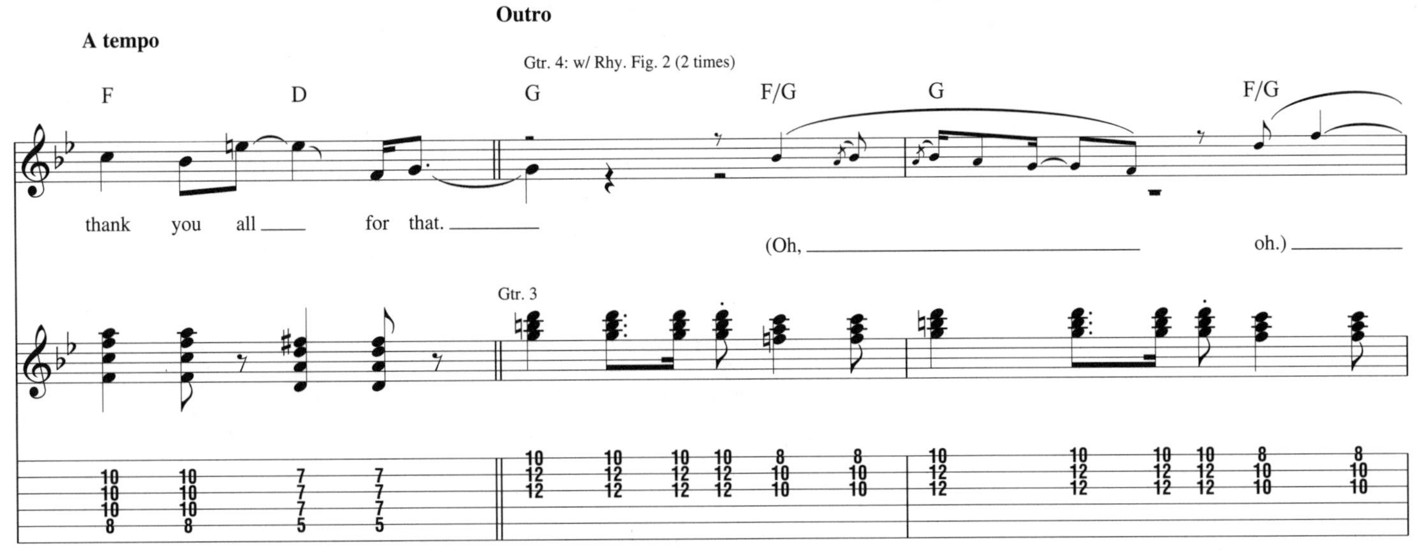
A tempo
Outro
Gtr. 4: w/ Rhy. Fig. 2 (2 times)
F D G F/G G F/G
thank you all for that.
(Oh, oh.)
Gtr. 3

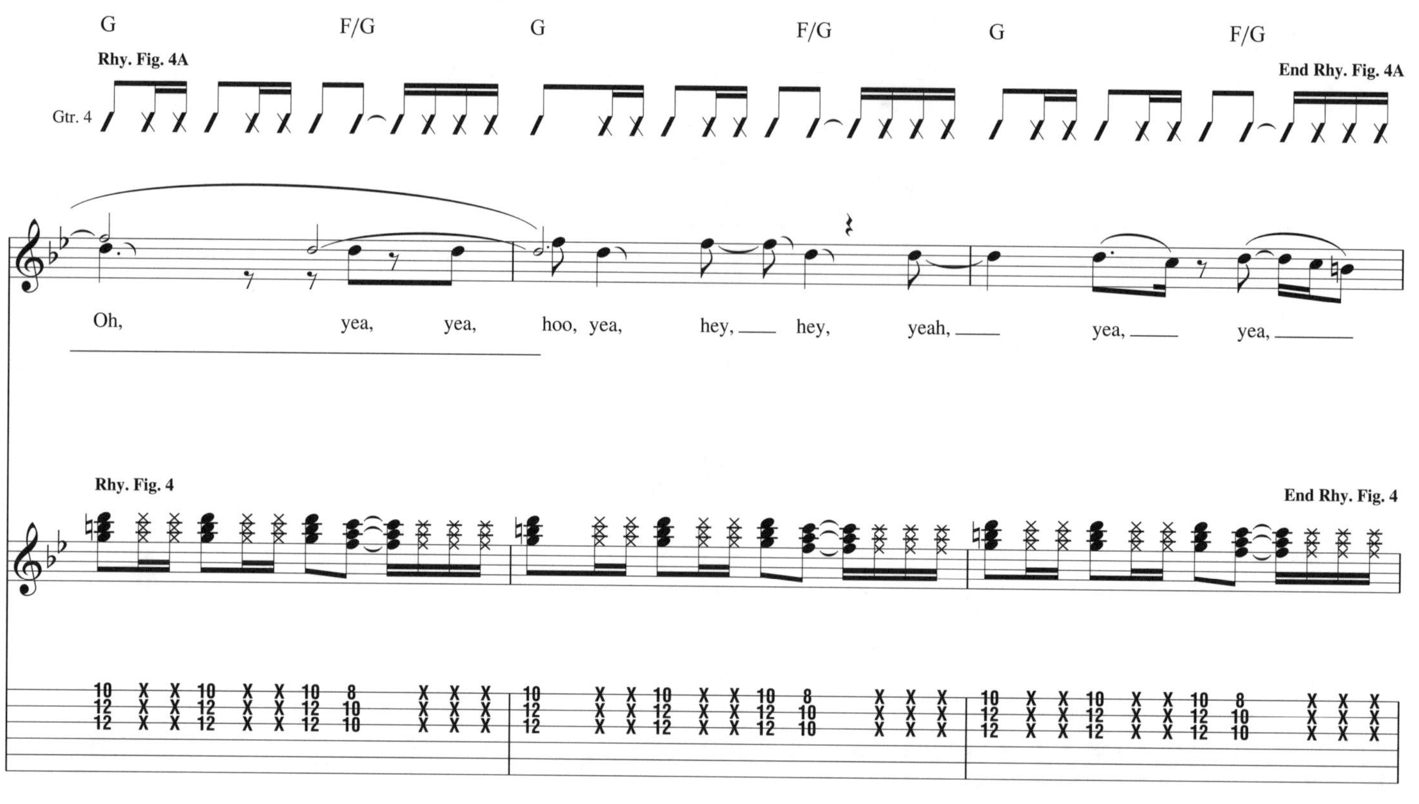
G
F/G
G
F/G
G
F/G
Rhy. Fig. 4A
End Rhy. Fig. 4A
Gtr. 4
Oh, yea, yea, hoo, yea, hey, hey, yeah, yea, yea,
Rhy. Fig. 4
End Rhy. Fig. 4

Begin fade
Gtrs. 3 & 4: w/ Rhy. Figs. 4 & 4A (3 times)
G
F/G
G
F/G
G
F/G
hey, come on, whoa, hey, come on, yea, hey, come on,

G
F/G
G
F/G
G
F/G
hey, hey, come on, hey, hey, come on, hey, hey, come on,

Fade out
G
F/G
G
F/G
G
F/G
hey, hey, come on, hey, hey, come on, hey, hey, come on.
(Yeah, oh, yeah, yeah.)

Song for Jeffrey

Words and Music by Ian Anderson

Gtr. 2: Open G tuning:
(low to high) D-G-D-G-B-D

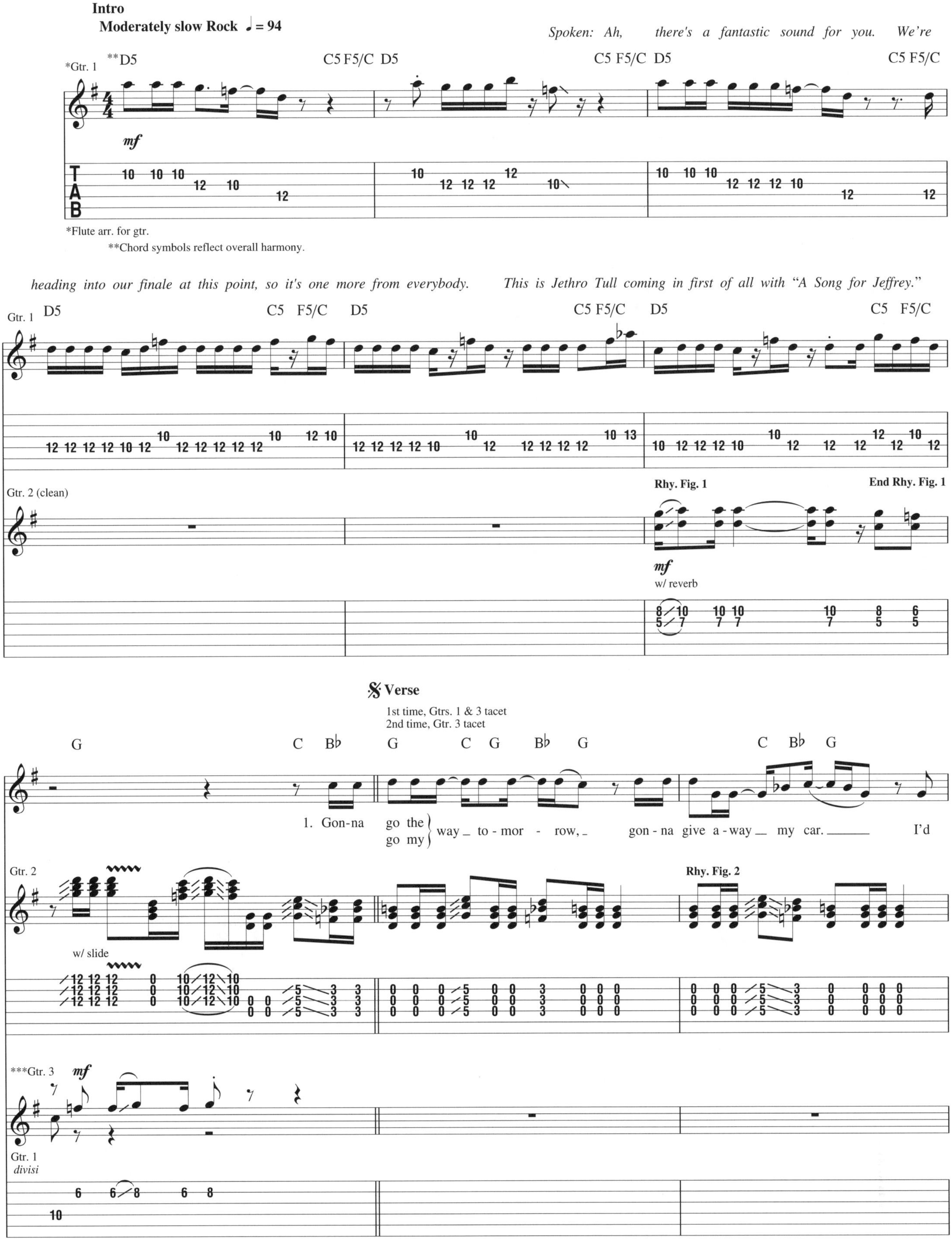

Intro
Moderately slow Rock ♩ = 94

Spoken: Ah, there's a fantastic sound for you. We're

*Gtr. 1 **D5 C5 F5/C D5 C5 F5/C D5 C5 F5/C

mf

*Flute arr. for gtr.
**Chord symbols reflect overall harmony.

heading into our finale at this point, so it's one more from everybody. This is Jethro Tull coming in first of all with "A Song for Jeffrey."

Gtr. 1 D5 C5 F5/C D5 C5 F5/C D5 C5 F5/C

Gtr. 2 (clean)

Rhy. Fig. 1 End Rhy. Fig. 1

mf
w/ reverb

*** Harmonica arr. for gtr.

C G B♭ G F G C G B♭ G
take you a - long with me, but you would not go so far. Don't see what I do not want to see, you don't
Gtr. 2
End Rhy. Fig. 2
Gtr. 2: w/ Rhy. Fig. 2
C B♭ G C G B♭ G F G
To Coda
hear what I don't say. Won't be what I don't want to be. I'll con - tin - ue in my way. Don't
Chorus
F G F G
cease to see where I'm a go - in'. Don't cease to see where I'm a go - in'. Don't
Gtr. 2
let ring
let ring
F G C B♭
cease to see where I'm a go - in' to. I don't want to.
Gtr. 2
let ring
let ring
Gtr. 3
1/4

Bridge
Gtr. 3 tacet
G C B♭ C F E♭ B♭
Ev - 'ry day I see the morn - in' come on in the same
Rhy. Fig. 3
w/o slide
1/4
F G F G G C
old way.
Gtr. 2
w/ slide
End Rhy. Fig. 3
*Use 2nd & 3rd fingers in conjunction with the slide.
Gtr. 2: w/ Rhy. Fig. 3
C F E♭ B♭ F G F G G G
Tell my - self to - mor-row brings me things I would not dream to - day.
Flute Solo
Gtr. 1
D5 D F C
Gtr. 2
w/o slide
slight P.M.
w/ slide

D
F
C
D
F
C
D
F
C
Interlude
Gtr. 1 tacet
G
C
B♭
G
C
B♭
G
C
B♭
Gtr. 3
1/4
1/4
1/4
Rhy. Fig. 4
Gtr. 2
D.S. al Coda
Coda
Chorus
G
C
B♭
F
G
2. Gon - na
cease to see where I'm a go - in'. Don't
End Rhy. Fig. 4
Gtr. 2
let ring

F
G
F
G
cease to see where I'm a go - in'. Don't cease to see where I'm go - in' to. I don't want
Gtr. 2
let ring
let ring

Gtr. 2: w/ Rhy. Fig. 4
C Bb
G
C Bb
to.
Gtr. 3
let ring
1/4
1/4

Outro
Gtr. 2: w/ Rhy. Fig. 1 (4 times)
Gtr. 3 tacet
G
C Bb
G
C Bb
D5
C5 F5/C
Gtr. 1
1/4
1/4

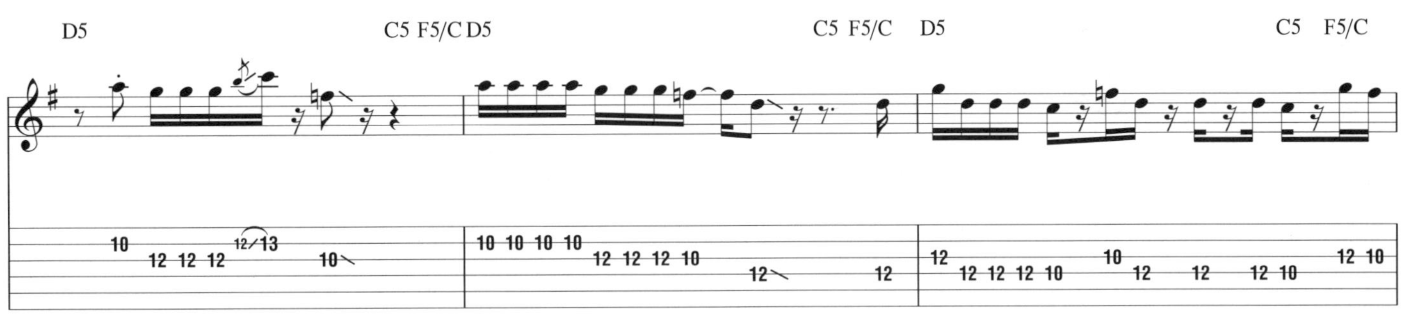
D5
C5 F5/C D5
C5 F5/C
D5
C5 F5/C

Gtr. 2 tacet
D5
C5
F5/C
D5
C5 F5/C D5
C5 F5/C
Gtr. 1
Gtr. 2
D5
C5 F5/C D5
C5 F5/C
D5
C5 F5/C D5
C5 F5/C
p
D5
C5
G
B♭
Gtr. 1
mf
let ring
Gtr. 2

Fat Man

Words and Music by Ian Anderson

* Open G5 tuning, capo XII:
(low to high) D-G-G?-D?-G?-D

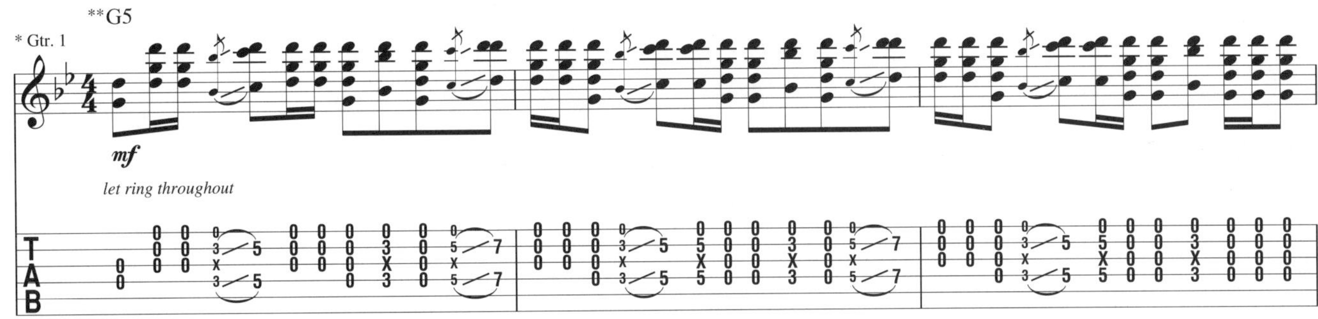

*Mandolin arr. for gtr.

**Chord symbols reflect implied harmony.

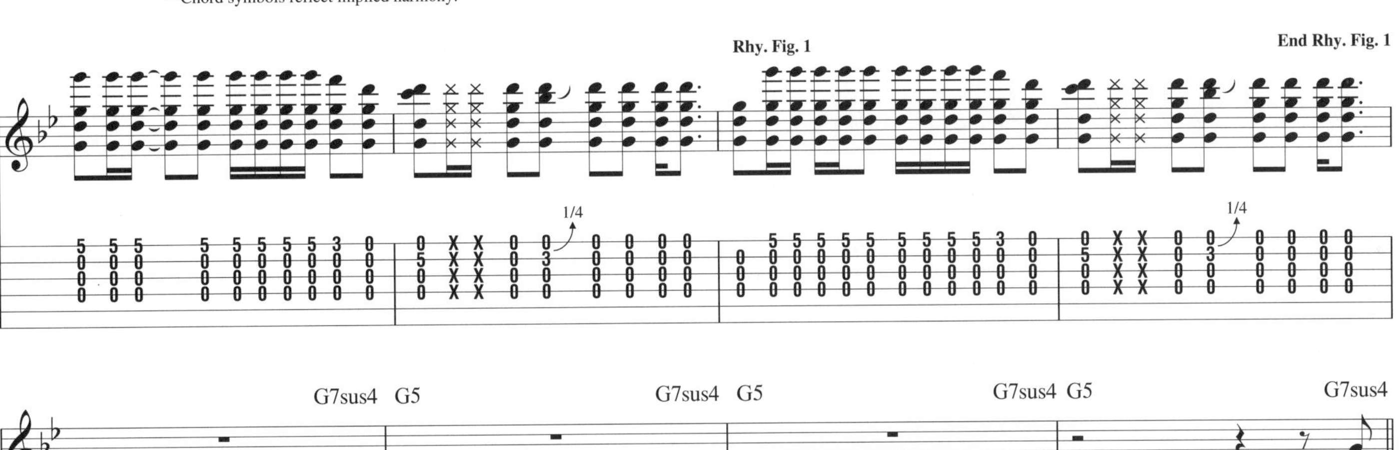

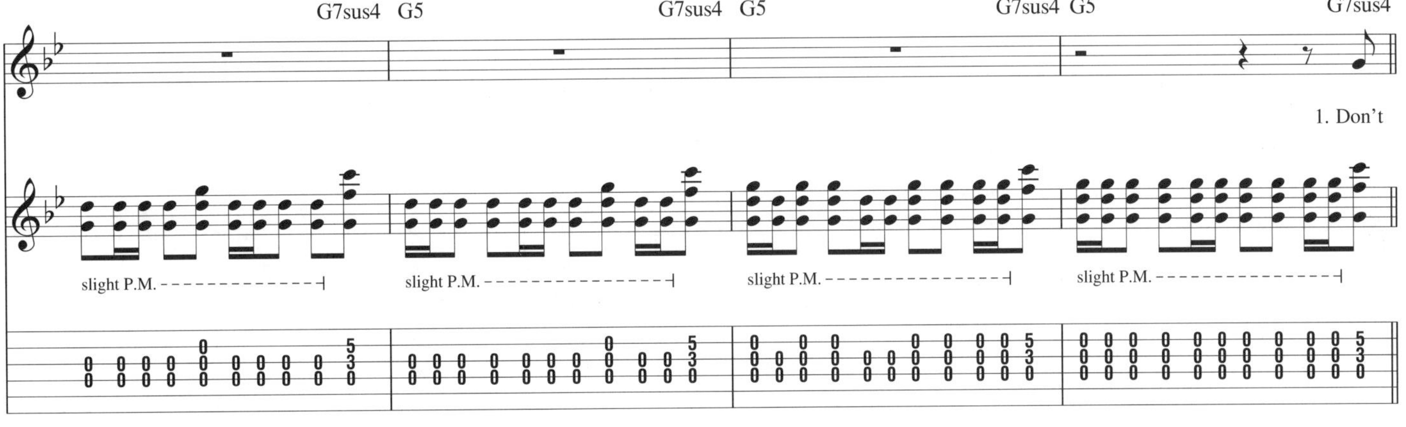

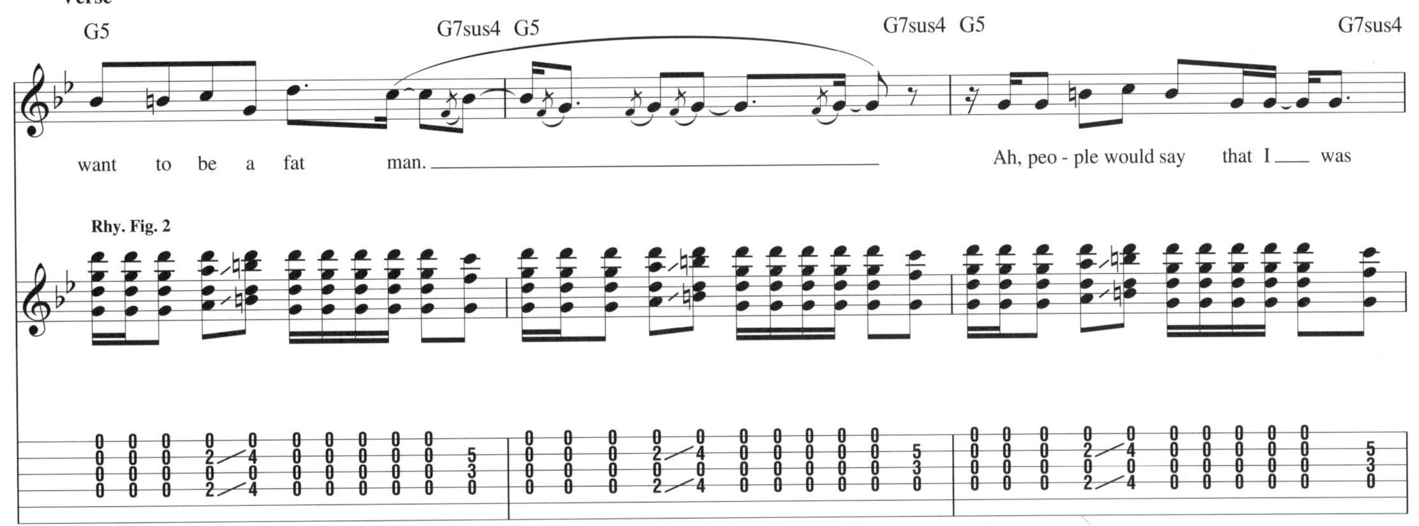

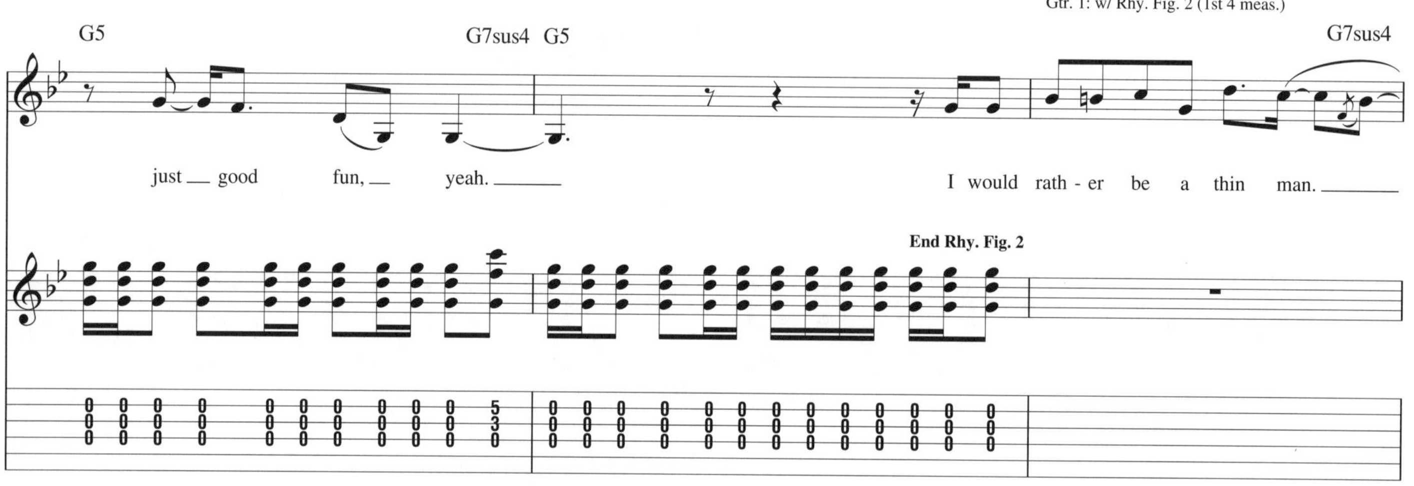

Gtr. 1: w/ Rhy. Fig. 2 (1st 4 meas.)
G5
G7sus4 G5
G7sus4
just good fun, yeah.
I would rath - er be a thin man.
End Rhy. Fig. 2

G5
G7sus4 G5
G7sus4 G5
G7sus4
I am so glad to go on be - ing one, yeah.

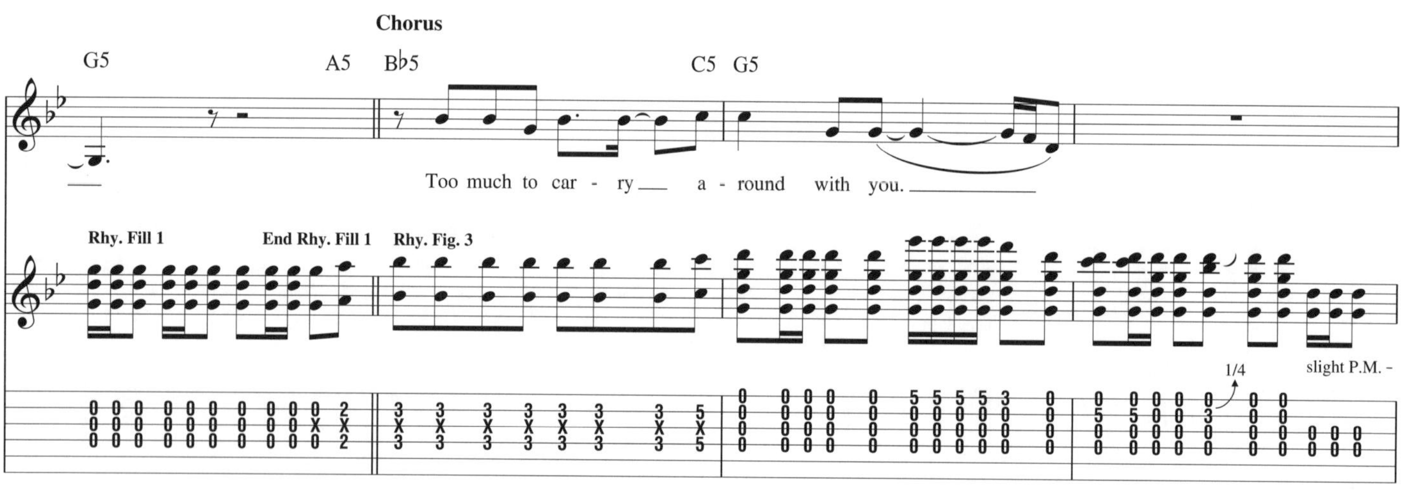

Chorus
G5
A5 B♭5
C5 G5
Too much to car - ry a - round with you.
Rhy. Fill 1
End Rhy. Fill 1
Rhy. Fig. 3
1/4
slight P.M.

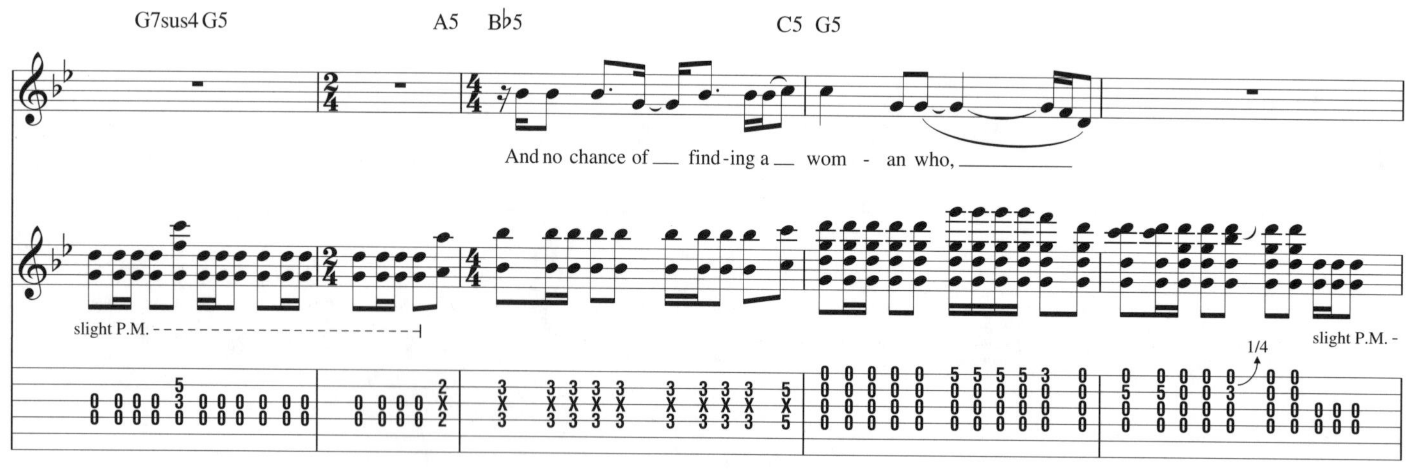

G7sus4 G5
A5 B♭5
C5 G5
And no chance of find-ing a wom - an who,
slight P.M.
1/4
slight P.M.

G7sus4 G5
A5
B♭5
G5 Em
F
Em
G5
ah, will love you in ___ the morn - ing and, ah, all the day - time too. _
slight P.M.
Bkgd. Voc.: w/ ad lib. humming (next 6 meas.)
Woo!
End Rhy. Fig. 3
Interlude
Gtr. 1: w/ Rhy. Fig. 1 (2 times)
G5
Gtr. 1
Drum Solo
G7sus4 N.C.
1/4
G5
2. I don't
*slight P.M.
*Gradually lift P.M.

Verse
Gtr. 1: w/ Rhy. Fig. 2
G5 G7sus4 G5 G7sus4 G5 G7sus4 G5 G7sus4
want to be a fat man. Have not the pa-tience to ig - nore all that, yeah.
Gtr. 1: w/ Rhy. Fig. 2 (1st 4 meas.)
G5 G7sus4 G5 G7sus4 G5 G7sus4
I hate to ad - mit to my - self half of my prob-lems came from
Chorus
Gtr. 1: w/ Rhy. Fill 1
Gtr. 1: w/ Rhy. Fig. 3
G5 G7sus4 G5 A5 B♭5 C5 G5
be - ing fat, yeah. I won't waste my time feel - ing sor-ry for him.
G7sus4 G5 A5 B♭5 C5 G5
I see the oth - er side through be - ing thin.
G7sus4 G5 A5 B♭5 G5 Em F Em G5
Roll us both down a moun - tain and I'm sure the fat man would win.
Bkgd. Voc.: w/ ad lib. humming (next 9 meas.)
Eee!
Outro
Gtr. 1: w/ Rhy. Fig. 1 (3 1/2 times)
G5
A tempo
Gtr. 1
D5/G G G5
rit.
1/4
1/4

Bouree

Music by Ian Anderson

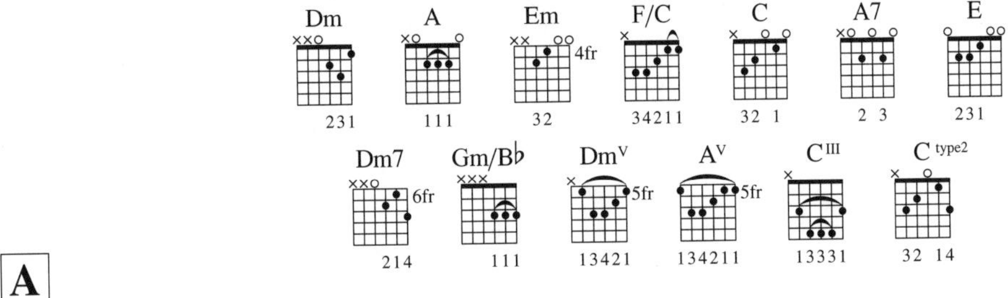

A

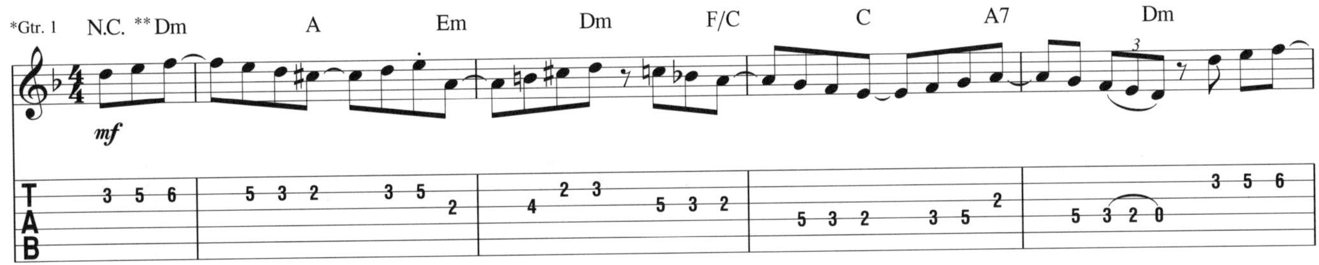

*Flute arr. for gtr.

**Chord symbols reflect implied harmony.

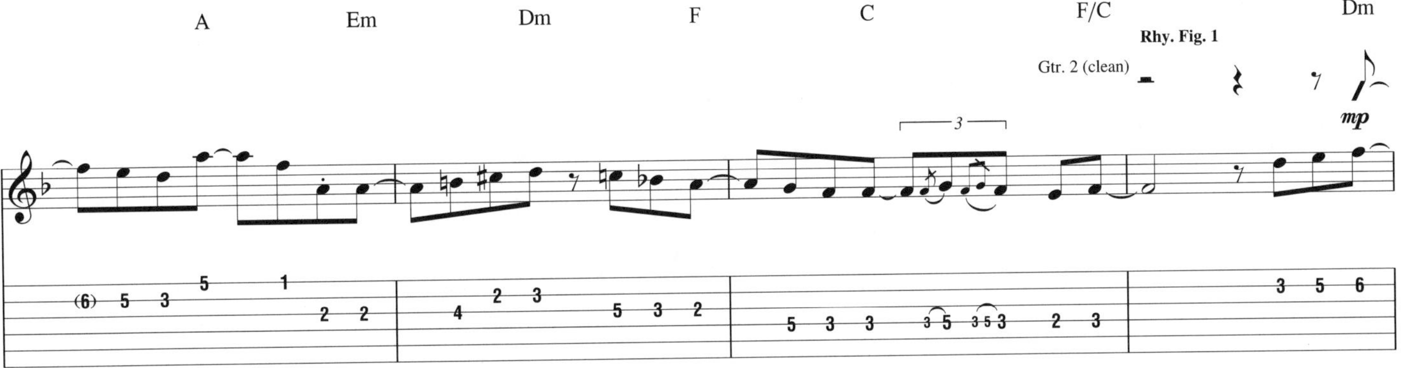

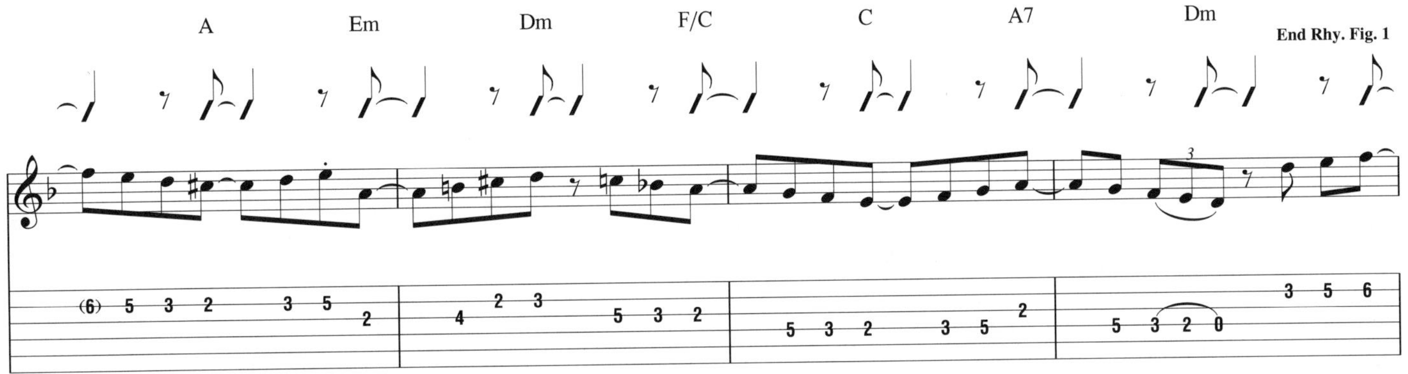

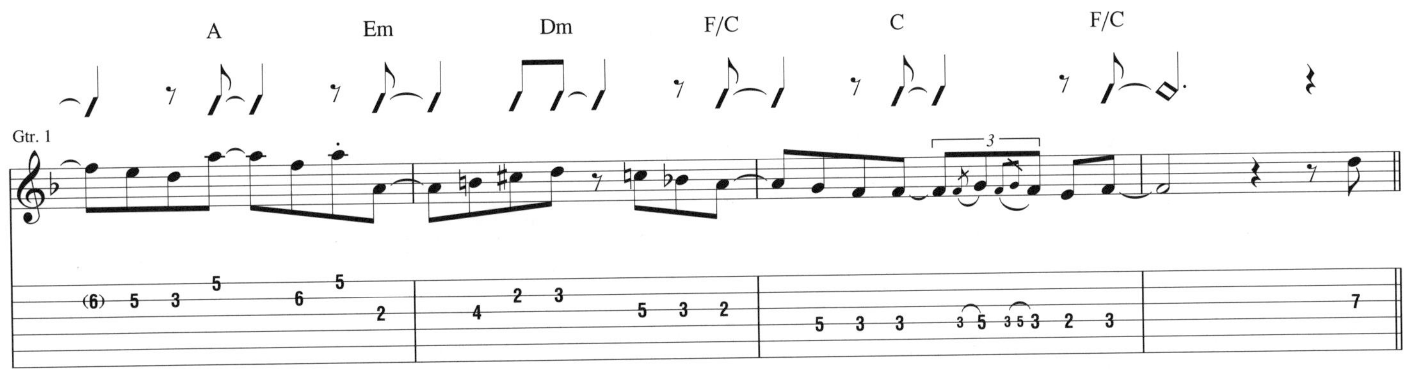

B
Dm
A
E
Dm
F/C
C
A7
Dm
A
E
Dm
F/C
C
F/C
1/2
Dm
A
C
Dm
C
Dm
A7
Dm
A
C
Dm
C
Dm
A7
Dm
C
Dm
Gr. 2 tacet

Dm7
Gm/B♭
Dm7
A C Gm/B♭
④ ③
7fr 5fr
Dm7
Gm/B♭
Dm7
Gm/B♭
Dm^V A^V C^III Dm^V C^III Dm^V A^V Dm^V
A^V C^III Dm^V C^III Dm^V

D
Gtr. 1 tacet
Gtr. 1
*Gtr. 3
divisi
*Bass arr. for gtr.
E
Gtr. 2 tacet
let ring

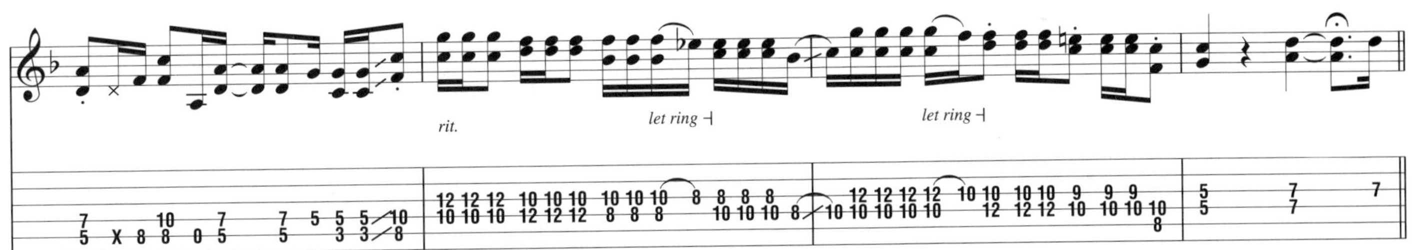
rit.
let ring
let ring

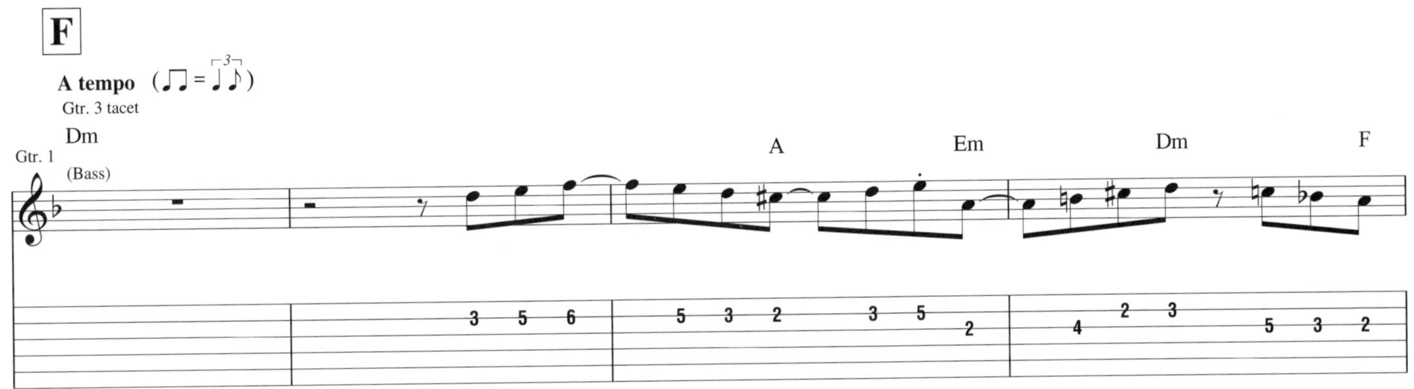
F
A tempo
Gtr. 3 tacet
Dm
Gtr. 1
(Bass)
A
Em
Dm
F

C
A7
Dm
A
Em
Dm
F

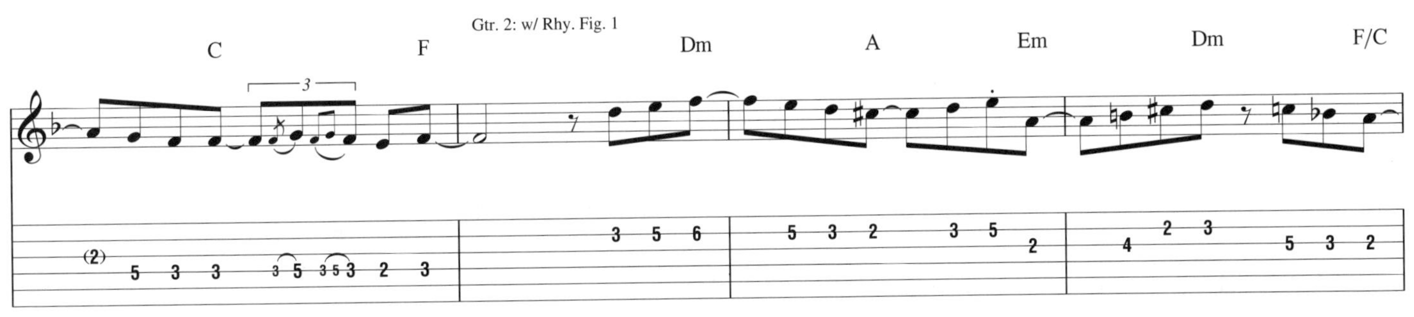
Gtr. 2: w/ Rhy. Fig. 1
C
F
Dm
A
Em
Dm
F/C

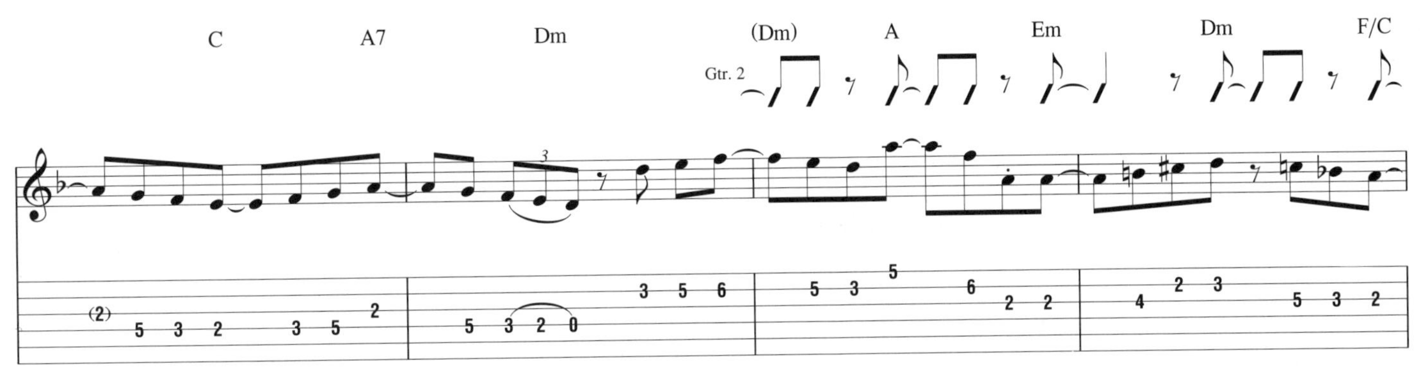
C
A7
Dm
(Dm)
A
Em
Dm
F/C
Gtr. 2

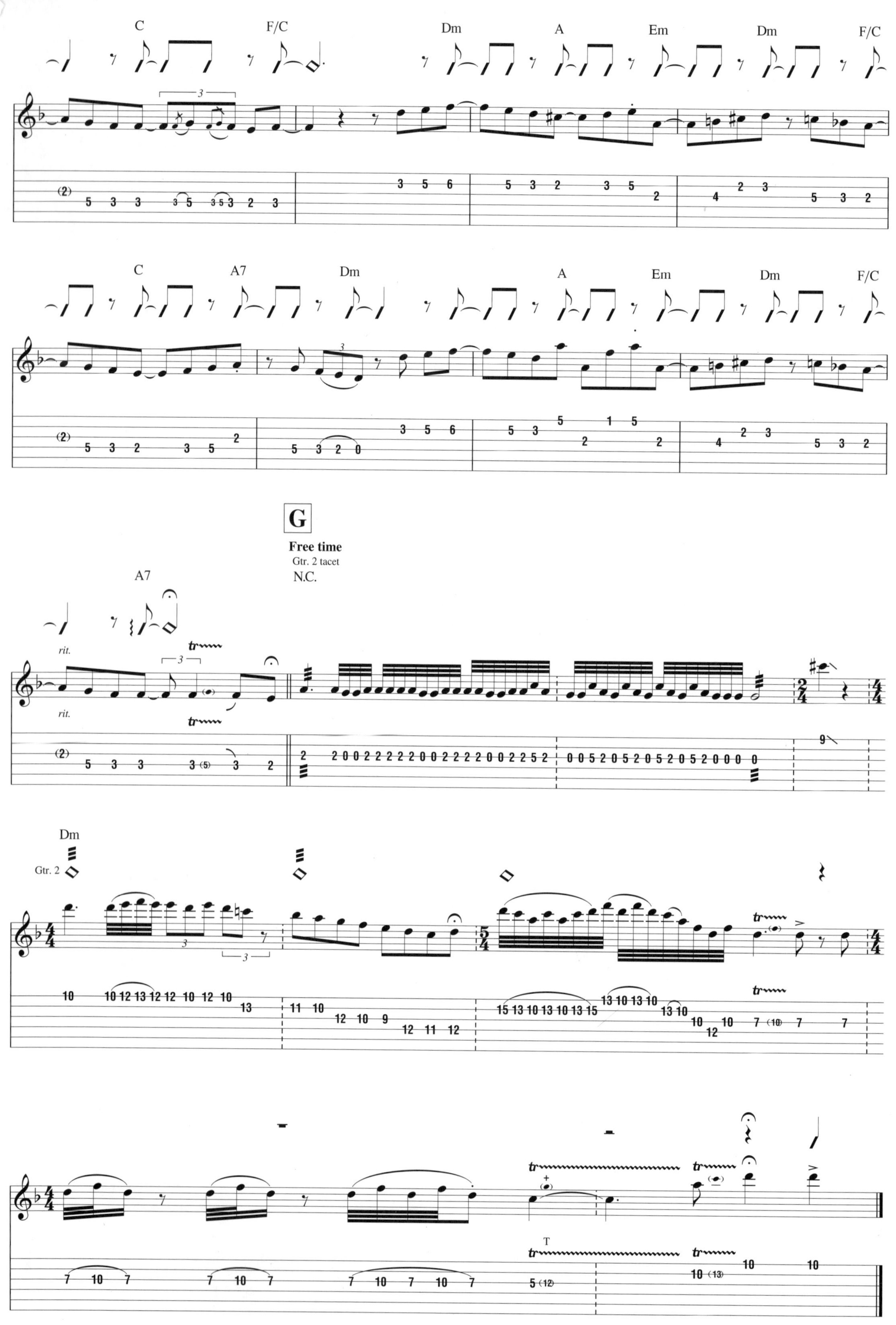
C
F/C
Dm
A
Em
Dm
F/C
C
A7
Dm
A
Em
Dm
F/C
G
Free time
Gtr. 2 tacet
N.C.
A7
rit.
rit.
Dm
Gtr. 2